Theodor W. Adorno (1903–69) was one of the foremost philosophers and social theorists of the post-war period. Crucial to the development of Critical Theory, his highly original and distinctive but often difficult writings not only advance questions of fundamental philosophical significance, but provide deep-reaching analyses of literature, art, music, sociology and political theory.

In this comprehensive introduction, Brian O'Connor explains Adorno's philosophy for those coming to his work for the first time, through original new lines of interpretation. Beginning with an overview of Adorno's life and key philosophical views and influences, which contextualizes the intellectual environment in which he worked, O'Connor assesses the central elements of Adorno's philosophy.

He carefully examines Adorno's distinctive style of analysis and shows how much of his work is a critical response to the various forms of identity thinking that have underpinned the destructive forces of modernity. He goes on to discuss the main areas of Adorno's philosophy: social theory, the philosophy of experience, metaphysics, morality and aesthetics; setting out detailed accounts of Adorno's notions of the dialectic of Enlightenment, reification, totality, mediation, identity, nonidentity, experience, negative dialectics, immanence, freedom, autonomy, imitation and autonomy in art. The final chapter considers Adorno's philosophical legacy and importance today.

Including a chronology, glossary, chapter summaries, and suggestions for further reading, *Adorno* is an ideal introduction to this demanding but important thinker, and essential reading for students of philosophy, literature, sociology and cultural studies.

Brian O'Connor is Associate Professor of Philosophy at University College Dublin, Ireland. He is the author of *Adorno's Negative Dialectic* (2004) and editor of *The Adorno Reader* (2000).

Routledge Philosophers

Edited by Brian Leiter
University of Chicago

Routledge Philosophers is a major series of introductions to the great Western philosophers. Each book places a major philosopher or thinker in historical context, explains and assesses their key arguments, and considers their legacy. Additional features include a chronology of major dates and events, chapter summaries, annotated suggestions for further reading and a glossary of technical terms.

An ideal starting point for those new to philosophy, they are also essential reading for those interested in the subject at any level.

Hobbes
A. P. Martinich

Leibniz
Nicholas Jolley

Locke
E. J. Lowe

Hegel
Frederick Beiser

Rousseau
Nicholas Dent

Schopenhauer
Julian Young

Freud
Jonathan Lear

Kant
Paul Guyer

Husserl
David Woodruff Smith

Darwin
Tim Lewens

Aristotle
Christopher Shields

Rawls
Samuel Freeman

Spinoza
Michael Della Rocca

Merleau-Ponty
Taylor Carman

Russell
Gregory Landini

Wittgenstein
William Child

Heidegger
John Richardson

Forthcoming:

Plato
Constance Meinwald

Hume
Don Garrett

Dewey
Steven Fesmire

Habermas
Kenneth Baynes

Smith
Eric Schliesser

Mill
Daniel Jacobson

Nietzsche
Maudemarie Clark

Brian O'Connor

Adorno

Routledge
Taylor & Francis Group

LONDON AND NEW YORK

First published 2013
by Routledge
2 Park Square, Milton Park, Abingdon, Oxon, OX14 4RN

Simultaneously published in the USA and Canada
by Routledge
711 Third Avenue, New York, NY 10017

*Routledge is an imprint of the Taylor & Francis Group, an
informa business*

British Library Cataloguing in Publication Data
A catalogue record for this book is available from the British
Library

Library of Congress Cataloging in Publication Data
O'Connor, Brian, 1965-
Adorno / by Brian O'Connor.
p. cm. -- (Routledge philosophers)
Includes bibliographical references (p.) and index.
1. Adorno, Theodor W., 1903-1969. I. Title.
B3199.A34O26 2012
193--dc23
2012011988

ISBN: 978-0-415-36735-6 (hbk)
ISBN: 978-0-415-36736-3 (pbk)
ISBN: 978-0-203-01983-2 (ebk)

Typeset in Joanna and DINOT
by Taylor & Francis Books

Printed and bound in Great Britain by
TJ International Ltd, Padstow, Cornwall

For Eileen

Contents

Acknowledgements

During my time preparing this book I was fortunate to receive a great many helpful comments on my interpretations of Adorno and of critical theory more broadly. I am grateful in particular to Eileen Brennan (as ever and always), Maeve Cooke, Gordon Finlayson, Roger Foster, Fabian Freyenhagen, Espen Hammer, Jared Millson, Danielle Petherbridge, Henry Pickford and Michael Rosen. Timo Jütten read insightfully through various drafts of all the chapters.

I thank Brian Leiter for inviting me to contribute to the *Routledge Philosophers* series.

The award of a University College Dublin President's Research Fellowship for 2010–11 was very much appreciated as it enabled me to make considerable progress towards completion of this book.

Abbreviations

All of the following are works by Adorno:

AP	'The Actuality of Philosophy'
AT	*Aesthetic Theory*
CIR	'Culture Industry Reconsidered'
CM	*Critical Models*
DE	*Dialectic of Enlightenment*
EMR	'Education for Maturity and Responsibility'
FCM	'On the Fetish-Character in Music'
GS	*Gesammelte Schriften*
HF	*History and Freedom*
HTS	*Hegel: Three Studies*
IPD	'Introduction' to *The Positivist Dispute in German Sociology*
IS	*Introduction to Sociology*
INH	'The Idea of Natural History'
JA	*The Jargon of Authenticity*
LSS	'On the Logic of the Social Sciences'
MCP	*Metaphysics: Concept and Problems*
ME	*Against Epistemology: A Metacritique*
MM	*Minima Moralia: Reflections from Damaged Life*
ND	*Negative Dialectics*
NL I	*Notes to Literature*, Vol. I
NL II	*Notes to Literature*, Vol. II

P	*Prisms*
PMP	*Problems of Moral Philosophy*
PNM	*Philosophy of New Music*
S	'Society'
SER	'Sociology and Empirical Research'
TPC	'Theory of Pseudo-Culture'

Chronology

1903	Theodor Wiesengrund Adorno born, 11 September, in Frankfurt.
1918	First meeting with Siegfried Kracauer.
1921	Graduates from secondary school, the Kaiser-Wilhelm Gymnasium, in Frankfurt.
1921–23	Studies Philosophy, Psychology, Music and Sociology at the University of Frankfurt. First meeting with Max Horkheimer, then a lecturer at the university (probably 1921).
1923	First meeting with Walter Benjamin.
1924	Doctorate in Philosophy from the University of Frankfurt, directed by Hans Cornelius, on the topic of Husserl's phenomenology.
1925	Moves to Vienna to study composition with Alban Berg and piano with Eduard Steuerman.
1926–27	Back in Frankfurt, works on his (first) Habilitationsschrift, directed by Hans Cornelius, on the topic of the Unconscious in Husserl. Completes a text but does not submit it.
1931	Completes a (second) Habilitationsschrift, directed by Paul Tillich, on the topic of Kierkegaard's concept of the aesthetic which is submitted. The work is accepted by the Frankfurt faculty. Gives his inaugural

	lecture ('The Actuality of Philosophy') as the holder of a *venia legendi*.
1931–33	Privatdozent (lecturer) in Philosophy at Frankfurt.
1933	Publication of his first book, *Kierkegaard: Construction of the Aesthetic* (his *Habilitationsschrift*). Forced out of the university by the Nazi Government's Anti-Semitic legislation.
1934–38	Moves to England, settling in Oxford as a registered advanced student. Works on a book on Husserl's phenomenology.
1937	Marries Margarete 'Gretel' Karplus in London.
1938	Moves to New York, becoming a member of the Institute for Social Research under Horkheimer's directorship. Begins work on the Princeton Radio project.
1942	Follows Horkheimer to California to begin collaborative writing work with him.
1944	With Horkheimer he completes the first edition of *Dialectic of Enlightenment*. Joins the Berkeley research team working on the Authoritarian Personality project.
1949	*Philosophy of New Music*. Returns to Germany, becoming a Professor of Philosophy at Frankfurt and continuing member of the Institute for Social Research (now refounded in Frankfurt).
1950	Publication of the *Authoritarian Personality*.
1951	*Minima Moralia*.
1952	*In Search of Wagner*.
1955	*Prisms*.
1956	*Dissonances: Music in the Administered World*. The book he had begun in Oxford is published: *The Metacritique of Epistemology (Against Epistemology)*.
1958	Becomes director of the Institute for Social Research. *Notes on Literature I*.
1959	*Soundfigures*.

1960	*Mahler: a Musical Physiognomy.*
1961	*Notes on Literature II.* Speaks with Karl Popper at a conference of the German Society for Sociology which initiates the 'Positivist Dispute' in social theory. Lectures in Paris on material that would form a substantial part of *Negative Dialectics*.
1962	*Introduction to the Sociology of Music.*
1963	*Hegel: Three Studies; Interventions; Quasi una fantasia.*
1964	*Jargon of Authenticity; Moments musicaux.*
1965	*Notes on Literature III.*
1966	*Negative Dialectics.* Radio Lecture, 'Education After Auschwitz'.
1967	*Without Model: Parva Aesthetica.*
1968	*Berg: Master of the Smallest Link; Impromptus.*
1968–69	Relations with the Student Movement deteriorate; in 1969 the Institute for Social Research is occupied and his lectures at the university are disrupted.
1969	*Catchwords: Critical Models II.* Completes an advanced draft of *Aesthetic Theory*. Death, 6 August, in Visp, Switzerland.

One
Adorno's life and philosophical motivations

Adorno's engagement with the German Philosophical tradition is profound. The central concepts of his philosophy are developed through critical confrontations with Kant and Hegel in particular and are sharpened considerably in his trenchant assessments of the phenomenological school. The great philosophical systems seem to frame his conceptual reference points. Yet Adorno's philosophy is by no means an academic response to the achievements of his predecessors. Informing his considerations of so many of the notable thinkers of the modern tradition is his interest in the most basic of human needs, happiness. Adorno reminds us that philosophy was once openly motivated by the need to conceptualize the 'good life', a life in which human beings might live freely, flourish as persons, relating fulfillingly and without preconditions to others (MM 15). It is through the good life that happiness might be attained. For Adorno happiness would be genuine experience, in deep contrast to the forms of experience we must go through and internalize in order to preserve ourselves within the distinctive conditions of modern society.

Adorno understands the social world to be normatively structured in such a way as to preclude the possibility of happiness: it is the world of 'damaged life' (the subtitle of *Minima Moralia*). He attempts to return philosophy to the question of the good life in a negative way only as he does not believe that the task of philosophy can be to develop a theory of happiness or to sketch out a plan for human flourishing. Adorno never goes further than elusive characterizations of these ideals, fearful that specifying them would serve only to narrow them and thereby contradict their unlimited potential. Rather, some sense of the possibilities of experience is gained through the criticism of various philosophical endeavours to construct theories of experience. Uncovering the ways in which those constructions are distorting offers us a glimpse at what has been denied. This is not, though, a matter of looking for errors in reasoning by any given philosopher. Adorno holds that philosophical distortions are determined by the cultural and normative conditions within which philosophy operates. But the philosophers of the modern age do not recognize the profound influence of social norms on their accounts of experience. If philosophy is therefore to contribute to the possibility of happiness it must work against its established models, models which unwittingly reproduce the socially prevalent norms that obstruct the possibility of genuine experience. For Adorno, then, philosophy is not exclusively a logical-analytical enterprise, but an historical one too. A constituent part of its validity is its self-conscious responsiveness to its socio-normative environment.

It was the extraordinary circumstances of Adorno's philosophical development – shaped largely by the traumas of German history and by an intellectual environment outside the academy – that brought him to think of philosophy as an enterprise that must work against itself in order to retain its capacity to understand the world. We can begin to understand the origins of and motivations behind this conception of the vocation of philosophy by looking at the experiences that would contribute to Adorno's uncommon intellectual formation.

1. Life and philosophical development

Theodor Wiesengrund Adorno was born in Frankfurt on 11 September 1903.[1] His father, Oscar Wiesengrund, was a cultured and prosperous wine merchant who had abandoned the Jewish faith into which he was born in favour of assimilation, converting, later in life, to Christianity. Maria Calvelli Adorno della Piana, a German of Corsican background, was Adorno's mother. She was a Catholic and Adorno was baptized in accordance with her religion. As a young man Adorno used Wiesengrund Adorno as his surname, but he decided when registering in the United States to abbreviate his full name to Theodor W. Adorno.

Before marriage Adorno's mother had sung professionally. Her sister (Agathe), who lived with the Wiesengrunds, was a renowned pianist. Together they provided a formative environment for the young Adorno. His old friend, Max Horkheimer, noted that Adorno's artistic mother and aunt 'were of crucial importance for his education'.[2] While still at Gymnasium (High School) he studied at the local conservatory, taking piano as his instrument. And music was among the subjects he selected as an undergraduate. After attaining a doctoral degree in philosophy – at the age of 21 – he moved, for six months, to Vienna in order to study composition under Alban Berg and piano with Eduard Steuermann. Adorno took composition seriously, steadily producing a number of works throughout the 1920s and 30s.[3] Many of his compositions are identifiably within the style of the so-called Second Viennese School (the group of early twentieth-century composers who comprised Arnold Schoenberg's circle, which included Berg and Anton Webern). Although Adorno decided against attempting composition as a full-time occupation, music would absorb a substantial part of his life's work. He wrote polemically and provocatively on the classical, post-classical and modernist traditions of music. Among his longer studies are books on Wagner, Mahler, Schoenberg, Stravinsky, Berg and an unfinished study of Beethoven. Considerations of virtually every development in contemporary music can be found in Adorno's collected works, about a third of which are devoted to music. His talent, training and achievements both as a composer and more especially as a theorist give us every reason to believe that he could have enjoyed a successful career solely as a distinguished writer on music. However, he chose instead to pursue philosophy as his profession, which he never perceived as entirely separable from his theoretical reflections on music. In a letter to Thomas Mann he wrote:

> I studied philosophy and music. Instead of deciding exclusively for one subject or the other, I have always had the feeling that my real vocation was to pursue one and the same thing in both of these different domains.
>
> (Adorno and Mann 2006: Letter 11, 5 July 1948)

Adorno discovered his fascination for philosophy some years before enrolling as an undergraduate. The circumstances of his earliest serious encounters with philosophical thinking are remarkable. His family arranged for the teenage Adorno to have weekly meetings with Siegfried Kracauer, an accomplished cultural theorist. In an essay on Kracauer, included in his *Notes on Literature*, Adorno, at sixty years of age, looked back on what those meetings contributed to his philosophical development. He wrote:

> For years Kracauer read the *Critique of Pure Reason* with me regularly on Saturday afternoons. I am not exaggerating in the slightest when I say that I owe more to this reading than to my academic teachers. Exceptionally gifted as a pedagogue, Kracauer made Kant come alive for me. Under his guidance I experienced the work from the beginning not as mere epistemology, not as an analysis of scientifically valid judgments, but as a kind of coded text from which the historical situation of the spirit could be read, with the vague expectation that in doing so one could acquire something of the truth itself.
>
> (NL II 58–59)

This passage acknowledges a great debt because what it attributes to Kracauer was to become a characteristic feature of Adorno's own philosophical approach. Adorno analyses the logic and arguments of the great works of the modern German philosophical tradition in order to uncover their deepest normative assumptions and unreflecting embrace of the models of reason found within the societies in which those works have emerged. Access to the 'truth' of these works could be gained only through analysis of their form: their patterns, processes and contradictions. Complementing Kracauer's interpretative philosophy – albeit in strikingly different ways – were Georg Lukács' *Theory of the Novel* and Ernst Bloch's *Spirit of Utopia* which also influenced Adorno in these early days. Although Adorno would later find himself on difficult terms with both Lukács and Bloch he forever valued their special capacity to give philosophical analysis an historical orientation without losing it in a history of ideas.

Adorno does not appear to have imported the historical style of analysis into his formal studies at the University of Frankfurt. It is not known whether he, at that time, even considered any attempt to do so as appropriate to the institutions of academic philosophy. His doctoral dissertation, entitled *The Transcendence of the Material and Noematic in Husserl's Phenomenology*, is described by his faithful editor, Rolf Tiedemann, as merely 'philosophy of the school', that is, of the school – such as it was – of Adorno's neo-Kantian supervisor Hans Cornelius (GS 1 376). Following his return to Frankfurt from Vienna, Adorno undertook a further work of academic philosophy, a *Habilitationsschrift* required to be eligible for a permanent teaching position within the German university system. The title of the work, completed in 1927, is *The Concept of the Unconscious in the Transcendental Theory of Mind*. In its Preface Adorno stated, with some exaggeration, that his study was aligned with the basic system of Cornelius (GS 1 81). This claim undermined the originality of the work, and Adorno, warned that his putative examiners would find only Cornelius in it, decided against submitting it for assessment. This work is, in fact, both more creative and of more significance in the evolution of Adorno's thought than is commonly appreciated.[4] Nevertheless, it is surprisingly unmarked by the distinctive philosophical style of analysis that Adorno had already gained from Kracauer.

It was at around the time of his abortive *Habilitationsschrift* that Adorno made the acquaintance of Walter Benjamin. This relationship was to be of enormous importance to Adorno, both philosophically and personally. Their correspondence, from 1928 to 1940 (in 1940 Benjamin, in fear of imminent arrest by the Nazi authorities, took his own life) reaches astonishing levels of complexity. They sympathetically press each other into ever richer theorizations of their latest positions. Under Benjamin's influence Adorno began to think more deeply about the problematic relation of philosophical and other forms of theoretical conceptualizations to reality itself. Particular and individual moments – traditionally neglected because of theory's preference for the general and universal – were instead interpreted as illuminations of reality. Benjamin, Adorno wrote, 'was impelled to break the bonds of a logic which covers over the particular with the universal or merely abstracts the universal from the particular' (P 230). The effort to rescue the particular from overbearing systems would, as we shall see, take on a humanistic objective.

In 1931 Adorno presented a wholly new *Habilitationsschrift* to the Frankfurt faculty. Published in 1933, with the title *Kierkegaard: Construction of the Aesthetic*, the work is unapologetic in its disregard for academic expedience. It was dedicated to Kracauer. Some continuity with the earlier *Habilitationsschrift* can be observed, though it is free of all interest in Cornelius. Adorno sought to reveal the inevitable 'contradictions' and 'aporias' that attend a philosophy built upon a pure space of subjectivity, or, in the case of Kierkegaard, inwardness. However, the influence of Benjamin is overt and the book has an entirely different 'methodology' to any work of philosophy Adorno had written before. Adorno develops his reading of Kierkegaard's notion of the 'aesthetic' through a series of loosely connected chapters in which various parts of Kierkegaard's texts are assembled in unfamiliar ways in order to allow them to express their central historical content. The book contained Adorno's first use of Benjamin's notion of a 'constellation' of concepts. Since the specificity of an object cannot be captured by the general and universal determinations provided by concepts, we must articulate it within a constellation of concepts. These concepts together – never individually and never directly – point us towards the object. The senior member of the committee charged with assessing the *Habilitationsschrift* was Paul Tillich, and in his report he noted an element of the analytical style which – although he perhaps did not know it – acutely picked up on a distinctive aspect of Benjamin's influence. He wrote that the truth at which Adorno's philosophy aimed lay 'in the interpretation of the tiniest facts of each historical moment' (quoted in Wiggershaus 1994: 93). Benjamin, in a project which Adorno enthusiastically encouraged, attempted in just that way to read off the history of nineteenth-century Paris through an examination of the arcades that had survived the modernization of the city. Adorno later described this sensibility in Benjamin, in which 'small or shabby objects like dust and plush' become visible, as a process of attentiveness to

> … everything that has slipped through the conventional con-
> ceptual net or to things which have been esteemed too trivial by
> the prevailing spirit for it to have left any traces other than those
> of hasty judgment.
>
> (P 240)

Adorno's inaugural lecture as a holder of a *venia legendi* (permission to teach at a university), given in 1931, was less adventurous and obscure than the Kierkegaard book. In a quite programmatic way it set out a number of principles and positions from which Adorno was never to withdraw even as his conception of philosophy developed. The lecture, 'The Actuality of Philosophy', specifically criticized formalism, positivism, phenomenology and irrationalism on the basis of the differing ways in which, allegedly, their methodologies are unable to grasp the specific nature of particular, historical reality. Adorno dismisses naturalistic methodologies and proposes, in line with his historical conception of theory, that philosophy take on an interpretative dimension (a radical hermeneutics, in effect).

It was during the period of Adorno's post-doctoral studies that he first met Max Horkheimer. Horkheimer was a member of the committee that accepted Adorno's (Kierkegaard) *Habilitationsschrift* (and indeed had conveyed to Adorno the Faculty's concerns about the 1927 effort). In 1931 Horkheimer took up the directorship of Frankfurt's Institute for Social Research and was at the same time appointed Professor of Social Philosophy at the university. The Institute had been established in 1922 thanks to a substantial private endowment (made by Felix Weil). Its Marxist leaning purpose was the study, through the combined use of theory and empirical investigation, of the relationship between social behaviour and economic structures. Horkheimer was the Institute's second director and his fellow researchers – during his early years there – were Erich Fromm, Leo Lowenthal and Friedrich Pollock. Under Horkheimer's influence, and through his exceptional theoretical abilities, the Institute developed the type of enquiry that soon came to be known as 'critical theory'. Critical theory endeavoured to bring together philosophy, sociology, economics, law and empirical research in order to overcome the supposed blind spots from which the disciplines suffered when working purely within their own boundaries. Horkheimer's programmatic essay 'Traditional and Critical Theory' expresses the early ideals of the Institute: to break the traditional academic division of intellectual labour and thereby to uncover the oppressive, determining forces of capitalism.[5] This critical enterprise was to contribute to emancipation from those forces.

The ideological orientation of the Institute made it an enemy of the National Socialists who, not long after they assumed power, ordered its closure. It then began a period of migration within Europe before re-establishing itself in New York. During its exile the membership of the Institute expanded. It was joined by the philosopher Herbert Marcuse and, in New York, by Adorno. Adorno, prior to the war, had held no position at the Institute and was therefore not involved in its large-scale research projects. However, he was a frequent contributor to the Institute's journal (*Zeitschrift für Sozialforschung*), in which he published some of his seminal essays on the sociology of music.

Adorno's own migration began as a direct consequence of the Nazis' 1933 Civil Service Law. This law excluded 'non-Aryans' from positions within the civil service, whose branches included university professorships (his *venia legendi* was rescinded). The 1930s became for Adorno a period not only of career uncertainty but of some degree of institutional isolation. He travelled to London to explore the possibility of an academic position there, an effort which proved fruitless. However, he accepted the surprising advice of enrolling at the University of Oxford as an advanced – that is, doctoral – student. His status as a student at least gave him a legitimate reason to be in England and, perhaps, some preparation for professional entry to the British academic system. He tried to make the most of these largely inappropriate circumstances. The official topic of his research was a critique of Husserl's phenomenology, nominally supervised by Gilbert Ryle, of whom Adorno spoke positively. Published eventually in 1956, in heavily revised form, as *The Metacritique of Epistemology* (though the existing English translation is called *Against Epistemology*), it is a more conventional enterprise than the Kierkegaard book. Echoing the first *Habilitationsschrift*, Adorno attempted to reveal the antinomies of a philosophical system that fails to accommodate itself to the material conditions of experience. All in all, Oxford was not a happy place for Adorno. Separated from his fiancée Margarete 'Gretel' Karplus, whom he would marry in London in 1937, and detached from the Frankfurt philosophical community, he found himself in the midst of few who could sympathize with him personally or philosophically.[6]

It was in the course of Adorno's Oxford years that Horkheimer succeeded in re-establishing the Institute in New York. Horkheimer was anxious to protect the Institute from disadvantaging perceptions of being a left-wing entity and he directed its members to avoid the use of politically charged concepts (i.e. those of historical materialism). Criticisms of Fascism and National Socialism were conducted more or less without any overt reference to the anti-Capitalist commitments that had launched the Institute in Germany. This prudent decision served the Institute well as its refoundation in Frankfurt after the war was funded by the American governing authorities who tasked it with the responsibility of exploring and exposing the cultural roots of National Socialism. Horkheimer was able to bring Adorno to New York by gaining for him a senior research position at the Princeton Radio Project (directed by Paul Lazarsfeld). The project, which Adorno joined in 1938, was engaged in an empirical study of the radio listening habits of Americans. Adorno was both untrained for that form of research and also deeply suspicious of it. It was not, however, the last such project with which he would be involved. In 1944 he became one of the four-member team responsible for the monumental University of California, Berkeley *Authoritarian Personality* inquiry (published in 1950) which investigated the complex relationship between authority and prejudice. The project's theoretical sophistication was largely due to Adorno. In the preface to a later edition of the *Authoritarian Personality*, two of Adorno's fellow researchers – Daniel Levinson and R. Nevitt Sanford – noted that Adorno's contribution had 'led to an expansion and deepening' of the work (Adorno, Frenkel-Brunswick, Levinson and Sanford 1982: v). Upon his return to Germany Adorno directed a number of enquiries into the perceptions of Germans of their guilt and responsibilities for the Nazi era.[7] Wherever these projects involved pre-prepared sets of questions, Adorno refused to allow their aggregated findings to speak for themselves. They had to be interpreted as individual expressions within a social totality that was often invisible to those responding to the questionnaires. In accounting for the determining power of the social totality on human behaviour Adorno used all such concepts as seemed appropriate to him, ranging from psychoanalysis and classical sociology to idealist philosophy.

On the grounds of ill-health Horkheimer moved in 1941 from New York to southern California. Adorno soon followed him as they were planning a collaborative book project. Among a remarkably

gifted group of European émigrés who preceded Adorno to Los
Angeles was Arnold Schoenberg, whom Adorno had known from
Vienna and whose conception of music he had combatively cham-
pioned in a number of published pieces. Thomas Mann was also
there. Adorno would be of no small use to Mann who at that time was
writing *Doctor Faustus*. The novel's central character, Adrian Leverkühn,
is a fictional modernist composer whose techniques Mann had
borrowed from Schoenberg, with the help of Adorno's expert guidance.
Looking back on the creation of *Doctor Faustus*, Mann acknowledged
Adorno's 'exceptional technical knowledge and intellectual attainments'
(Mann 1961: 37). Even after he had officially resettled in West
Germany, Adorno would return to California several times in the early
1950s both for academic projects and with a view to completing the
residency requirements for American citizenship.

The work that would turn out to be the most significant
achievement of Adorno's time in America was *Dialectic of Enlightenment*
(1944), completed with Horkheimer in Los Angeles. *Dialectic of
Enlightenment* fundamentally redefines the philosophical basis and
scope of critical theory. Adorno and Horkheimer set out to explain
the twin developments of instrumental reason and of capitalism as
historical processes which began with the promise of emancipation:
emancipation from nature, from blind force, from dependency and
from authority. Yet history has witnessed, they claimed, the collapse
of all of these Enlightenment ideals into new forms of control,
domination and myth. They offer a radical account of the evolution
of our modern sense of individuality and find it to be a process of
self-abnegation and cruelty. The resources of psychoanalysis are
enlisted in their narrative. Stupefying popular culture – in a chapter
clearly authored more or less entirely by Adorno – is interpreted as
consonant with the limited form of rationality that enables capitalist
societies to reproduce themselves. The analytical perspective
Adorno and Horkheimer develop through the examination of reason,
capitalism and individualism is used to tackle the social pathology
of Anti-Semitism. The themes and the rhetorical power of the book

continue to disconcert its readers. *Dialectic of Enlightenment* seems to offer a perspective from which the totality of Western society can be mercilessly criticized. It was understood, by radical movements some twenty years after its first appearance, as a diagnosis that should lead necessarily to transformative action, even though Adorno himself never placed any such confidence in the revelatory power of philosophy. The expectations that seemed to be raised as much by the narrative force of *Dialectic of Enlightenment* as of its claims would return to haunt Adorno.

Adorno's standing philosophical commitments to history and particularity took on a new significance for him as he attempted to orient philosophy towards engagement with the catastrophe of the Holocaust. The neglect of particularity, which concerned him ever since his reading of Benjamin, was not simply a methodological problem: it was truly a normative one. When a system declares some feature of reality to be inessential or irrelevant it is an act of violence against that feature: it is an attempt to exclude it from reality by excluding it from significance. As we shall see, the image of Auschwitz – the encapsulation of the human cost of the violence of system and identity – pervades Adorno's post-war writings.

In 1949 Adorno left America in order to take up a professorship at Frankfurt and a position at the Institute for Social Research, now restored to Germany. *Minima Moralia* – a book of reflections in personal and theoretical ways on the status of the good life – was (in 1951) the first work of philosophy he completed upon his return from exile (and the first of his many books to be published by Suhrkamp). It was only in the 1950s that he began to achieve what he regarded as satisfactory articulations of his deepest theoretical commitments.[8] The Introduction to the revised Oxford manuscript, published as *Metacritique of Epistemology: Studies in Husserl and the Phenomenonological Antimonies* (1956), and 'The Essay as Form' (1958) (which will be discussed in the next section) consider, in a variety of approaches, the relationship between experience and theory and the relationship between theory and history. These concerns also form the core of Adorno's magnum opus, *Negative Dialectics* (1966). The great work of aesthetics that absorbed him until his death, *Aesthetic Theory*, remained unfinished. He continued to write on music, producing books and numerous papers in this period, as well as dozens of essays on literature. His abiding worries about empirical social research led him to the forefront of a debate on method in social theory in which he found himself in opposition – in a conference of the German Sociological Society in 1961 – to a supposed adversary, Karl Popper.[9] While Adorno was pursuing all of these intensely abstract and academic projects, he also took up the role of public intellectual. In a series of radio lectures, in particular, he sought to stimulate post-war Germany to reflect on the socio-cultural commitments which had led to its not so very distant embrace of National Socialism. He challenged the public to consider whether German society was yet capable of realizing autonomous individuals who had the moral strength to withstand participation in mass movements.

It is worth noting the striking contrast between the lectures of the social democratic public intellectual who thought a mature society could be realized through education and debate and the co-author of *Dialectic of Enlightenment* who appeared to find no hope in any of the social arrangements produced by Western history. The student activists of the restive 1960s were beguiled by the latter, and were keenly disappointed by the absence in him, as he stood before them, of the inspiring radicalism they had taken from his earlier work. Adorno was unsympathetic to any form of revolutionary action, interpreting it as blind to its own motives and naïve about its likely consequences. When he took the side of the authorities against an apparent student occupation of the Institute in 1969 his lectures were targeted for disruption and protest. Seeking escape from the febrile atmosphere in Frankfurt he and his wife travelled to Zermatt in the Swiss Alps. Whereas relaxation was advised, to recuperate from a stressful and unmanageable year at the university, Adorno instead undertook a strenuous trip to the Matterhorn. Suffering from pains he was sent for observation to a hospital in

Visp near to Zermatt where, on 6 August 1969, he suffered a fatal heart attack.

2. Fundamental commitments and philosophical style

Although Adorno distanced himself from the activism of his students he maintained that philosophy itself could be a space for radical resistance. Authentic philosophical thinking is, for Adorno, a form of opposition, a form of acting which is independent of the intellectual conventions which demand compliance with the everyday processes of society. A great deal of philosophy, he held, also follows those conventions. Adorno often referred to authentic philosophical thinking as autonomous – it is capable of operating independently of the prevalent forms of social rationality – and spontaneous. It is spontaneous in that it does not conform to any defined procedure. Philosophy should, he contended, operate without the constraint of having to regulate itself under its traditional imperatives, the most destructive of which requires thinking to arrange its concepts according to prescribed rules. In a lecture of May 1963, to a student audience at the University of Frankfurt, Adorno declared: 'I belong to a generation that grew up in violent rebellion against the very concept of philosophical systems, and whose entire way of thinking was defined by that rebellion'. He went on: 'we had to break free from too much order and too much security' (PMP 20). Adorno devoted his philosophical career to uncovering the myriad of ways in which systems limit the kinds of explanations that philosophers could develop. As constraints on the direction of philosophical thinking, systems become an obstacle to objectivity. Fittingly, he described the last great philosophical work he was to complete in his lifetime – *Negative Dialectics* – as an 'anti-system' (ND xx).

Adorno interpreted philosophical systems as the effort to force reality to conform to concepts, principles, laws and relations that are developed in advance of any open examination of reality. He certainly

never held that there is some 'immediate' grasp of reality that our
conceptual activities somehow impede. That is the core thesis of
philosophical irrationalism, which he repeatedly criticized. What is
at issue for him, rather, is the assumption that reality will ultimately be captured through the right system or the right procedure.
This may seem like a mischaracterization of how philosophy goes
about its business. But many of the most influential theorists within
modern philosophy, and modern science too, emphasize the need
to establish the principles of the enquiry before the enquiry itself
can begin. They are concerned with directing enquiry, as economically as possible, towards what is essential. Important too is
that the result can be reproduced by anyone who follows the same
procedure. The outcome of a properly undertaken investigation is,
effectively, a neat fit of reality to our modes of enquiry. No knowledge that has not been confirmed through the enquiry can be
accepted. Adorno's worry, though, is that reality takes on the character
of the mode of enquiry that revealed it. If, for instance, our methodology advises us to break down reality into separable component
elements it will, in its analyses and conclusions, naïvely take reality
to be fundamentally atomized.

This tendency to explain reality through method is, according to
Adorno, driven by a desire for *identity* in modern theory. The distance
between our knowledge and reality itself is entirely closed when we
think we have succeeded in framing reality within our concepts
and by means of our methods. Adorno's idea of, what he calls, the
nonidentical addresses the spaces that systems simply cannot consider.
The nonidentical does not lie beyond us. It is not a mysterious,
transcendent otherness. Adorno's claim is that it is outside the reach
of the generalizations with which our systems of enquiry – among
them, philosophy, sociology, psychology, empirical science – operate.
The nonidentical is also lost to the social generalizations that
inform daily politics (about class, gender, race, religion etc.).

The prestige of systemization has prevented philosophy from
engaging with the kind of experience that should matter to us: that

which Adorno, as we have noted, associates with happiness. Everyday experience, he holds, has become manipulative and instrumental. Success and even survival in contemporary society appear to demand these attributes. This state of affairs, Adorno believes, bears the character of *reification*. Reification is the reduction of potentially transformative possibilities of experience into control, strict self-regulation and self-delimitation. The agent becomes thinglike without dynamic relations to the surrounding environment (the stem of reification being 'res', thing, as '*Ding*' is the stem of the German *Verdinglichung*). What Adorno diagnoses as reified experience is simply assumed by the various philosophical theories that he subjects to criticism. (Reification is discussed in greater detail in Chapter 2 below.) The aggrandizing theories of the subject – from Descartes to German Idealism and Phenomenology – taking their material from their historical situations, repeat at the most abstract level what is, in fact, part of the condition of social reality. Philosophy represents experience as a process in which the world is constructed by the methods and systems of the philosopher. This is reification because the philosophical agent is closed off from transformative reflection: consistent application of the method or system is the essence of the agent's business.

Nonidentical experience – experience that is not distorted or reduced to manipulation – involves, by contrast, openness to the objects – people, the things of nature – that we encounter. Experience in this sense does not seek to confirm to us what we already think reality is: that can generate only a 'tautology', Adorno claims (ND 54). Method and system are therefore alien to it. In nonidentical experience the individual thinks and conceptualizes in a way that is responsive to the objects with which the individual is engaging. The individual does not attempt to constitute the world. But nor is experience passive: it is an active process of interaction in which the articulations of the subject are challenged and refined. The answer to reified 'constitutive' subjectivity is not, as the irrationalists demand, the denigration of the subject. Rather subjectivity realizes its real capabilities as it recreates itself in a responsive relationship to the things of the world. It is to that conception of a truly experiencing subject that Adorno is referring when he declares:

> To use the strength of the subject to break through the fallacy of constitutive subjectivity – this is what the author [Adorno himself] felt to be his task ever since he came to trust his own mental impulses.
>
> (ND xx)

Adorno's conception of experience influences the very way in which he writes philosophy. Just as, for him, philosophy must reject the thesis of the 'constitutive subject' as a principle of experience, the philosopher cannot behave as a constituting subject. This commitment guides Adorno's own philosophical approach or style. By style I do not mean a mannerism or idiosyncrasy, but rather how Adorno, in his writings, thinks through philosophical problems. Adorno's texts are his efforts to develop, without a system, the appropriate concepts for specific topics and to deal with them in their particularity. And his position on any given topic is the totality of those concepts. The positioning of those concepts around the matter under analysis is a 'constellation' of concepts which, as we have seen, Adorno adopted from Benjamin. As Adorno, near the very end of his life, noted of this philosophical process:

> ... from my theorem that there is no philosophical first principle, it now also results that one cannot build an argumentative structure that follows the usual progressive succession of steps, but rather that one must assemble the whole out of a series of partial complexes that are, so to speak, of equal weight and concentrically arranged all on the same level.
>
> (AT 365, editors' afterword)

The greater the series the closer it comes to expressing the particularity of the object. The constellation, however, is not another technique for achieving identity between knowledge and the object: it does not subsume the object, but attempts to develop the complex within which it can be articulated without reducing it to a general example of something. It is a process of construction which is responsive to the object.

Although the early influences on Adorno's philosophical development – all of which crystallized in the Kierkegaard book – are also prevalent in his post-war work Adorno, as noted above, is a philosopher in the wake of Auschwitz. His style embodies what he regards as the correct response to the failure of modernity's supposedly superior sense of reason and morality to stand in the way of prejudice and destruction. After Auschwitz philosophy must finally become the critical self-reflective activity of reason it always claimed to be. In this form it should no longer try to create the world after its own image. As he put it: 'Auschwitz confirmed the philosopheme of pure identity as death' (ND 362). Philosophy must instead be a process of thinking about how our concepts, as we apply them, distort the objects of which we are attempting to gain knowledge. Philosophical thinking in this sense – free of systematic and methodological imperatives – is, to use a term employed frequently by Adorno, 'unregimented'. The thinking individual, or subject, does not try to impose an order on the object: the individual is open to where experience of the object – generated through the effort to know that object in its particularity – might lead. Although Adorno finds examples of radically autonomous experience in aesthetic modernism – which we will discuss in Chapter 6 – philosophy alone for him is capable of providing us with an opportunity for a style of thinking that avoids identity and for which an unregimented openness allows, what he called, 'full, unreduced experience in the medium of conceptual reflection' (ND 13).

One of Adorno's most important explanations of philosophy as *the movement of thought* – a notion he takes from Hegel – is found in 'The Essay as Form'. In that work, which is itself an example of the genre it explores, Adorno advocates the essayistic approach to theoretical writing as it 'does not play by the rules of organized science and theory, according to which, in Spinoza's formulation, the order of things is the same as the order of ideas' (NL I 10). The essay is not, in other words, a treatise, methodically executed. It is an '*essai*', an attempt, driven by the 'mobile' intellect (NL I 20). No fixed principle, Adorno argues, can govern a reflective consideration of things. The thinker may attempt to anticipate the shape of the investigation by committing in advance to a definitive mode of procedure. But this, Adorno claims, is to assume the 'separation of form and content' (NL I 5). That is the mistake of thinking that the content of the enquiry – what the enquiry has produced as knowledge – is not determined by the form of the enquiry. By contrast, the essay has an 'antisystematic impulse' in that it 'introduces concepts unceremoniously, "immediately", just as it receives them' (NL I 12). Against tradition, Adorno grants the essay the capacity for precision over the clearly delineated, methodologically exact treatise.

He explores Descartes' instructions (in the *Discourse on Method*) on the correct way for rigorous enquiry to proceed. Descartes' carefully adumbrated methodological sequence is intended to enable us to avoid error and provide us with a path to certainty through a reliable procedure. Yet it is, Adorno claims, 'no longer able to demonstrate its own validity or self-evidence' (NL I 16). The method stipulates what the conditions of a successful enquiry must be, namely, that it must be pursued in the way the method specifies. What is not demonstrated in this ultimately internal criterion of success is whether the certainty that systematic thinking achieves is, at the same time, objective knowledge.

Adorno often described the style of essayistic thinking as 'dialectical'. It is, though, dialectical in a very specific sense. In Hegel's philosophy 'dialectics' is a moment of thought in which an initial judgment suffers from what at first appears to be a debilitating self-contradiction: what is described in a judgment – an object – appears to contain significances that the concept that is applied to it, in the judgment, cannot accommodate. (Hegel, however, is accused by Adorno of turning dialectics into a method, designed to help us achieve a complete systematization of all the apparent contradictory and opposed notions that philosophy and science have generated.) Adorno uses the term 'dialectical' as the illuminating experience of contradiction. Hence the name he was to give to his philosophy, *negative dialectics*. In dialectical thinking the object is allowed to speak against the finality of our conceptualizations. It operates, then, with a sense of obligation to the object: the obligation to deal with the object on its own terms. Adorno actually speaks of this disposition as '*Schuld*', which means both 'guilt' and 'debt'. It is a consciousness of what our concepts fail to say about the object and it is the obligation that the knowledge of that failure places on us to think ever more about the object in its particularity. Adorno writes: 'Dialectics is the consistent sense of nonidentity. It does not begin by taking a stand-point. My thought is driven to it by its own inevitable insufficiency, by my guilt of what I am thinking' (ND 5). He also conceives of this attitude as based on a love of things (reacting against a dismissive remark of Hegel's who alleged that Kant's thing-in-itself was a product of 'a tenderness for the things of this world'). He writes that to 'love things' is to relate to 'what is distant and different' (ND 191). The affective dispositions of love and guilt, not the pure logic of philosophical rationality, drive the immersion in objects as they are. And this is the historical burden for philosophy in light of the legacies of reification and destruction.

The commitment to the idea of unregimented philosophical experience enabled Adorno to fit naturally within the version of social theory that Horkheimer had proposed in the 1930s. Adorno's analyses move fluidly among traditional disciplines whenever any one of them presents opportunities for a more insightful conceptualization of the matter at hand. He dismissed the assumption that 'the value of a discipline is essentially determined by whether it is pure' (IS 124–25). Purity here is simply another constraint. He derides it as thinking in 'little boxes' (IS 124). According to Adorno, 'philosophy fulfils itself only where it is more than a speciality' (CM 21), that is, when it does not limit itself to its ascribed domain. This resonates with the idea – which we saw above – that for Adorno philosophy must abandon the security given to it by its own preconceptions: that it must be a system, or have a worked out method or speak about objects as pure abstractions but never about particulars.

Because Adorno's writings are essayistic in form they present the interpreter with substantial challenges. If we extract the core propositions from his texts we lose sight of the movement of thought that generated them. Indeed, Adorno implicitly warns us against taking the traditional scholarly approach to his works. Only philosophy that is without the experiential dimension – by which he means systematic philosophy – can be reported, he claims. Its controlled production can be reproduced without a loss of content. Authentic philosophy, by contrast, is inseparable from its original expression. He writes: 'Essentially, therefore, philosophy is not reportable (referierbar). If it were, it would be superfluous; the fact that most of it can be reported speaks against it' (ND 34–35, translation modified). The very process through which Adorno's philosophy unfolds – the philosophical disposition that inhabits its use of concepts – cannot be translated. Furthermore, offering an account or report of Adorno's philosophy involves re-presenting it in ways that Adorno himself deliberately avoided. The interpreter in trying to elucidate Adorno's difficult thought threatens to undermine it by looking for an implicit or underlying system that it does not possess. As Adorno explained:

> I would think it contemptible were I to formulate my ideas in terms of 'firstly', 'secondly' and 'thirdly', since this would amount merely to the pretence of a systematic treatment that is inappropriate to the subject-matter. What I am trying to do instead is to lead you undaunted over the rough ground in pursuit of the ideas and reflections which in my view represent the actual movement of philosophical thought.
>
> (PMP 23)

There is, nevertheless, a further consideration. Adorno's concepts and arguments may well have been forged through a process of dialectical reflection, but they were understood by Adorno himself as decisive interventions in the philosophical discussions of his times. The decision to publish a philosophical text – a decision Adorno was frequently willing to take – involves interrupting the 'movement of thought' (even if only temporarily). The text then stands as a philosophical statement and is subject to critical evaluation and, typically, its author's defence. A central objective of this book is to make clear just how deeply Adorno had thought through his most significant philosophical positions and to articulate justifications for those positions that are not in every case explicitly stated in his writings. This may require us to take lightly Adorno's claims about the inextricability of content from its form of presentation, but the reward may be to see more clearly and immediately the power and ongoing significance of Adorno's philosophical work.

Further reading

(1) Adorno's Life and Intellectual Context

Claussen, D. (2008) *Theodor W. Adorno: One Last Genius*, trans. R. Livingstone, Cambridge MA / London: Harvard University Press.
Jäger, L. (2004) *Adorno: A Political Biography*, trans. S. Spencer, New Haven CN / London: Yale University Press.
Jay, M. (1996) *The Dialectical Imagination: A History of the Frankfurt School and the Institute of Social Research 1923–50*, 2nd edn, Berkeley CA: University of California Press.
Müller-Doohm, S. (2005) *Adorno: A Biography*, trans. R. Livingstone, Cambridge: Polity Press.
Wiggershaus, R. (1994) *The Frankfurt School: Its History, Theories and Political Significance*, trans. M. Robertson, Cambridge: Polity Press.

(2) Adorno's Philosophical Motivations

Jay, M. (1984a) *Adorno*, London: Fontana.
Schweppenhäuser, G. (2009) *Theodor W. Adorno: An Introduction*, trans. J. Rolleston, Durham NC: Duke University Press.

Two
Society

An objective of Adorno's critical theory is to locate the determining influences of historical conditions on the ideas and practices found in contemporary society. The scope of intellectual phenomena he examines is broad, ranging from everyday beliefs to the key concepts of the most sophisticated productions of human culture. In considering the ideas contained in works of philosophy and art – literature and music in particular – Adorno rejects a common view that theoretical and aesthetic works possess timeless truths that stand above the influence of history or society. What those works express can be made intelligible, he argues, only if we see them as articulations of the deepest beliefs that are specific to the society in which they have been produced. Adorno does not hold the simple view – made notorious by vulgar Marxism – that art and philosophy mirror society. As only interpretative engagement with specific intellectual phenomena can uncover, society is present in different artefacts in differing ways. At one extreme we can see the naïve embodiment of social norms in, for example, positivist philosophy, in which the processes of everyday rationality are abstractly reproduced. At the other extreme, modernist art expresses a critical resistance to social norms (a claim to which we shall return in Chapter 6 on Adorno's aesthetic theory). To characterize it generally, then, Adorno's critical theory, in its interpretation of cultural phenomena, is ultimately an effort to bring to light the active influence of society.

We have already seen, in Adorno's biography, that he was – for a philosopher, at least – well informed about sociological theory and its methodologies from his university education, famously through his practical experience of empirically grounded psychological surveys on the authoritarian personality and also through his post-war work at the Institute for Social Research. Nevertheless, his social analysis is essentially philosophical. Even in writings nominally devoted to social theory – for example, *Introduction to the Sociology of Music* (1962) – Adorno avails little of the materials of the sociological tradition. Instead, his investigations of society are pursued through philosophical categories. Directing philosophical analysis towards social phenomena has placed Adorno's philosophy at odds with the model of philosophy as the practice of pure reason, elevated above history. In looking at Adorno's formative experiences we have seen why he came to regard the historicization of philosophical analysis as necessary. And from another disciplinary perspective a philosophically infused social theory has seemed to some (as we shall see) to operate outside the space of what can be verified by any existing sociological method. In that regard it appears to be merely philosophy.

What gave Adorno a preference for the philosophical approach to social theory was that philosophy took seriously the possibility of there being a difference between appearance and reality or essence. Existing sociological method, he claimed, examined only appearance. 'Dialectics', as he calls his own interpretative approach, 'will not allow itself to be robbed of the distinction between essence and appearance' (IPD 11). In Adorno's theory this means showing how a supposedly given fact – an appearance, be it epistemological, metaphysical or sociological – is mediated by something that does not appear. To seek the reality behind appearances is, he claims, 'to give a name to what secretly holds the machinery together', the machinery of society (SER 68). The conventional options furnished by sociology cannot, for Adorno, get at the mediatedness of facts nor access the conditions that sustain and reproduce those facts. By conducting social analysis without the usual methodologies of the social sciences Adorno radically transforms the very business of social analysis. He questions given assumptions about the material social theorists are supposed to consider and about the variety of certainty that is possible in the interpretation of society. Social analysis proceeding without a prescribed methodology gains a freedom to engage with material in new ways. It tries to gain access to 'unregimented experience' (IPD 57). The methodology he vehemently opposes, positivist or empirical sociology, by contrast, is accused, among other things, of assuming that society can be made transparent by identifying and categorizing ready instances of general cases.

The development of an interpretative approach to social analysis – which might uncover the complex social character of any given phenomenon – is not the only task of critical theory. Critique also is vital. Critique involves showing that the influence of society is in some way problematic, that it somehow harms human well-being. In fact, devising an effective form of critique, in that sense, has been a challenge faced by Marxist social theory from its beginnings, the seriousness of which was only fully recognized by critical theory.[1] Adorno was keenly aware of the worry that radical social theory is a biased and therefore objectivity-lacking perspective on society. It is commonly charged with importing a set of easily disputable values with which to measure society. What Adorno proposes, in response, is 'immanent critique'. He undertakes immanent critique in order to reveal in an objectively compelling way what he reads as the essentially irrational nature of society. This is obviously a daunting aspiration, confronted as it is by any number of objections in principle. For instance: how can anything other than human behaviour be judged to be irrational? And why should we agree that society is anything more than a notion – simply a theoretical construction – and thereby not an appropriate subject for predicates (i.e. rational or irrational). Adorno, as we shall see, is quite conscious of the difficulty of making good the allegation of irrationality.

In this chapter we shall examine what Adorno means by society, explaining the various ways in which he characterizes it as a totality.

We shall turn then to two potent criticisms that Adorno's notion of totality has faced. The final part of the chapter will involve an examination of the idea of immanent critique.

1. The social totality

Adorno's form of social analysis is intentionally interpretative rather than scientific. It involves understanding what are taken as the disparate facts of society as formed through a broader context. This context is not a network of causes in which the effects of social conditions are directly evident. We cannot, Adorno holds, achieve the kind of clarity found in a scientific investigation of causes. This is because the formative conditions of social facts are elusive, lying behind the appearances whose character they influence. What Adorno's analyses try to show is that society gives facts their meanings. Those meanings shape the decisions we – social actors – make. Facts therefore have a particular social function. They are not truths that are independent of changing history. They serve a role in the social order in which they appear.

In 'Traditional and Critical Theory' Horkheimer had set the agenda of critical theory with the claim that the 'world which is given to the individual' – and which the individual takes simply to be the case – 'is, in its present and continuing form, a product of the activity of society as a whole' (Horkheimer 1999: 200). And it is not only 'facts' that are influenced by the whole. Horkheimer claims that the way human beings 'see and hear is inseparable from the social life-process as it has evolved over the millennia' (Horkheimer 1999: 200). This notion of the social preformation of the world experienced by individuals is adopted by Adorno.

The key category that Adorno employs (as did Horkheimer in 'Traditional and Critical Theory') in his interpretative social analysis – one which is found originally in idealist philosophy – is that of totality. He claims that in order to understand society we must analyse it as a totality rather than as a collection of disconnected facts. This means, for Adorno, that the multiple elements of society are in some kind of ongoing reciprocal arrangement. The existence of society as a totality in this sense is not obviously apparent to the everyday standpoint or indeed to organized empirical observation. Yet it is, for Adorno, a reality. He does not posit it as an interpretative heuristic, as something whose status concerns us only in so far as it assists our understanding. Rather, for Adorno, it is the case that society acts as a totality and it is only when we begin to read social phenomena as its moments that their deeper significance can be appreciated. This has obvious implications for how we are to understand ourselves and our possibilities. 'Damaged life' – our condition – is a life pursued within the space of the social totality in which our beliefs and decisions are directed by institutional norms which seem objective and reasonable. These, however, are the norms through which the social totality preserves itself.

Adorno argues that reflection on the investigative frameworks we bring to society and its phenomena is required if we are to produce an understanding of society that is not prejudiced or preformed by the framework. In taking this stance he positions himself specifically against what he refers to generally as positivist social analysis. His main contention is that society, as a totality, is not an object which can be grasped through any of the methodologies adopted by positivism. Social analyses that cannot accommodate the idea of totality – because it is inaccessible to their methodologies – are false, Adorno argues. They misrepresent society by failing to see what gives rise to its supposedly objective facts. In this regard they are *ideological* in that they effectively grant epistemological validity to society just as it appears, excluding investigation of what underpins that appearance.

There are many other theorists who take the broadly holistic approach. Social holism, similarly to Adorno's position, maintains that social facts are explicable as the products of general processes. A classical example of this is found in the hermeneutics of Wilhelm Dilthey. Dilthey holds that social facts are intellectual expressions of the life of a society, and that each society, as a cultural totality, is marked by its own, distinctive objective spirit. As those facts are essentially specific to the objective spirit of their society they can be made sense of only by reference to that society. They also allow us access to the character of the society – the objective spirit – to which they essentially belong. There is, however, a substantive difference to be developed between Adorno's notion of totality and social holism (of the kind just briefly described). For Adorno society has become a totality. Its totalistic character is not an inevitable or desirable development. (We will return to this when considering Karl Popper's criticism of Adorno.)

Adorno's thoughts on the totalistic operations of society fall into three strands: (1) facts are 'mediated' within a social whole or totality (facts cannot be explained as atomized units, separate from the processes of society); (2) the life of society is comprehensively determined by certain core beliefs (the seemingly disparate actions of individuals are, ultimately, guided by behaviour determining commitments); (3) society is a coercive totality or system (society is not an innocent collection of individuals in that it forces individuals into forms of life that serve society rather than the deeper interests of individuals). We must examine each of these in turn.

A preliminary though crucial issue needs to be mentioned before we turn to those different strands of analysis. That is the issue of how the social totality determines the activity of individuals and their productions. What is the process that produces a change in those individuals? Adorno specifically rejects the notion that social influence can be understood as some kind of *causality*. This separates his position from what he takes to be Marx's conception of the causal relationship between the base of society – its economic system – and its superstructure – its various institutions. A 'critique that operates with the unequivocal causal relation of superstructure and infrastructure', he contends, 'is wide of the mark' (ND 268). His core claim is that causality does not capture what really happens in the social process. There is no centre of society – a base – that *causes* the consciousness and behaviour of individuals. The search for causal sources, Adorno polemically argues, follows a scientific model which is inappropriate for the complex phenomenon of society. He writes:

> The more its concept heeds the scientific mandate to attenuate into abstractness, the less will the simultaneously ultra-condensed web of a universally socialized society permit one condition to be traced back with evidentiality to another single condition.
>
> (ND 267)

Rather than causality there is 'integration – where the universal dependence of all moments on all other moments makes the talk of causality obsolete' (ND 267). Although Adorno considers integration – in which phenomena take on the character of the totality – to be a quite different form of social determination to that which is captured by the notion of social causality does it not, in some way, look causal, a process in which individuals are made into one kind, rather than another? The reason we cannot think of this as causality, for Adorno, is that it takes place within a totality which operates as a self-sustaining system (as we shall see in more detail below). The notion of a causal process – of even a network of causes – does not describe the same processes as those that are supposedly characteristic of a system.

(1) Adorno claims that meaning is mediated by the social totality. Each part of society can be properly understood only as a part of a whole from which it gains its meaning. Hence, for Adorno, the contrary claim, that there are facts that can be adequately explained without a social context which determines them, is false. He writes: 'facts in society are not the last thing to which knowledge might attach itself, since they themselves are mediated through society' (LSS 112). It is only by reference to a determining social totality that we can understand what gives facts the objectivity they are perceived to possess in everyday experience. An example we

will consider in some detail in Chapter 5, on Freedom and Morality, is the notion of individuality. The form of individuality valued today – self-disciplined, rational, in competition with the world – is taken to be a natural fact about human beings: this form of individuality is what we, apparently, essentially are. If we think of individuality from the point of view of the social totality, however, we can begin to understand it as contributing to the preservation of the social totality in its current form. As Adorno claims: 'the whole survives only through the unity of the functions which its members fulfil' (S 45). And in that light, independent and competitive individuals turn out to be a particular form of human agency that is specific to contemporary, capitalist society.

It was noted above that totality is a philosophical category rather than one of sociology. Adorno thinks of it as philosophical in the sense of being a *speculative* rather than empirical idea. Speculation in this usage does not mean 'conjecture', as it does in ordinary language. It has the Hegelian sense of taking a perspective which is above the facts, as it is only from that perspective that the full significance of facts can be seen. Obviously enough speculative thinking is opposed to those methodologies that see themselves as scientific. Indeed, the development of sociology, Adorno claims, has been motivated by the supposed need to counteract the essentially ungrounded nature of speculative enquiry. But this comes at a serious cost, he holds: 'When scientific concept formation ... sets itself up as reason's antispeculative executor, its machinery has become unreason' (ND 314). It becomes unreason because it actually prevents social analysis from freely considering the relationship between facts and what it is that might sustain those relationships. For Adorno, as we saw in the previous chapter, any constraint on thinking is an obstacle to objectivity. Philosophy as speculative thinking, however, 'refuses to have its rules prescribed to it by organized knowledge' (CM 13).

The speculative character of the concept of totality is evident in the following passage:

For while the notion of society may not be deduced from any individual facts, *nor on the other be apprehended as an individual fact itself*, there is nonetheless no social fact which is not determined by society as a whole. Society appears as a whole behind each concrete situation.

(S 145, my italics)

An important implication of this, for Adorno, is that since mediation takes place in a totality something about the character of the 'totality' can be read off from phenomena which are formed within a mediated location. The specific character of the totality is imprinted on the individual thing: 'the individual phenomenon conceals in itself the whole society … ' (IPD 39). It is on the basis of this claim that Adorno, indebted to Benjamin, refers to the task of interpreting social facts as 'social physiognomy' (IPD 32, IS 48): through the right interpretation of what appears to us we can gain access to the character of those social conditions that give appearances their particular content.

(2) The second strand of Adorno's notion of totality brings us to a very distinctive commitment of the Frankfurt School variety of social theory: the effects of capitalist norms of the social whole. Adorno holds that the shared belief by individuals in the norms of capitalism influences their behaviour, even when those individuals appear not to be engaged in capitalist activities (e.g. when they are engaged in musical production, in philosophy, or in leisure pursuits[2]). In order to be an efficient agent of capitalism one must have internalized the 'rules of exchange', and these rules shape the general consciousness of the individual. By exchange Adorno means the system in which all phenomena – things, labour, time – become translatable into a pecuniary value. He calls this 'equivalence'. Once made equivalent in this sense phenomena can be bought or sold for the universal token, money. The rationality which is required for the effective operation of exchange – the capacity to translate the diverse objects of the world into fiscally equivalent phenomena – informs rationality

as a whole. It is a recurrent operation of rationality, undertaken throughout our ordinary lives, and it does not leave our ability to engage in broader and more ambitious exercises of reason untouched. The tendency to translate everything into abstract value – what it is worth – comes to determine individuals' perceptions of wider reality; it somehow weakens, Adorno believes, the capacity for qualitative discrimination. The difference between things is no longer specifiable in terms of what each thing uniquely is. Rather, abstract value becomes the pre-eminent measure. And since all objects – within exchange capitalism – must be valued they can be grouped together, mutually translatable through the medium of monetary exchange. Adorno puts it this way: 'Bourgeois society is ruled by equivalence. It makes the dissimilar comparable by reducing it to abstract quantities' (ND 7).

This situation, in which the world is reduced to equivalence, prevails, Adorno thinks, because it is supported by a common consciousness. Individuals, marked by the rule of equivalence, collectively perpetuate the system of exchange. Adorno claims, in fact, that socialization today involves becoming an effective agent of exchange. He sees it as 'the underlying social fact through which socialization first comes about' (IS 31). It is therefore a form of behaviour constitutive of the individual's social identity. What this means is that the very process of becoming an individual in a society which operates the exchange principle requires the individual to be integrated within the institutions of capitalism. The spontaneous behaviour of the 'normal' person will be framed by the institutional norms of capitalism. It is no surprise, then, that Adorno stresses the centrality of the effective norm of the belief in equivalence to the preservation of the social totality. It is 'the hinge connecting the concept of a critical theory of society to the construction of the concept of society as a totality' (IS 32).

If Adorno is right about the integration of individuals within the institution of capitalist exchange then the idea that society is simply the sum total of the individuals who live within it is naïve. It does not perceive that the consciousnesses of individuals are shaped by forces in some way external to them, by 'the totality which they form' (S 145). As Adorno writes:

> What really makes society a social entity, what constitutes it both conceptually and in reality, is the relationship of exchange which binds together virtually all the people participating in this kind of society.
>
> (IS 31)

The 'binding' involved is not a voluntaristic arrangement of individuals adopting the principle of exchange on pragmatic grounds. Rather, that principle seems natural – it is second nature – and it presents itself as an unavoidable law of social action. To act against it – were that possible – would be to act against one's interests in self-preservation.

Adorno does not want to say that society is independent of the individuals who form it. In the following statements we can see that he understands society to involve some kind of reciprocal determination between system and society:

> Social totality does not lead a life of its own over and above that which it unites and of which it, in its turn, is composed. It produces and reproduces itself through its individual moments ... System and individual entity are reciprocal and can only be apprehended in their reciprocity.
>
> (LSS 107)

Or:

> Society is a total process in which human beings surrounded, guided, and formed by objectivity do, in turn, act back upon society.
>
> (LSS 119)

These claims distinguish Adorno from what he takes to be the abstractions of Hegel's notion of *Geist* (spirit). *Geist* is understood as an agency that directs individual actions without itself appearing to be determined by individuals. But it can seem that although Adorno sensibly excludes – what we might call – the supra-agency of *Geist* in principle, the way in which he avoids it in practice is complex. The norm of the 'rule of equivalence', though human in origin, seems to be beyond the control of individuals, somehow taking on a power of its own, and serving as a condition of socialization. How then are 'system and individual' in a reciprocal relationship? What Adorno has in mind, in fact, is reciprocity not as mutual enhancement but as mutual enforcement. The rule of equivalence, central to our economic lives, makes it more likely that we will be inclined to think about the basic features of our experience in a quantitative manner. If that becomes a normal way of thinking about experience, however, then the rule of equivalence will begin to appear less artificial and quasi-natural. That human beings can 'act back upon society' does not mean, under the conditions of the social totality, that they act in ways that undermine the totalistic dynamic of society. Rather, they act back in ways that consolidate it. Reciprocity, in this way, deepens the power of the social norm of capitalist exchange and entrenches ever more deeply our identities as economic actors.

(3) The third strand of Adorno's notion of totality is found in the claim that society is a coercive system. The use of the term 'system' is a highly significant one for Adorno, as we have seen from his remarks about his deepest philosophical motivations. Drawing on his own often critical reading of the German Idealists he thinks of systems as coercive in that in systematic philosophy disparate objects are forced into an harmonious totality or whole. When woven into a totality their individualities are suppressed, he argues. This pursuit of systematic completion is, for Adorno, precisely what society too attempts to achieve:

> Society is a system in the sense of a synthesis of an atomized plurality, in the sense of a real yet abstract assemblage of what

is in no way immediately or 'organically' united. The exchange relationship largely endows the system with a mechanical character.

(IPD 37)

The implications of this coercive systematicity are devastating. Never far from Adorno's thinking is the reality of physical exclusion. Physical exclusion is directly motivated by the desire for an homogenous totality, for, as Adorno has primarily in mind, a *Volk*:

In the form of the exchange principle, the bourgeois *ratio* really approximated to the systems whatever it would make commensurable with itself, would identify with itself – and it did so with increasing, if potentially homicidal, success.

(ND 23, translation adjusted)

Adorno here draws an unusual connection between 'the system' – capitalistic integration – and the identity politics that motivated so many non-Jewish Germans and others to support the policies of the Nazis. This differentiates him, to some degree, from those interpreters of the Holocaust who see German Anti-Semitism as grounded in sentimental and romantic anti-modernist tendencies. (In Chapter 5 we will see Adorno's argument that the weakening of experience within capitalism undermines the conditions in which human autonomy might develop. Without that autonomy resistance to prejudice becomes difficult.)

Adorno warns against the term 'organism' to capture the processes of the social totality. After all, for conservative, nostalgic thinking the image of the organism is an appealing one. It implies collective purpose. Adorno refers to this thinking, however, as 'organicist ideology' (IPD 38). It imagines society as more or less frozen into various classes and estates, yet working in mutual harmony for the common good. All parts of the organism, it seems, are equally vital (though somehow never quite equally prestigious). Adorno differentiates the notion of society as totality from society as organism as follows:

> In this respect it [the notion of totality] is the exact opposite of all organicist or holistic conceptions of the kind which may perhaps be applied, with retrospective projection, to agrarian regions ... If one wanted to characterize the concept of society itself, then the notion of system, of an order imposed in a somewhat abstract way, would be far more adequate than the notion of organic wholeness.
>
> (IS 43)

What Adorno emphasizes, then, is that a system imposes an identity upon its parts. It turns individuals into moments of itself. Whereas in philosophical systems the diverse objects or concepts of the world are mischaracterized to make them fit together, in the case of the social totality individuals must really become its mere parts: its functionaries. As a totalistic operation, society leaves no space for a viable alternative to itself. Adorno writes:

> Behind the reduction of men to agents and bearers of exchange value lies the domination of men over men ... The form of the total system requires everyone to respect the law of exchange if he does not wish to be destroyed, irrespective of whether profit is his subjective motivation or not.
>
> (S 149)

There is another key way in which system and organism need to be differentiated. The proponents of the organic view see it as a natural law of social organization. And when society is understood as an organism certain styles of behaviour can be demanded in the name of social cohesion. Ideally, each individual should operate, willingly, as a part of the whole, recognized as the common purpose of all. This situation is one in which there is togetherness based on this commonality of purpose. In contrast, a system, Adorno argues, actually divides individuals from each other. It divides them even as it pushes them into a common behaviour. The rule of equivalence that facilitates exchange between all human beings is also the rule that separates them. As he explains:

> ... the totality within which we live, and which we can feel in each of our social actions, is conditioned not by a direct 'togetherness' encompassing us all, but by the fact that we are essentially divided from each other through the abstract relationship of exchange.
> (IS 43)

The system turns individuals into atoms who can, the claim goes, engage only in opportunistic relations with others.

2. Criticisms of Adorno's idea of totality

In the 1950s a debate developed, among German-speaking theorists, about which form of analysis was most appropriate to the task of understanding society. The two leading protagonists were brought together, in 1961, to address a conference in Tübingen. Karl Popper spoke for the side which endeavoured to give sociology a more rigorous, sometimes scientific formulation. Adorno, his opponent, regarded any such position as positivism with its inherent intellectual limitations, or worse, as the ideology of scientism. He was the key representative of the 'dialectical' position. The designation 'dialectical' was to indicate that it, unlike its positivist opponent, would be concretely responsive to particularity, while also conscious of the mediated place of the particular in the totality. The conference did not end the debate. The so-called 'positivist dispute in German sociology', which it further stimulated, continued throughout the 1960s, with renewed criticisms, defences and counter-arguments by the various participants. (In addition to Adorno and Popper, the debate was joined by Hans Albert, Ralf Dahrendorf, Jürgen Habermas and Harald Pilot.) It is from the 'positivist dispute' that a number of powerful criticisms of Adorno's conception of the social totality emerged. Two in particular are worth considering for a number of reasons. By seeing how those criticisms might be answered we gain a clearer view of the distinctive character of Adorno's position. It contrasts strikingly with that of his 'positivist' critics as well as with the holistic theory with which it was mistakenly associated. And the question of how well Adorno can be defended against those criticisms – by himself or others – obviously leads to an evaluation of this position. The first we will consider is Karl Popper's dismissal, in principle, of what he takes to be Adorno's social holism. The second comes from Hans Albert whose criticism of the unverifiability of the concept of totality forced Adorno to try to explain further his use of this idea.

Although Popper was by no means the kind of positivist to whom Adorno could strongly object – in the Tübingen debate, in fact, Adorno noted many similarities between his position and that of Popper – Popper himself was strongly inclined to take the fight to Adorno. The essence of his criticism of Adorno is that he offers yet another trivial social holism theory. He sets out Adorno's position as follows (I extract from the text):

(1) Society consists of social relationships.
(2) The various social relationships somehow produce society ...
(3) Among these relations are co-operation and antagonism; and since (as mentioned) society consists of these relations, it is impossible to separate it from them.
(4) The opposite is also true: none of these relations can be understood without the totality of all the others.

Comment: the theory of social wholes developed here has been presented and developed, sometimes better and sometimes worse, by countless philosophers and sociologists. I do not assert that it is mistaken. I only assert the complete triviality of its content.

(Popper 1976: 297)

Adorno is indeed committed in some way to the four claims Popper attributes to him, but there is more to his position – as we have seen – than the picture drawn by Popper leaves us with. The basis on which Adorno can be clearly separated from Popper's incomplete characterization is that for Adorno 'totality' is not innocent: the forms of influence that work upon individuals, and gather them into a totality, are contrary to their deepest interests, to their freedom: 'A liberated mankind would by no means be a totality' (IPD 12), he writes. Adorno's position is, on the basis of that claim, no standard holism. By arguing that the totality is a coercive force he understands his own position to be no instance of 'the trivial idea that everything is interrelated' (S 148). (It is not clear why both Adorno and Popper should consider that idea 'trivial'.) From Adorno's point of view that 'trivial' idea does not realize that 'bourgeois society' is 'now fully organized and driven to subsume everything as totality' (PNM 23). Holism, at least in its non-critical formulation, is neutral with respect to that idea of, what Adorno sees as, 'the imbalance of institutions over men, the latter coming little by little to be the incapacitated products of the former' (S 144). We are in a reality, Adorno claims, where 'humanity [is] fashioned into a vast network of consumers, the human beings who actually have the needs, have been socially pre-formed beyond anything one might naively imagine' (S 148). And for Adorno this represents 'the domination of the general over the particular, of society over its captive membership' (S 148). The network of humanity, then, is not, when situated in the social totality, simply one of interaction and mutual influence (as it might be, say, in a well-functioning family or circle of friends). It is a network of domination. And crucially, as we have seen, Adorno rules out the idea that there could be a good, life-enhancing form of totality.

We turn now to the second objection to Adorno's concept of totality. During the positivist dispute he was pressed on what was seen as a lack of justification for this concept. This criticism emerged, almost inevitably, as a direct result of Adorno's anti-positivist way of asserting the validity of the concept. His core claim, as we have seen, is that society as a totality is all pervasive. It influences every social fact, but it is not itself a fact among the others: facts are mediated within it. He writes: 'That society does not allow itself to be nailed down as a fact actually only testifies to the existence of mediation' (IPD 11). This supposes, of course, the truth of mediation. Hence, if the meaning of facts or concepts cannot be explained as, essentially, parts of a holistic system then the notion of totality cannot be supported. Adorno, in speculative mode, refuses to play along with what he calls the 'positivist criterion of a significant datum' (IS 34) as a way of justifying the notion of totality.

But what sort of justification can be provided if we are to abandon conventional, empirically evidenced based models? Adorno does not deny that the notion of totality is inaccessible to the sociologically authoritative form of demonstration:

> Probably no experiment could convincingly demonstrate the dependence of each social phenomenon on the totality, for the whole which preforms the tangible phenomena can never itself be reduced to particular experimental arrangements.
>
> (LSS 113)

Hans Albert criticizes Adorno on precisely this point: 'the untestability of Adorno's assertion is basically linked with the fact that neither the concept of totality used, nor the nature of the dependence asserted, is clarified to any degree' (Albert 1976: 175n). He accuses Adorno of justifying the concept merely with 'verbal exhortations'. But Albert's allegation of untestability is actually Adorno's point. What Albert sees as a lack of theoretical rigour and conceptual emptiness is exactly what Adorno defends as philosophy's best effort to articulate the complex social whole. For Adorno it is in the very nature of society that it cannot be pinned down to experimental arrangements. He replies to Albert's complaint in the following way:

> ... the 'untestability' does not reside in the fact that no plausible reason can be given for recourse to totality, but rather that totality, unlike the individual social phenomena to which Albert's criterion of untestability is limited, is not factual.
>
> (IPD 13)

Between Albert and Adorno there can be no meeting of minds. Adorno's reply brings us to the central issue that simply separates him, irreconcilably, from positivism. For Adorno the question is: must social theory be restricted to concepts and explanations that are verifiable either empirically or deductively? Adorno's answer is obviously in the negative.

Yet must not some form of justification be provided? Some 'plausible reason' offered? Rejection of positivism is no licence for any alternative. Ultimately, what commits Adorno to the notion of totality is not that it can be methodologically validated, but that it enables him to explain what he understands to be the patterned behaviour of individuals (i.e. their tendency to act under the rule of equivalence, the variety of ways in which they regulate their actions, and that the commonality of their behaviour is no coincidence or accident) as well as the socio-historical context of intellectual phenomena in general:

> Without the anticipation of that structural moment of the whole, which in individual observations can hardly ever be adequately realized, no individual observation would find its relative place.
>
> (LSS 10/)

No individual observation would be understood, in other words. As he also puts it: 'the dialectical concept of totality is intended "objectively" namely, for the understanding of every individual observation' (IPD 14). To certain kinds of theorists this thesis would be vulnerable to the classic objection: where do we begin our search for the evidence which would establish the truth of the hypothesis? We cannot assume a concept of totality without assuming something about its character, but in so far as we determine its character in some way we leave ourselves open to the charge that our preconceived notion will interpret particulars in a prejudicial way, one which serves to confirm the hypothesis.

Adorno, in fact, differentiates his form of social analysis from that procedure in which a hypothesis is put forward which can thereafter be confirmed or rejected, in varying degrees, depending on how well the observed corresponding behaviour of the phenomena supports it. The strength of the hypothesis over other hypotheses seeking to explain the same phenomena will be its capacity to say more about those phenomena. Adorno rejects that procedure on the grounds of its inappropriateness for social analysis. He writes: 'Concepts such as that of hypothesis and the associated concept of testability cannot be blithely transferred from the natural to the social science' (IPD 42). He believes that the hypothesis/testability procedure is mistaken about the character of, we can call it, social material. Social material – e.g. the operative rules of the totality, beliefs which regulate our behaviour even though we do not realize we hold them – is quite unlike material objects or events that can, indeed, be used to test empirical hypotheses. To assume that social material is a species of physical material is already to have reduced it to something easily understood. The correct approach requires that 'the material – the phenomena – is interpreted in accordance with its own predetermined structure' (IPD 7). Were interpretation of social phenomena to be pursued in this way no conclusions could be drawn in advance. Phenomena would be taken not under imposed 'catalogues of hypotheses or schemata' but in accordance with their individuality and the particular way in which they take on the determinations of the totality. Adorno's project is not precisely to show simply that there is a social totality but that there is a social totality the influence of which marks its multifarious moments. Interpretation should uncover the character of this influence.

Adorno's interpretative form of social analysis does not provide criteria for its own success in the way that positivist methodologies do. Adorno undertakes a quite different, though less certain, notion of social enquiry. As interpretation its findings are not like those of scientific research, which must meet specified standards of certainty. Their certainty is accepted when those findings are seen to have been produced through strict procedures. Interpretation, however, does not operate according to any pre-established procedure. This is why Adorno writes that dialectics 'is unable to take its claim to truth as guaranteed' (IPD 9). In taking this approach to social analysis, Adorno's thinking is consistent with one of his earliest statements on the need for interpretation, given the objective situation in which philosophy finds itself. Interpretation is appropriate as the world which we are attempting to understand does not present itself as an intelligible and easily classifiable unity. Rather, the world as we confront it appears, Adorno claims (in his inaugural lecture of 1931), like a text which is 'incomplete, contradictory and fragmentary' (AP 31). Its nature and its elements are obscure. For Adorno this means that the 'indestructible and static' (AP 31) forms with which positivist methodology investigates the world actually render the world, falsely, into those forms. Adorno does not object to the procedures of the exact sciences *per se*, except when they are imported into the domain of theory: 'Plainly put, the idea of science is research; that of philosophy is interpretation' (AP 31). This interpretative approach is not one in which we might find the facts, as though they were simply waiting to be observed (like a scientific discovery). Rather, interpretation means uncovering the forms of thought which shape our world and which are at work, often unknown to the agents who are shaped by them, in the production of social phenomena: 'The task of philosophy is ... to interpret unintentional reality ... ' (AP 31). The social theory that emerges from this framework, from a defence of 'the unquestioned authority of the institution of science' (IPD 67), will have to be free of the 'illusion' of certainty (IPD 58). As we have seen, however, Adorno is very far from drawing the conclusion that the uncertainty of his approach should lead us to think that a theory of society is no longer possible. It is imperative that theory continues to make sense of society, but it simply cannot do so by importing scientific models.

3. Immanent critique of society

The critical dimension of Adorno's social theory is found in his efforts not only to explain the behaviour influencing operations of the totality, but to show, indeed, that those operations are objectionable. As we have seen, his conception of the totality is to be distinguished from social holism theory on the basis that for Adorno the totality is antagonistic to human beings. Social holism theory, by contrast, is descriptive, not normative. Critical theory must be critical as well as interpretative, then. It must show that society, in its current form, is normatively problematic. But how can Adorno make good on such a demanding objective, involving as it does an overview of society as a whole?

In fact, justification of the critical perspective – of showing that society is criticizable – is one of the central tasks of Adorno's critical social theory. For Adorno it means demonstrating that the claims that critical theory makes about the allegedly irrational nature of society are themselves rational. A rational criticism, in this case, is one that seeks to make an argument that is compelling even to those who do not enter into the discussion with the same sets of worries as the social critic. In this respect it makes an appeal to human beings willing to consider any argument which comes with no positional preconditions. Criticism cannot meet that requirement if it is the expression of a moral standpoint which not everyone can be expected to share. After all, there have been social critics since the beginning of civilization who, through their preferred normative frameworks, found society to be morally abhorrent.

Adorno's concern with the rational foundations of critique stems from his awareness that Western Marxism has all too often asserted the would-be truths of its own perspective from ideal or utopian vantage points. It is not difficult to see why those vantage points have been assumed: if existing society really is a debased thing, held together by norms that go against the better interests of human beings, surely we have to go outside – transcend – existing society for alternative norms. The problem with this move, however, is that utopian or ideal assertions are not difficult to characterize as arbitrary, as based on a conception of society that is merely the product of a philosophical imagination. From the perspective of the society which is subject to critique, utopian assertions will appear as *extra-normative*. They are extra-normative in that they are grounded in some space which lies entirely outside any norms that might have appeal to the individuals at whom the consciousness-raising exercise of critical theory is aimed. Adorno's term for extra-normative criticism is 'transcendent'. Writing against it he says: 'The transcendent critic assumes an as it were Archimedean position above culture and the blindness of society' (P 31). And in so far as criticism is transcendent or extra-normative it cannot persuade because it employs norms that lie outside the society that is criticized. Indeed, Adorno points out that the notion of a transcendent perspective is, in any case, illusory in that it falsely thinks itself free of the effects of reification and the other social conditions it strives to expose. It congratulates itself on an imaginary purity: 'The choice of a standpoint outside the sway of existing society', according to Adorno, 'is as fictitious as only the construction of abstract utopias can be' (P 31). The essential difficulty, then, is the unmediated nature of transcendent criticism.

Adorno endeavours to develop a form of critique in response to the failure of transcendent criticism. If successful, critical theory cannot be dismissed as just another ideological representation of society since its criticisms will be seen to be justified by arguments not embedded in a loaded critical perspective. Its arguments will therefore need to avail of norms which are meaningful to those whose society is subject to critique.

If critique of this kind is possible there must be norms even in an allegedly 'total' society that somehow are not saturated by that society.

They remain recognizable as norms we might act upon in spite of the potent formative influence of the institutions which constitute the social totality. The task of critique is to bring these norms into play with the possibility of being persuasive to people in that society. In fact there are two kinds of norms at work in the form of critique Adorno develops: (a) the norm of rational consistency and (b) the indeterminate norms of freedom and happiness. Adorno never held the view that formal processes of reason are reducible to context. In an often overlooked remark he writes that nothing 'but a childish relativism would deny the validity of formal logic and mathematics and treat them as ephemeral because they have come to be' (ND 40). (Adorno is very likely to be thinking of Nietzsche here.) As we shall see, this thought underpins his effort to develop a form of critique that is neither transcendent nor based on the social norms he wishes to uncover.

It is through immanent critique, Adorno proposes, that we can avoid illusory, transcendent critique. According to Adorno, immanent critique involves an examination of the coherence of a position by assessing it through its own values (this is the norm noted as (a) above). There can be no appeal to standards that are alien to the position criticized. He writes:

> If an assertion is measured by its presuppositions, then the procedure is immanent, i.e. it obeys formal-logical rules and thought becomes a criterion of itself.
>
> (ME 25)

That is to say, it is possible to make an assessment of a society using as criteria values it would recognize as its own. In this way, immanent critique will avoid transcendence and the attendant illusion of social detachment. This bare definition of immanent critique raises a question, though. Is Adorno not making a doubtful equivalence between the notion of logical consistency and ethical-normative questions (i.e. whether this is a good society)? In theory, a perfectly self-consistent society might be utterly vicious. And, conversely, it can hardly be a requirement of a decent society that all its norms be harmonious. In fact, Adorno attempts to bridge the space between the logical and the normative through the notion of the irrational society, that is, a society which is both inconsistent and normatively objectionable.

An immanent critique of society is a critique of those beliefs which hold society together. These are beliefs given by society to the individual who, Adorno claims, conforms to those beliefs. It is in this way that society sustains and reproduces itself. Adorno puts it strikingly when he writes that 'conformity has replaced consciousness' (CIR 236). Conformity, however, is irrational in that it can succeed only, in Adorno's account, when the individual holds contradictory beliefs which constrain that individual's self-realization. Contradictoriness is therefore the mark of irrationality for Adorno. An example of this is what Adorno sees as the contradiction between the concept of freedom and the restricted life-choices open to the individual: 'a contradiction like the one between the definition which an individual knows as his own and his "role", the definition forced upon him by society ... ' (ND 152). It is a contradiction between one's sense of identity, one's self-valued individuality, and the very real phenomenon of the identity one must also possess as a socialized actor. Were individuals to insist on a society free of this contradictoriness, society as it stands would be imperilled. This is because, Adorno argues, society needs these contradictions: they are required for it to persist in its present shape. So it is because society functions with these contradictions at its centre that Adorno describes it as irrational: irrational in the sense of being both inconsistent and normatively objectionable. He writes:

> By calling this society irrational I mean that if the purpose of society as a whole is taken to be the preservation and the unfettering of the people of which it is composed, then the way in which this society continues to be arranged runs counter to its own purpose, its *raison d'être*, its *ratio*.
>
> (LSS 133)

Ultimately, it is only when society is viewed as a whole that its essentially contradictory nature comes into view. Its irrationality, Adorno claims, remains imperceptible to non-dialectical thinking. According to Adorno, the positivist form of social analysis, looking merely at facts rather than society's interconnectedness, cannot perceive the irrationality of society: 'dialectical contradiction expresses the real antagonisms which do not become visible within the logical-scientistic system of thought' (IPD 26). And, again:

> ... the cognitive ideal of the consistent, preferably simple, mathematically elegant explanation falls down where reality itself, society, is neither consistent nor simple, nor neutrally left to the discretion of categorial formulation ... Society is full of contradictions and yet determinable; rational and irrational in one, a system and yet fragmented ... The sociological mode of procedure must bow to this ...
>
> (LSS 106)

Adorno is influenced in his formulation of the very idea of immanent critique by Hegel's notion of 'determinate negation'. In Hegel's *Phenomenology of Spirit* determinate negation is a productive negation which emerges from the experience of failure. To put this in the Hegelian idiom, it is the experience of contradiction between our beliefs. Specifically, it is a contradiction between our concepts of an object and how the object appears to us (what we take it to be in that appearing). Contradiction, for Hegel, emerges only when we are willing to reflect on the constituent elements of our knowledge claims. He characterizes this process as a 'labour of the negative' (Hegel 1977: 10). This negativity is not, however, an end in itself. It is, as noted, productive in that it brings insight into the naïvely held commitments which turn out to be contradictory. This is why the negation is determinate: it has a 'content', Hegel says. The essential element of determinate negation that Adorno adopts for immanent critique is that we can make ourselves consciousness of naïve contradictoriness without the introduction of criteria of truth from outside. That Hegel ultimately sees determinate negation as a moment within the progressive systematization of our beliefs certainly distinguishes it quite significantly from Adorno's notion of immanent critique, which is, in the end, purely critical. In Hegel we can move beyond the determinate negation to a newer understanding of our epistemic commitments. In that sense we move beyond the initial contradiction. For Adorno, however, those contradictions are embedded in history: critique can reveal them, but they persist until society itself has moved beyond them. The only function critique can perform is to reveal that irrationality (contradictoriness): it cannot go with Hegel in thinking that critique is already a step beyond the state of affairs criticized. As Adorno puts it, 'What is negated is negative until it has passed. This is the decisive break with Hegel' (ND 160).

Adorno, perhaps confusingly, warns at one point against an exclusively immanent critical approach. He writes:

> The alternatives – either calling culture as a whole into question from outside under the general notion of ideology, or confronting it with norms which it itself has crystallized – cannot be accepted by critical theory. To insist on the choice between immanence and transcendence is to revert to the traditional logic criticized in Hegel's logic.
>
> (P 31)

This statement might seem to undermine Adorno's own notion of immanent critique, but it is important to understand what lies behind it. In fact, it makes more complex the notion of what 'immanent' means in immanent critique. Pure – that is, undialectical – immanence would involve taking a culture entirely from the perspective of those who experience it. But since that perspective is the problem – it is uncritically involved in the world – critical theory adopts a perspective beyond it: the critical perspective.

Nevertheless, that perspective is not transcendent in the way utopian criticism is said by Adorno to be transcendent. It does not import norms which the position criticized would consider alien. But that tells us that Adorno does not believe that society is absolutely lost, i.e. that no trace of a wholesome notion of human and communal flourishing can be found from within it. The problem is, rather, that these notions have been misdirected in that they are framed in terms of the needs of capitalism. It is here that the indeterminate norms of freedom and happiness (noted as (b) above) are at work. The forms of success – of a good life – that are peculiar to a capitalist society shape perceptions of what human flourishing might be. But this society does not ask whether the ways in which the deepest human needs, which it claims to satisfy, might actually be inhibited by the institutions within which the satisfaction of those needs is to be pursued. That question, though, is precisely the kind that an immanent critique must follow. Critique does not adopt a perspective that is alien to the position criticized. At the same time it seeks to release the potential that the position criticized somehow inhibits. The contradictions that emerge through immanent critique point to a need for a non-contradictory reality in which the ideals of human beings – freedom and happiness – might be realized, without institutional structures. They cannot be made determinate – institutionalized – without subverting their meaning to us. In this way, then, Adorno negotiates the dichotomy between immanence and transcendence.

Immanent critique as a special form of critique is – it has to be – a form of social interpretation too. Society is not, as Adorno himself has argued, a collection of facts that can be set out in propositions. Indeed, as we have seen him argue (particularly during the positivist dispute) society is a totality which does not reveal itself as such. Its operations are not visible to any conventional form of criticism. He writes:

> … this resistance of society to rational comprehension should be understood first and foremost as the sign of relationships

between men which have grown increasingly independent of them, opaque, now standing off against human beings like some different substance. It ought to be the task of sociology today to comprehend the incomprehensible, the advance of human beings into the incomprehensible.

(S 147)

What makes society what it is, in other words, is not apparent, not encounterable in facts at least. This means that what we adumbrate as both the claims and the practices of society are interpretations, with all the disputability that interpretations bring with them. Yet we have to be able to identify the prevailing ideas of society − its conception of the good, its institutions − before we are in any position to assess with confidence the consistency or inconsistency of its commitments. Again, however, the question is whether the seemingly unending conflict of interpretations will encourage us to revert to a methodology which brings certainty by closing off features of social reality or whether the capacity of interpretation to acknowledge the complexity of social reality validates it as the only appropriate approach. We have seen Adorno's reasons for taking the latter direction in spite of the precariousness of its results.

Summary

Adorno's critical theory is an attempt to identify the damaging social influences at work in social phenomena. Although his approach incorporates sociological concepts, his critical theory is ultimately grounded in philosophy. It is his view that philosophy has preserved the distinction between appearance and reality, and that distinction is vital if we are to claim, as Adorno does, that society determines social phenomena (the appearances of society). By adopting this distinction, Adorno takes himself to be positioned against empirical or positivist methodologies which hold that the investigation of appearances is sufficient to describe the life of society. Adorno insists that interpretation – which tries to locate the reality which influences those appearances – is required by social theory.

He conceives society as a totality. Society is not a collection of disconnected facts. Rather facts (what things supposedly are) are interconnected – mediated – by the social totality, the character of which impresses itself on each fact. In this respect Adorno's position is dialectical. This idea of the social totality has three aspects. First, facts and meanings are mediated through the totality and are not atomized units. A speculative notion of enquiry is proposed to allow theory to gain access, free from the methodological limits of positivism, to the processes of mediation. Second, forms of human behaviour are determined by the social totality in which they are located. The practice of exchange in capitalism – the ability to engage in this practice being fundamental to socialization – influences human interactions more broadly. Conformity of behaviour is produced by the life-determining practices of the social totality. Third, the social totality has a coercive dimension in that it obliges all of those who live within it to adopt its norms for the sake of self-preservation. It is a system, not an organism. Individuals become parts of this system. Adorno rejects causal explanation in his account of the processes of the social totality because what is at work in social processes is the integration of phenomena into a complex which cannot be broken down into a series of causes.

Adorno's notion of the social totality has been dismissed as simply another social holism. However, what Adorno is claiming is that society has become a totality: it is now a coercive system. Adorno is therefore adopting a critical stance on current society's holistic life processes. The difficulty of giving experimental evidence for the operations of the social totality seems to disqualify it from serious social theory. Adorno defends his entitlement to use the notion of totality on the basis that it is not intended as an empirical concept, and that its influence on facts is evident in the behaviour of those facts and individual moments.

Adorno's critical theory not only interprets but criticizes society. Critique involves an investigation into the conditions of society that can be shown to distort or deform the possibilities for human flourishing. Adorno proposes that social criticism should become immanent critique. The alternative is transcendent critique which involves assessing social arrangements in accordance with how they meet some standards of the good life which are independent of society. No such standpoint can be defended, Adorno argues. For that reason social criticism should begin within society, and explore whether society meets its own standards (i.e. its claims to provide the context for freedom). Immanent critique is in this regard a variety of determinate negation. Critique opens up the prospect that society might come to a consciousness of the limitations of its processes. Immanent critique, it is argued, is nevertheless a problematic procedure in that it requires interpretation in order to assemble its case, and that may seem to deprive it of compelling force.

Further reading

Cook, D. (2004) *Adorno, Habermas, and the Search for a Rational Society*, London / New York: Routledge, chapters 2 and 3.
Hammer, E. (2005) *Adorno and the Political*, London: Routledge, chapter 4.
Rose, G. (1978) *The Melancholy Science: An Introduction to the Thought of Theodor W. Adorno*, London: Macmillan, chapters 3 and 5.

Three
Experience

The key critical issue in Adorno's account of the social totality is, as we have seen, the contention that contemporary society constrains the possibilities of human experience. In Chapter 1 the characteristics of distorted experience were briefly noted. A concern with the condition of experience is not confined to Adorno's social theory. In fact, this concern occupies a considerable portion of his purely philosophical work. He develops a distinctive theory of experience which provides him with a basis for the critical claim that experience need not take its current historical form.

The topic of experience has occupied a crucial role in the evolution of modern philosophy. The modern tradition is defined, against its predecessors, by its distinctive theorizations of experience. The efforts of the empiricists to determine the component parts of experience and the relationships between those parts are well known. And historically significant too is the transcendental project, reacting against empiricism, in which certain necessary conditions of experience are identified, often as a refutation of scepticism about the certainty of some dimension of experience. Aspects of these classical epistemological endeavours can be found at work within Adorno's philosophy. He too discusses the fundamental parts of experience – e.g. subject, object, concept, judgment – and he likewise tries to demonstrate that experience rests on specifiable conditions. These are conditions which, as transcendental philosophy holds, cannot be ignored or rejected without an attendant loss of theoretical coherence (by the rejecter). Adorno's conception of experience, then, does not operate in isolation from mainstream approaches.

At the same time, Adorno's investigations are driven by a quite new agenda. The task of the philosophy of experience can never simply be dissection or justification of experience, or both. Rather, for Adorno, philosophy must try to understand the potential of experience and, thereby, offer us a critical perspective on experience in its current socio-historically determined forms. When Adorno speaks of experience he is referring to the contours of how individuals interact with each other and with their environment (of other people and nature). In the fullest operation of experience subject and object interact without coercion or dominating intentions.

This chapter will begin with an outline of Adorno's notion of the relationship between reification and epistemology. We will then turn to a general account of Hegel's conception of experience in so far as it relates to the position Adorno advances. We will see that, in fact, Adorno's position is a materialist modification of Hegel's theory. The general framework of Adorno's theory of subject-object mediation will then be examined. The theory of mediation allows Adorno to develop a set of ideas about the identity and nonidentity of subject and object in experience, the topic of the final part of this chapter.

1. Reification and epistemology

As we have seen, Adorno holds that experience has, under the conditions of modernity, become 'reified'. Reified experience is a distortion of subject-object interaction: it is not genuine experience as such. Adorno, in common with other theorists who hold that there is reification, defines it negatively or contrastively. Reified experience is experience in which the subject adopts an instrumental relation, rather than a responsive one, to other things. Reification, as Joseph Gabel puts it, is 'a way of being-in-the-world' (Gabel 1975: 152). And that way is one in which the world is understood as comprising discrete and limited objects. In a reified world objects are delimited, or 'thing-ified'. An environment of reification is one in which objects are given fixed and limited identities. This, according to Adorno, allows them to be simply manipulated and instrumentalized by the subject. But this form of relating to objects inhibits the subject's experience as it engages with 'things' without openness to the possible richness of objects. Objects are, rather, experienced as familiar since they are shaped for use by the manipulating subject. The subject, Adorno argues, expects them to be amenable to its projects. As he puts that thought: 'subjectification and reification do not merely diverge. They are correlates' (ND 91).

Now one might well think that 'manipulation' and 'instrumentali-zation' are simply pejorative terms for what are, in fact, natural, evolutionarily achieved ways of dealing with our complex environment. Those who are troubled by the phenomenon of reification typically respond to that kind of contention, however, by identifying it precisely as a contention of a reified consciousness. A reified consciousness does not appreciate that it is, in fact, part of a social process which normatively informs its beliefs and actions. It takes that process, again, to be quite natural. As Adorno explains the general principle:

> I mentioned the concept of reified consciousness. Above all this is a consciousness blinded to all historical past, all insight into one's own conditionedness, and posits as absolute what exists contingently. If this coercive mechanism were once ruptured, then, I think, something would be gained.
>
> (CM 200)

Individuals, presumably, would become aware of the network of dependencies that constitute their identities, and would also deal with the world not as a given, but as an historical process. The essence of the problem of reification for Adorno is that it does not allow us to see our world – comprising subjects and objects – as a socio-historical development. Instead, it takes the world to be made up of limited things whose interactions seemingly follow a purely natural, given course.

In setting out his account of non-reified experience Adorno, as mentioned, adopts concepts from the epistemological tradition but it will be clear that the critique of reified experience places Adorno's philosophy in a difficult relationship with that tradition. Adorno argues that epistemology as a discipline of philosophy should not be abandoned even though it does not, as it stands, cognize the problem of reification. Alternative approaches to the theory of experience exist, but epistemology, even in its problematic forms, is to be preferred because it attempts to discuss experience as a structure of related moments (i.e. of subject and object). As he writes, 'criticizing epistemology also means ... retaining it' (ME 27). Its commitment to understanding experience as some kind of interaction is not misguided in principle even though, according to Adorno, it has never understood that interaction correctly.

By contrast, the allegedly non-rational analyses of experience, considered by Adorno, posit a oneness of subject and object. This is supposed to be some kind of original, organic, indefinable whole that has somehow been shattered by the appearance of conceptual analysis. According to that view, subject and object are merely the products of a sundered unity. This position is obviously suspicious of reason, which it sees as a disruption of experience. Adorno finds these commitments at work in Heidegger's 'fundamental ontology' and in romanticism. He dismisses them both as irrationalisms. For Adorno, the problems of irrationalism push us back towards epistemology, because it, at least, attempts to address the separable though mutually dependent moments of experience. As Adorno claims, today 'as in Kant's time, philosophy demands a rational critique of reason' (ND 85). Nevertheless, epistemology can provide this critique only if it is transformed in its fundamental character. To its legitimate descriptive dimension – identifying the components and structure of experience – must be added a normative dimension, one that can both diagnose the ways in which experience has become reified and propose a model for emancipated – genuine – experience.

Adorno brings into focus what he considers the deficiencies in contemporary experience by analysing a variety of philosophical models. He gives foundation to his contention regarding the 'withering of experience' (MM §33, 55) under the conditions of modernity – its reification – by exploring specific philosophical theories of experience. This may seem oddly academic: why would a critical theory of society regard the analysis of abstruse treatises as an important way of revealing the reality of reified experience? The answer lies in Adorno's thesis – gained originally from Kracauer – that philosophy is the purest expression of the rational commitments that we have. As Hegel famously puts it: 'philosophy is its own time comprehended in thoughts' (Hegel 1991a: 21). Philosophical positions unknowingly operate with the use of the deepest rational commitments of their societies, commitments about the basic shape of the world and the relations within it. When they describe experience they go about it with preconceptions of how the world is divided up and about the ways in which those divided parts interact. These preconceptions are socially influenced. Only through – what Adorno calls – *metacritique* can we gain access to the socio-historical commitments of epistemology. In a reified social world, Adorno thinks, reified relations are reproduced in philosophical theories. The effects of reification are manifest in a variety of forms. The following are the main features of reified experience: reduction of the object to a manipulable thing; reduction of the subject to that of manipulator; comprehension of the current form of relations as natural. Phenomenology, transcendental idealism and empiricism or the positivist tradition are subjected by Adorno to particularly strong critique, as these positions, in his view, offer accounts of experience which presuppose precisely what he decries as reified relations. Hence a critical engagement with contemporary philosophy seems to be an effective way of reaching into the condition of contemporary experience.

This engagement changes the character of philosophy into an interpretative exercise: we must interpret and reconstruct the forms of social rationality as they entangle themselves in the philosophical texts we are reading. This is to be distinguished from crude sociologistic critique which labels texts under some given sociological category: e.g. Descartes' cogito is merely the bourgeois personality, or Nietzsche's nihilism simply the expression of societal decadence. Such readings can be found in, among other places, the philosophical encyclopaedias of the era of Soviet Europe. In Adorno's hands, interpretation involves understanding what prevents a text from being successful, that is, from achieving its aims, and tracing that failure back to the problematic social norms it embodies. The incoherence – or contradictoriness – of those norms cannot permit the production of a coherent philosophical text. Important philosophical works, for Adorno, are those that have, with the highest sophistication, endeavoured to present us with a theory of experience in which there is no tension between subject and object yet in which, nevertheless, that tension inevitably becomes apparent.

In Chapter 1 we saw that Adorno's philosophical output consists, to a large extent, in engagements with major philosophical figures. The book length study of Husserl's phenomenology, the long chapter on Heidegger in *Negative Dialectics* and his intermittent assessments of empiricism are mainly hostile. His approach to other philosophers – particularly Kant, Hegel and even Kierkegaard – is generally more constructive: he sees them as problematical philosophers, but nevertheless as philosophers with theses that contain the potential to provide us with compelling insights. A comprehensive study of Adorno's philosophy would have to negotiate the details of his individual works of criticism as it is by means of his critiques of philosophical texts that his account of experience emerges: those texts exemplify certain kinds of errors or are latently innovative. The readings of different philosophers are genuinely specific. A critical framework is not simply imposed on the philosopher in question. Hence the particulars of those critiques are bound to be interesting to any interpreter of Adorno. It is not, however, possible to do justice to Adorno's works of criticism within the space of this book. Instead, this account of his philosophy of experience will extract the main ideas from those critical engagements.

2. An Hegelian conception of experience

According to Adorno, as noted above, reified subjects act instrumentally. It was also claimed that reification is not a natural state of affairs. Yet, what would non-reified experience be like? Adorno does, in fact, provide a substantive account of the theoretical basis of non-reified experience. This account is quite at odds with experience as explained by empiricism. He does not undertake an investigation of the supposed mechanisms through which discrete bits of the material world come, by means of physical and psychical causality, to be represented in the mind. He proposes, rather, an account of the possibility of a dynamic interaction between subject and object in which, in differing ways, both sides are transformed by the process. (In the section below on Mediation we can see this in some detail.)

The core of this dynamic theory can, according to Adorno himself, be found in Hegel's groundbreaking model. Indeed, as Adorno notes:

> These days it is hardly possible for a theoretical idea of any scope to do justice to the experience of consciousness, and in fact not only the experience of consciousness but the embodied experience of human beings, without having incorporated something of Hegel's philosophy.
>
> (HTS 2)

It is therefore useful to consider those aspects of Hegel's model which Adorno found so compelling.

Hegel argues – primarily in the *Phenomenology of Spirit* – that experience is a process of intellectual transformation in which the basis of our commitments to the concepts we employ is put to the test. Motivating this conception of experience is Hegel's dissatisfaction with accounts of human action which think of our relationship to the world as instrument-like. According to those theories – ranging, in Hegel's account, from empiricism to Kantian idealism – knowledge is an instrument that allows us to gain access to the world. In this arrangement, however, the subject is separated from the very things it is to experience.

According to Hegel, the unreflective consciousness – the perspective of any ordinary agent, or 'natural consciousness' (Hegel 1977: 49) – has many conceptual commitments which it never examines. When tested, though, these commitments will turn out to be insufficient. They are nothing more than generalizations which fall short of the specificity of the object they judge. Moving beyond those generalizations is, according to Hegel, experience. Experience is, in this way, a process of intellectual evolution. From this simple characterization of Hegel's idea we can see that it is quite unlike classical empiricist and materialist theories of experience which hold that we passively register the world outside us. They do not account for experience as something we undergo. For Hegel, by contrast, experience is an intellectually active process, replete with the examination or self-scrutiny of our commitments. And it is in the course of that process that we move into a deeper understanding of the adequacy, or otherwise, of the concepts we employ.

This process is not a business of pure conceptual analysis. Nor is it an exercise in trying to sort through and take an inventory of the concepts that we actually hold. Neither of these approaches contains an experiential dimension. What is involved, rather, is a process in which the objects which our concepts name are, in a way, allowed to 'talk' (as Adorno puts it (ND 28)). For that to become a possibility, though, alertness to the reach and limits of the concept over the object is required on our part. The experiential dimension is the realization that the concept does not in fact encompass the object in the ways we had previously thought or expected. It may even occasion, if we are properly responsive to the object, the adoption of a more adequate intellectual framework – consciousness in the Hegelian terminology – through which we judge such objects.

The experience of the insufficiency of our concepts for a particular experience is, fundamentally, an experience of contradiction. Adorno describes it as 'the animating contradiction' (HTS 53) in that it unsettles our fixed assumptions or judgments about an object. But what is the motive force that leads us to respond to – rather than to ignore – a state of contradiction? The answer is 'reason' (Hegel 1977: 52). Reason obliges us to change our concept when a contradiction has been encountered. Hegel writes: 'Consciousness must alter its knowledge to make it conform to the object' (Hegel 1977: 54). The use of 'must' points to the compulsion of reason. The term 'dialectics' encapsulates this process in which contradiction has an animating role. Hegel thereby describes experience as the 'dialectical movement of consciousness' (Hegel 1977: 55). This description strongly ties experience with responsivity. Responsivity is emphatically not passivity. In passivity the subject simply receives, whereas in responsivity the subject (dialectically) reacts and adjusts: it alters its knowledge. Responsive experience means experience never at rest.

Another influential feature of Hegel's theory can be found in the notion of determinate negation (which we briefly considered in relation to Adorno's notion of immanent critique). What Hegel wants to capture with this notion is that a productive contradiction reveals something specific about the limits of our conceptualization. The contradiction intimates failure in a materially informative way. He contrasts the disposition of determinate negation with that of scepticism. Scepticism effectively holds that the failure of some particular mode of justification entails the impossibility of justification in general. It thereby stops with the contradiction, unaware, it seems, that the contradiction obliges reflection on our commitments. A central pillar of Hegel's thinking here is that we ought not to hold

contradictory commitments. Determinate negation is the way
beyond contradiction since it involves reflection on the failure and
a revision of the conceptual framework. Scepticism, as Hegel
understands it, cannot see beyond its own framework and hence
remains fixed in its concluding contradiction. This notion is of
great significance to Adorno who notes that 'the concept of determinate negation ... sets Hegel off' from Nietzsche's 'irrationalism'
(HTS 77–78). What is being alleged of Nietzsche here is that he
grants final authority over experience to the subject. With that
power the subject – its judgments, its concepts of the object –
cannot be overturned by experience. Contradiction does not impact
on a Nietzschean subject.

An implication of the idea of determinate negation is the notion that
consciousness – the knowing agent – can correct itself. Significantly
too, the process of correction is not imposed by any external authority.
Even though the corrective comes about by response to the object
the subject must decide whether it is ready to adopt a new perspective.
This is a radical innovation: consciousness is not isolated in the
space of its own self-certainty. It has a capacity for self-correction
which involves an alteration in its perspective or intellectual framework. Hegel recognizes that this process of correction involves the
surrendering of beliefs in which we make the kind of investment
which can only painfully be abandoned. Hence he describes it as a
process in which 'consciousness suffers this violence at its own
hands: it spoils its own limited satisfaction' (Hegel 1977: 51).

Experience, with its dynamic of self-correction, has implications
not only for the knowing subject and its catalogue of beliefs and
concepts. The object which is the focus of the enquiry is also
changed, as Hegel argues, in that the way in which it comes to be
understood through the increasing sophistication of our grasp of it
reveals it in new dimensions. In this sense it is a changed object:

> ... in the alteration of the knowledge, the object alters for it
> too, for the knowledge that was present was essentially a

knowledge of the object: as the knowledge changes, so too
does the object, for it essentially belonged to this knowledge.

(Hegel 1977: 54)

Given that the subject's beliefs are challenged and transformed in
this process and that the object in some respect comes to be
understood in new ways we can think of Hegel's account as one in
which the subject-object relationship is dynamic and its elements
mutually determining.

Adorno's considerable regard for Hegel's innovative contribution
to the conceptualization of experience is evident from a great many
remarks. He nevertheless argues – in *Negative Dialectics* and also in the
slightly earlier *Hegel: Three Studies* – that Hegel's actual deployment of
his conception of experience is constrained by a deeper commitment to developing these categories in a systematic order. Hegel
holds that determinate negation is the logical path of intellectual
progress. It leads to a transformation of our understanding, forcing
us into a distinctive new way of understanding what we do when
we think we are making knowledge claims or expressing beliefs.
This, according to Hegel, actually leads to a system of concepts:
'The necessary progression and interconnection of the forms of the
unreal consciousness will by itself bring to pass the *completion* of the
series' (Hegel 1977: 50). For Adorno, however, systematicity is, as
we have seen, a prejudice about the order of experience and is therefore at odds with the openness and the exposure of consciousness to
revision that is characteristic of the ideal – Hegel's own – definition
of experience as dialectical. The essence of Adorno's accusation is
that experience is, as Hegel rightly argued, driven by responsivity
to objects, one in which we attempt to articulate them. That is the
promise but not the reality of Hegel's position. By constraining
dialectical experience within systematicity, however, the dynamic
elements are distorted and forced to a conclusion. Indeed, they
cease to be elements of experience, precisely in that they are geared
towards a predetermined outcome.

The 'negative' which is the moment of insight into our failure to encapsulate an object may be the basis of a more complex knowledge of how we relate to objects. And that moment may even lead to a new level of sophistication in our ways of relating. What cannot be assumed, however, is that it will produce a positive outcome – a new standpoint – and certainly not, Adorno repeatedly argues, that it can be an element of a further series of negations ending with a complete system of concepts. This system would be identical with the object since it would no longer be at odds with it. That is, the full range of concepts, and their interconnectedness, which would encapsulate an object, would be established. Experience would therefore cease. Ultimately this Hegelian agenda is a false one, pursued, according to Adorno, only by distorting experience itself into a sequence with purely logical values:

> The negation is not an affirmation itself as it is to Hegel.
>
> (ND 158)

> At each new dialectical step, Hegel goes against the intermittent insight of his own logic, forgets the rights of the preceding step, and thus prepares to copy what he chided as abstract negation: an abstract – to wit, a subjectively and arbitrarily confirmed – positivity.
>
> (ND 159)

Adorno considers his position to be a more consistent appreciation of the logic of determinate negation than Hegel's ultimately systematized version. The negation arises in the experience of objects. There can be no assurance that anything more than a consciousness of our failure to encapsulate the object is possible. No forward step is guaranteed. In his discussions of this difficulty, Kant, in fact, often turns out, for Adorno, to be the more insightful thinker. Although there are many reasons why Adorno finds the transcendental theory of experience objectionable – it is an abstraction of experience, a categorization-driven model, he argues – it nevertheless develops important ideas about where the reach of the subject ends. The idealists – including Hegel – could not accept the Kantian idea of a world that would not ultimately conform to reason or to the labours of the subject, but this is precisely what Adorno valorizes in Kant. Kant can make sense of the distinction between the *thing-in-itself*, as that aspect of the subject which is 'liberated from the subjective spell', and the *object*, as that which 'is "posited" by the subject' (CM 254). This distinction is a materialist counterweight to the Hegelian idealist notion of the possible encapsulation of objects by a system. The materialist dimension is that of objects which do not ultimately conform to our modes of knowledge (Kant). A materialist (i.e. non-idealist) dialectical conception of experience is one which emphasizes the subject's open-ended, non-systematic relations to objects. It is, for this very reason, that Adorno terms his philosophy a 'negative dialectic' in contradistinction to the constructive, system directed dialectic of Hegel. Adorno, as we shall see in more detail in the following sections, understands objects as irreducibly particular and therefore not encompassable by concepts which are, by their nature, universal. Experience, for Adorno, will be, then, the uninhibited and restless commitment by the subject to understanding, not to encapsulating, the object.

3. Mediation

The basic commitments of Adorno's conception of experience are found in the Kantian-Hegelian position sketched out above. What remains to be explored is Adorno's account of the differing ways that subjects and objects enter into interaction and how that interaction can be a transformative one. His account, as we shall now see, is offered within a theory of mediation. (The implications for this theory for the notion of what subjects and objects are will be examined in a separate section.)

A curious feature of the term 'mediation' (*Vermittlung*) is that although it is Hegelian in origins Hegel himself did not use it to designate subject-object interaction. Hegel actually employs the term mediation to explain a number of the key dimensions of his logic, not his conception of experience. The most important of the senses he gives it is that it is the intellectual mechanism by which we proceed from contingency to necessity, from the contingency of the world to its dependence on a necessary being, God: 'this elevation is a *passage* and *mediation*' (Hegel 1991b: §50, 96). Adorno's use of the term is really, as Michael Rosen points out, that of philosophical ordinary language (Rosen 1982: 176).

Furthermore, the meaning of the term mediation in the subject-object relationship is not the same as its usage in the notion of social mediation. Whereas Adorno's analysis of the subject-object relationship concentrates on the experience of interaction with another, social mediation refers to the social basis of significant facts. There is a suggestive connection between the two ideas of mediation: both are directed against the naïve ideas of given subjects and given objects. Adorno does not, however, write them into a single theory.

Mediation is not, in Adorno's philosophy, a term for a purely logical relationship between subject and object. The very idea of a subject or of an object does not immediately entail the other by way of definition. Rather, Adorno claims that we cannot account for experience without locating it within the interactivity of subject and object. And this will mean that understanding the experience one has as a subject will make reference to the objects with which one is engaged as well as the manner in which one has engaged with them. Obviously, the idea that experience is the product of some kind of subject-object interaction is far from novel. What distinguishes Adorno's position from most others is that for him this interaction must be a transformative one. The idea that transformation is possible through this interactivity implies that the process has the potential to affect profoundly what subjects and objects are. As he writes: subject and object 'constitute one another as much as – by virtue of such constitution – they depart from each other' (ND 174). This is

a significant statement in that it points to two important features of
the transforming subject-object interaction: first, that subject and
object are mutually determining and, second, they are not at the
same time identical. That is, the very operations of mutual determination are possible only because there is a difference between
subject and object. These characteristics of mutuality and difference
lead Adorno to refer, à la Hegel, to this mediational relationship as
the 'dialectics of subject and object' (ND 115).

A further entailment of the theory of mediation is that the relationship between subject and object is never immediate. Immediacy,
as Adorno understands it, would involve the direct, non-conceptual
relationship of subject to object, one of identity (to be explained in
further detail below). The thesis of immediacy, in this way, denies
the mediation of subject and object, holding rather that there is
some sort of experience in which subject and object cannot be
differentiated. For Adorno this is no innocent philosophical notion.
In reality, immediacy means a reduction of subject to object: the
object is somehow immediate to the subject as opposed to being
something to which the subject attempts to 'adjust' through its
conceptual activity. Adorno sees the thesis of immediacy, then, as
tending towards the primacy of the subject in experience. He
writes: 'The duality of subject and object must be critically maintained
against the thought's inherent claim to be total' (ND 175). Whereas
Adorno wants to establish that the structure of experience is dynamic
interactivity, the immediacy thesis falsely excludes that possibility. As
he writes, against Heidegger in this instance, 'We cannot, by thinking,
assume any position in which that separation of subject and object
will directly vanish, for the separation is inherent in each thought'
(ND 85). Should that assumption be made, Adorno contends, it is
simply a case of the subject doing 'violence' to the object by
making the object identical with itself.

The thesis of immediacy, though, has surely more to be said for
it than that it is merely a Trojan horse for subjectivist philosophy. It
might be argued that Adorno's theory of mediation hardly captures

the phenomenology of experience. Do we really experience objects as elements within an overall process of mutual transformation? It seems, instead, to be the case that we experience objects directly or immediately. Adorno does not actually deny this. His contention is, in fact, that what we take to be simply given, as immediate, is actually the product of a complex process of engagement through conceptualization. Immediacy is explicable through mediation. He invokes Hegel to express this idea: 'Hegel taught that whenever something new becomes visible, immediate, striking, authentic, a long process of formation has preceded it and it has now thrown off its shell' (P 155). And he also acknowledges that to explain experience simply as mediation would be to fail to recognize the experience of immediacy. He writes: 'One can no more speak of mediation without something immediate than, conversely, one can find something immediate that is not mediated' (HTS 59). The theory of mediation does not deny the apparent directness of experience, but shows that it is, in fact, the product of mediation. And as it is a product, our relation to objects – however immediate the experience – can never be described as one of identity.

Another issue we need to visit is how the theory of mediation contributes to critical theory. How does it allow us to make a normative assessment of current experience? What we have seen of the theory so far seems to suggest that it is epistemological rather than normative (i.e. relating to the way in which experience ought to operate). Indeed, the following passage appears to confirm that Adorno's interest in mediation is essentially epistemological:

> There is nothing that is not mediated (*Vermittelt*), and yet, as Hegel emphasised, mediation must always refer to some mediated thing, without which there would be no mediation. That there is no mediated thing without mediation, on the other hand, is a purely privative and epistemological fact, the expression of our inability to define 'something' without

mediation, and little more than the tautology that to think
something is to think.

(ND 171, translation adjusted)

Mediation is in this account a fundamental structure of experience.
It relates to the conceptual or definitional activity which – in that
distinctive Hegelian way – characterizes experience. How are we to
locate a normative element in this? Adorno's position is complex.
He cannot hold that we need to make experience 'mediational'.
After all, his point appears to be that it already is ('an epistemological
fact'). The contention seems to be, rather, that we need to recognize that experience is, actually, mediational. This says, in effect,
that the basic structure of experience is not distorted, but that we
somehow fail to cognize the scope of what it allows us to do.

To explain this demand let us recall, from above, Adorno's
remark about reification:

> I mentioned the concept of reified consciousness. Above all this
> is a consciousness blinded to all historical past, all insight into
> one's own conditionedness, and posits as absolute what exists
> contingently. If this coercive mechanism were once ruptured,
> then, I think, something would be gained.

(CM 200)

Adorno is saying here that our conditionedness is a fact, even
though reification obscures our perception of it. By becoming
conscious of our conditionedness, however, we develop a changed
sensitivity to our historical being. And that allows us a quite different,
presumably more sophisticated appreciation, of the possibilities of
our agency. Similarly, awareness of the mediational basis of experience should involve a new understanding of the manner in which
we relate to objects and how, again presumably, that relating can
become more sophisticated. If we simply take ourselves to be related
externally to objects then we will, through a lack of self-understanding,

be deprived of latent forms of experience. And vitally we will not see experience as our opportunity for transformation.

4. Subject and object

We have seen that for Adorno a mediational theory of experience produces a new explanation of subject-object interaction. The reification of experience involves a failure to recognize that subject and object 'constitute one another'. Of course the ways that subject and object determine each other differ. As Adorno puts it: 'Due to the inequality inherent in the concept of mediation, the subject enters into the subject altogether differently from the way the object enters into the subject' (ND 183). Adorno regards the subject as the 'How' and the object as the 'What' of the mediational process (CM 249). Adorno's explanations of how this process works in respectively differing ways – for the subject and the object – is rich in detail. And a powerful critical perspective with which to judge the history of the philosophy of experience is developed through those explanations. This section will look at the specific functions of mediating subjects and objects. As Adorno's thesis about the role of the object in mediation is the driving element of his theory we should begin with it.

Object Mediation. The function of the object as the 'What' of the mediational process is developed by Adorno into the thesis of what he calls the 'priority (*Vorrang*) of the object' (see ND 183–86) (I have used the term 'priority' instead of the translator's 'preponderance'). There are two reasons why it can be recognized as having priority. First, it is our effort to relate to the object that *stimulates* experience. The subject must go beyond itself – to the object – in order to experience. Adorno writes:

> What we may call the thing itself (*Sache selbst*) is not positively and immediately at hand. He who wants to know it must think more, not less, than the point of reference of the synthesis of

the manifold, which is the same, at bottom, as not to think at
all … The experiencing subject strives to disappear in it.

(ND 189)

Second, throughout experience the subject cannot arbitrarily determine
that it has successfully engaged the object. The business of declaring
the truth of an experience is not a unilateral power of the subject.
Conceptualization fails if it does not meet the object. Adorno notes:

> That the subject may not simply content itself with the mere
> adequacy of its judgments to the state of affairs judged derives
> from the fact that judgment is not a mere subjective activity,
> that truth itself is not a mere quality of judgment; rather, in
> truth something always prevails that, although it cannot be
> isolated, cannot be reduced to the subject.
>
> (HTS 39)

The object's priority does not, of course, place it outside the mediational process. Adorno explains: 'That the object takes priority even
though mediated itself (*selbst Vermittelten*) does not cut off the subject-object dialectic' (ND 186, translation adjusted). It is part of
that 'dialectic' and therefore not to be read as it is by traditional
materialism. Materialism takes the object to be prior, in a sense, as
pure givenness: the sheer presence of the object which comes
before any conceptualization and which stands as the irreducible
material element. Adorno specifically rejects this idea:

> The reduction of the object to pure material, which precedes all
> subjective synthesis as its necessary condition, sucks the object's
> own dynamics out of it; it is disqualified, immobilized, and
> robbed of whatever would allow motion to be predicated at all.
>
> (ND 91)

Understood as givenness we could not explain the *stimulation* by the
object of experience. Were the object simply givenness it would not

be part of a subject-object mediation because as something devoid of properties – a 'poor and blind form' (ND 187) – there would be nothing to mediate. Adorno argues further that this form of materialism – sheer givenness – is, despite its intentions, actually consistent with a subject-oriented starting point. It understands the object as a stripped down and empty thing, as the 'residue' when all conceptualizations and determinations are somehow subtracted (ND 187).

From Adorno's rejection of the notion of the object as a given we can anticipate why the empiricist version of experience, which itself seems to be committed to the responsivity of the subject to the object, does not accurately capture the correct sense of the priority of the object. Adorno notes: 'for all its sensualistic reduction of things, empiricism registered some of the object's priority' (ND 187). In empiricism, however, experience is, Adorno holds, a matter of the subject passively registering the object under certain categories of intelligibility. Empiricism, as Adorno understands it, naïvely takes experience to be a relation between two fixed sides: the subject and the object available in its totality. What the conception of experience that Adorno is developing insists upon is that experience is a process of transformation through mediation. So although empiricism and other forms of materialism may seem also to maintain the priority of the object thesis – as brute objectivity or as fixed states-of-affairs to be mirrored – they locate that priority outside the dialectical process of experience.

Subject Mediation. The priority of the object thesis does not, as Adorno puts it, mean placing 'the object on the orphaned royal throne once occupied by the subject' (ND 181). That priority is not a matter of giving to the object what the idealist tradition par excellence had given to the subject. The priority of the object, then, should not deprive subjectivity of agency. In fact, Adorno claims that our understanding of agency is enhanced by the priority of the object thesis, as he formulates it. As the subject is never in passive relation to the object, receiving information from it in the way that classical empiricism describes, it is the 'How' of experience. In experience the subject adjusts towards the object in order to come to know it: to conceptualize it. This is a power in the subject as it requires, what Adorno calls, 'unfettered strength and candid self-reflection' (ND 31) to act with flexibility.

Adorno's thought here contains the core of a radical theory of action. The idea is that the acting – mediating – subject is rational precisely in its efforts to respond to the object objectively, a responsivity that cannot be pre-determined. Rationality ceases when knowledge becomes a matter of the subject applying categories to an object, that is, of classification. (To give this some concrete illustrations: the notion that individuals can be psychiatrically categorized from a set of scientifically pre-established options is, as we know, rather crude and dangerous. And, correlatively, to think that the activity of slotting things into established categories is a realization of our full rational potential is obviously mistaken.) The notion that rationality is a feature of action sharply contrasts with the idea of 'constitutive subjectivity' (a notion we considered in the context of Adorno's general philosophical project), of a world maker imposing its will and agency on a totally pliable environment. A responsive, dialectical subject is free in that it has the capacity to be transformed through the very experience to which it actively contributes. Transformation is acutely denied, by contrast, to constitutive subjectivity as it is a fixed agency manipulating the world in accordance with its own determinations.

As the 'How' of mediation the subject – 'the necessary and painful exertion of the knowing subject' (ND 31) – brings the world of objects and of nature to articulation. Adorno claims, in this regard, that idealism, which ultimately misconstrued subjective agency as the creater of experience, nevertheless correctly proposed the vital idea that 'the reality in which men live is not unvarying and independent of them. Its shape is human and even absolutely extra-human nature is mediated through consciousness' (ME 28). More strikingly he endorses a Hegelian idea,

... that nothing whatsoever exists outside what is produced by human beings, that nothing whatsoever is completely independent of social labor. Even nature, seemingly untouched by labor, is defined as nature by labor and to this extent is mediated by it.

(HTS 68)

The notion that nothing exists 'outside of what is produced by human beings' might seem to align Adorno with the claims of constitutive subjectivity after all. But this needs to be clarified. Adorno himself declares that the subject 'is the agent, not the constituent' of objects (CM 254). What is meant then by human production cannot be equivalent to constitution. And we have seen why this is the case in Adorno's notion that the object is no mere given: were it pure potential its actuality would be entirely a matter for subjectivity. We can, though, think of the facts of our world as produced by human beings. Indeed as Nicholas Rescher notes:

Our knowledge of fact always reflects the circumstances of its being a human artifact. It is always formed through the use of mind-made and indeed mind-invoking conceptions and its concepts inevitably bear the traces of its man-made origins.

(Rescher 1993: 188)

But this does not require us to also hold that our facts bear no relation to the objects about which we form facts. The human activity of fact-making is an effort to conceptualize the object, and in Adorno's account this conceptualizing is responsive to the object. 'The cognitive utopia would be to use concepts to unseal the non-conceptual with concepts, without making it their equal' (ND 10). (When we turn in Chapter 6 to Adorno's aesthetic theory we will consider his idea of mimesis. Mimesis is imitative experience, imitative in the sense that the subject tries to make itself like the object. Arguably, Adorno moved towards the idea of mimesis in order to provide deeper grounding for the dynamic of subject-object mediation.)

5. Identity and nonidentity

It is for the idea of nonidentity that Adorno is perhaps best known
within twentieth-century philosophy. His account of nonidentity
and the attendant criticisms of identity thinking are, in fact, direct
corollaries of the mediation theory we have just examined. Adorno
contends that identity thinking – in its various forms – is a distortion
of the potential of experience, and it is one which is uncritically and,
indeed, unknowingly adopted by epistemological misconceptions
of experience. Identity thinking understands experience to be a
process in which the subject can effectively identify objects in the
sense of fully determining them through the concepts which are
applied to them: identity thinking, he claims,

> says what something comes under, what it exemplifies or repre-
> sents and what, accordingly, it is not itself. The more relentlessly
> our identarian thinking besets its object, the farther will it take
> us from the identity of the object.
>
> (ND 149)

Adorno sees identity thinking as a form of behaviour which cuts
the subject's experience of the object down to one of the supposedly
all-encompassing concepts or categories supplied by the subject.
This is to be rejected: 'To define identity as the correspondence of the
thing-in-itself [or object] to its concept is *hubris*' (ND 149). This
hubristic tendency, however, marks the history of modern philosophy.

The range of philosophies adjudged guilty of this is wide. There
is positivist philosophy – epitomized, Adorno thinks, by the empirical
social science we discussed in the previous chapter – which, Adorno
claims, understands knowledge as a process of categorization: the
object is known when 'identified' by the appropriate category. Adorno
attacks this as the aggressive application of 'wretched cover-concepts
that will make the crucial differences vanish' (ND 152). These cover-
concepts claim, somehow, to identify what is essential in the object.

Whatever falls outside their range is of no significance to them. Adorno describes this as nothing but the 'omnipotence of the subjective concept' (ND 85) in that the object does not, in that form of concept application, mediate the subject. In this way conceptualization is imposition 'from outside' (ND 145).

Idealism, another alleged subject-driven theory of experience, also assumes that experience involves the subject's identity with the object. The specific move of idealism is to understand the object to be some kind of expression of the consciousness of the subject (as we saw in the discussion of constitutive subjectivity). Adorno speaks of this feature of idealism as an all-consuming system which cannot allow anything to have the dignity of independence. Subjective idealism in particular seeks to explain what we experience as the object – the not-I – as in all significant respects the produce of consciousness. In this way 'self-preserving thought' (ND 23) makes the object identical with itself. This reflection brings Adorno to perhaps his most striking metaphor: 'The system is the belly turned mind, and rage is the mark of each and every idealism' (ND 23). It is, he goes on, 'rage at nonidentity' (ND 23) which it cannot permit.

While Adorno's targets might appear guilty of a very deep philosophical mistake it transpires that there is a specific moment even in the process of non-coercive knowledge which is identity-driven. Adorno claims, perhaps surprisingly, that 'we cannot think without identifying. Any determination (*Bestimmung*) is identification' (ND 149, translation adjusted). He also notes that the 'will to identity works in each synthesis. As an a priori task of thought, a task immanent in thought, identity seems positive and desirable' (ND 148). Now if there is an 'identity' agenda in all epistemic acts the basis of Adorno's disagreement with so-called identity philosophy becomes more complicated. If discourse cannot take place outside the constraints of what he calls the identity 'compulsion' (ND 157) then what is the basis of his criticism of identity? It looks as though the criticized positivists and idealists are simply explaining what thought does, as even Adorno acknowledges: it necessarily identifies. And his alarming claim that 'to think is to identify' (ND 5) appears to deny the possibility of the openness thesis that is central to the conception of experience that Adorno is proposing. If thought inclines towards identity, that is, towards fixing the characteristics of the object, how can the openness thesis be sustained?

We have to distinguish here between non-coercive and coercive – let us call them – attitudes of identity. In contrast to the coercive attitude – the one Adorno finds in modern society and in its philosophy – the non-coercive attitude attempts to close the gap between it and the object, without the authority of preconceived categories. It seeks to bring the object nearer by understanding the object on the object's terms. Hence he writes that 'the ideal of identity must not simply be discarded' (ND 149). Identity thinking, after all, expresses an ideal moment, namely, a 'togetherness of diversity' (ND 150), 'affinity' (ND 270), 'a pledge that there should be no contradiction, no antagonism' (ND 149). It is, in other words, a state of affairs in which a thing might be fully experienced without being dominated. This utopian possibility is 'rational identity' (ND 147). Adorno's critique of identity thinking, then, is not of 'rational identity', but of the coercive attitude which, in the ways we have seen above, force an identity onto the object. Nevertheless, identity, in whichever variety, is an objective of experience. Our appropriate response to the prevalent form – coercive identity – is not to move directly to 'rational identity'. Such a recommendation would show no understanding of our historical conditionedness. Rational identity would be possible only were the antagonistic conditions of modernity to be overcome. As Adorno puts it: 'If no man had part of his labor withheld from him any more, rational identity would be a fact, and society would have transcended the identifying mode of thinking' (ND 147). The step beyond coercive identity under current historical circumstances is, in essence, to begin to think our way out of coercive identity. Adorno proposes, in this regard, the idea of nonidentity thinking as expressive of the critical and historically appropriate possibilities of experience (to be discussed below).

In undistorted experience the subject relates to the object in the manner of, as Adorno puts it, 'nonidentity through identity' (ND 189). Why is it, though, that our efforts at identity – conceptualizing the object – actually also generate the experience of nonidentity? And how can the effort of the subject to 'disappear' in its experience of objects be rewarded with nonidentity, a term which seems to suggest the impossibility of that disappearing? To understand how we experience 'nonidentity through identity' we need to remember that Adorno thinks of objects as irreducibly particular. He speaks of 'nonidentical individuals' (ND 146). Our concepts categorize objects in general ways, yet they can never, as experience intimates, achieve identity with the object. The concept 'cuts short what the particular is and what nonetheless cannot be directly named, and replaces it with identity' (ND 173). The experience of nonidentity is not an experience of alienation from the object: it does not, in other words, intimate the absolute otherness of the object. Coming to know something is to know it in its specific particularity, something which classificatory concepts can never give us. What we see from this is that our epistemic labours are always object directed, yet reflective experience constantly alerts us to the gap between our concepts and the object in its real complex particularity.

Adorno's claims about the relationship between concepts and non-conceptuality are expressed in different ways. His core idea is the anti-idealist thesis that to 'refer to non-conceptualities ... is characteristic of the concept' (ND 12). Concepts 'mean beyond themselves' (ND 12) (Adorno quotes Emil Lask with that phrase). But he also confusingly speaks of the 'non-conceptual in the concept' (ND 12). What is problematical about that formulation is not alone its paradoxicality but its conflict with his claim that concepts refer to non-conceptuality (as opposed to containing it). Adorno presents his core idea a great deal more effectively when he frames the relationship of concepts to non-conceptuality within a theory of judgment. For instance: 'every judgment ... carries with it the claim to predicate something that is not simply identical with the mere concept of the subject' (ND 71): our *judgments* are conceptualizations of non-conceptual entities, objects. Hence judgments of experience contain conceptual and non-conceptual moments. They are a form of thought in which the concept does refer beyond itself to the object. It is through judgment alone that concepts can be referential (otherwise they stand merely as a lexical form). What is actually going on in subject-object mediation is the process of getting a judgment right: of finding the right concept to refer to the object, thereby adjusting to the object and also redefining it in so far as it is referenced by us. So when Adorno claims that '[r]eflection upon its own meaning is the way out of the concept's seeming being-in-itself as a unit of meaning' (ND 12) he might be taken to suggest that 'reflection' would lead us to consider *judgment* rather than *concept* as that unit. It is, it seems, only within judgment that concepts take on that function of meaning 'beyond themselves'.

The non-conceptual dimension of objects is principally what Adorno is thinking of when he speaks about the nonidentity of our concepts and object. It is fair to say, though, that Adorno does not develop a systematic theory of nonidentity and nor does the above discussion of the problem of non-conceptuality capture the full range of significances of the term (see Thyen 1989: 204). The following are some representative statements from *Negative Dialectics* (many more to the same effect could be cited).

(i) *Nonidentity as the irreducible material 'something' of a judgment:*

By itself, the logically abstract form of 'something,' something that is meant or judged, does not claim to posit a being; and yet, surviving in it – indelible for a thinking that would delete it – is that which is not identical with thinking, which is not thinking at all.
(ND 34)

(ii) *Nonidentity as the non-fit of concept and particular or of subject and object:*

Reciprocal criticism of the universal and of the particular; identifying acts of judgment whether the concept does justice

to what it covers, and whether the particular fulfills its concept –
these constitute the medium of thinking about the nonidentity of
particular and concept.

(ND 146)

(iii) *Nonidentity as another name for contradiction:*

Contradiction is nonidentity under the rule of a law that affects
the nonidentical as well.

(ND 6)

(iv) *Nonidentity as an experience of being obliged to live within the constraints
of the social totality:*

In the unreconciled condition, nonidentity is experienced as
negativity.

(ND 31)

(v) *Nonidentity as the impulse for freedom:*

[Subjects] are free because their overpowering impulse – the
subject's nonidentity with itself is nothing else – will also rid
them of identity's coercive power.

(ND 269)

(Adorno makes this claim as a rejection of Kant's allegedly repressed,
super-ego driven concept of agency. This issue will be discussed in
detail in Chapter 5.)

(vi) *Nonidentity as the contradiction revealed through immanent critique:*

Totality is to be opposed by convicting it of nonidentity with
itself, of the nonidentity it denies according to its own concept.

(ND 320)

We can see from these various definitions that Adorno employs the
term nonidentity in varying senses, though not equivocally. What

connects them is that each statement instances some form of opposition to a specific type of identity. But there is something else at the centre of each of them. Their language alerts us to the rather serious fact that recognition of nonidentity is not just a matter of logic or epistemology. Adorno's critique of identity – in spite of those logical and epistemological dimensions – is ultimately normative: it is directed specifically at what ought not to be. His view of non-rational identity, as we have seen, is that it is coercive in that it forces an object or a particular to fit a category. And, for Adorno, this form of coercion is precisely what happens at the level of modern social organization. This is no coincidence. As we saw, Adorno holds to the Hegelian-Marxist view that the prevailing rationality of society is embodied – with the problematic exception of critical theory – in philosophy. The identity 'compulsion' in philosophy is therefore a symptom of the society in which it operates. The philo-sophical form follows social form. In the twentieth century – in the world that Adorno lived through – social organization was pursued catastrophically by means of the constitutional assertion of pure national identity. That assertion was the violent, physical exclusion of the particular, that is, of particular human beings who were defined as not compatible with the universal (the national ideal). Adorno forcefully aligns the historical reality with the philosophical tendency:

> Genocide is the absolute integration. It is on its way wherever men are leveled off – 'polished off', as the German military called it – until one exterminates them literally, as deviations from the concept of their nullity.
>
> (ND 362)

This disturbing statement gives us a vivid illustration of just what is at stake in the critique of identity thinking and in the recognition of nonidentity. It is never exclusively an academic dispute about the definition of terms, but is related directly to the possibility of a better world in which particularity can express itself. That claim lies at the very centre of Adorno's philosophy, and we shall revisit it in further contexts when we examine both Adorno's effort to reconceive metaphysics and to develop a new conception of moral action.

Summary

The central concern of Adorno's philosophy is experience. He develops a theory of experience which contains concepts that may appear to be familiar from the modern tradition of epistemology. However, he is primarily interested in providing a justification for his claim that experience, under current historical circumstances, is distorted. A critical normative dimension is therefore central to his theory of experience.

Adorno argues that experience has become reified. By reified experience he means that subjects relate to objects and to others merely as things to be manipulated. The subject sees itself as a manipulator of outer things, indifferent to the complexity and particularity of objects. Even though the modern tradition of epistemology is, according to Adorno, marked by this reified relation of subject and object Adorno holds that epistemology is nevertheless to be defended because it is an attempt to consider experience rationally. An irrational account of experience attempts to form subject and object into a primal oneness, whereas epistemology tries to locate the different elements of experience and to explain their individual operations. Criticizing contemporary philosophy is, for Adorno, a way of gaining access to the conditions and rationalizations of contemporary experience.

Hegel's account of the dialectical dynamic of experience is a critical influence on Adorno's theory. Hegel argues that consciousness – the subject – can go beyond its narrow conceptualizations of objects by experiencing them. Experience involves the subject coming to realize that its way of conceiving an object fails to capture the truth of the object and that it has been committed to the wrong way of knowing. This process should be transformative. In this respect it is a process of determinate negation because the result of coming up against the limits of one's conceptual commitments is not empty, but informative. However, Adorno argues that Hegel's position is compromised by its desire for systematicity and completeness. Genuine experience is openness to the object and holds no assumptions about how our experience of the object will conclude. Hegel's dialectic of experience is subverted because it is directed by the notion of an ultimate and complete conceptualization by the subject of the object.

Adorno explains the process of subject-object interaction as one of mediation. Subject and object mediate each other, but – obviously – in differing ways. If subject and object mediate each other then it follows that accounts of experience which claim that we are immediately related to objects are false: they do not recognize the degree to which subjects bring conceptuality to bear on the process. In the mediation process the object is the 'what'. It has 'priority'. Conceptual acts aim at the object and their truth claims must be grounded in the particularity of the object. At the same time the subject is not passive: it is the 'how' of mediation and does not simply register the object. Its descriptive acts are rationally driven efforts to articulate the object.

The theory of mediation explains why the notion of identity is a distortion of experience: it entails that the object cannot be collapsed into the concepts of the subject. Adorno finds identity thinking in a wide range of philosophies: empiricism which naïvely attempts to capture objects with cover concepts and idealism in which the object is nothing but the product of the subject. Identity is, though, a legitimate desire of experience: it means being with the object (rational identity). However, in the absence of the conditions in which rational identity could be achieved (we have, rather, a reified social world of separate and antagonistic elements) Adorno argues that we must look instead to the nonidentity in our relationship with objects. Our concepts might appear to encapsulate objects but concepts – more accurately judgments – also contain a reference beyond the identity the judgment seems to state. The process of nonidentity in experience is multi-faceted, including not only nonidentity of subject and object, but of the individual with society. The latter points to Adorno's considerations of the violence against particularity by ideological concepts (national or racial identity).

Further reading

Foster, R. (2007) *Adorno: The Recovery of Experience*, Albany NY: SUNY Press, chapter 1.

Jay, M. (1984a) *Adorno*, London: Fontana, chapter 2.

O'Connor, B. (2004) *Adorno's Negative Dialectic: Philosophy and the Possibility of Critical Rationality*, Cambridge MA / London: MIT Press, chapters 2 and 3.

Rosen, M. (1982) *Hegel's Dialectic and its Criticism*, Cambridge: Cambridge University Press, chapter 7.

Four
Metaphysics

In the previous chapter we saw that for Adorno undistorted experience is marked by its responsiveness to nonidentity. Unaffected by reification the genuinely experiencing agent is in a ceaseless process of reflection on the objectivity of its conceptualizations. The measure of that objectivity is the degree to which the subject has adjusted its knowledge towards the particularity of the objects with which it is engaging. These various claims about nonidentity are central to Adorno's description of the potential of human experience, a potential that cannot be realized within the normative order of contemporary society.

Nonidentity is, however, available to philosophical experience. Adorno understands his own philosophy, in its efforts to explore the contradictory moments of society and its phenomena, and to interpret the marginal and neglected, as the exercise of nonidentity thinking. (This, for him, is true also of Benjamin and, partially, of Hegel.) But what is the intellectual space which allows us to think nonidentically when philosophy finds itself located in an allegedly totalized society? The answer Adorno provides is a surprising one: the very possibility of nonidentity thinking rests in our metaphysical capacities. As we shall see, the idea of metaphysics that Adorno ultimately defends is developed through a radical reconceptualization of the traditional metaphysical enterprise.

1. Metaphysics and philosophy

Adorno was keenly aware that the philosophical currents of his time viewed metaphysics with outright hostility. The main focus of their rejection of the oldest discipline of philosophy is its explanatory procedure: it generates foundational entities which stand in dualistic opposition to the material and social world they supposedly explain (e.g. the Platonic forms, the God of scholasticism, the Cartesian Cogito, or Hegelian spirit). In its commitment to world-transcending entities, metaphysical philosophy is quite incompatible with a pre-dominant commitment of modern philosophy, naturalism. Broadly defined, naturalism holds that there is no feature of the world which cannot in principle be explained through the intra-worldly business of science. In so far as metaphysics takes itself to be a unique kind of activity necessarily different from the character or methodologies of those disciplines which yield empirical knowledge or hypotheses or logical-deductive propositions, it simply cannot be accommodated within the naturalistic framework. While it is most unlikely that Adorno was acquainted with the specific strand of naturalism influentially devised by Quine, there can be little doubt that he would have perceived it as scientism, given the unfriendly interest he took in the complementary positivist critique of metaphysics (by Schlick and Carnap, to whom he refers in a number of places).

The philosophical rejection of metaphysics is not exclusive to naturalism. In the historical materialist tradition of contemporary Western philosophy there is pointed opposition to the other-worldliness towards which metaphysics allegedly directs itself, an other-worldliness that shifts the foundations of the various normative and historical enterprises of our lives – our ethics, our politics – outside the human realm. This anti-metaphysical position emphasizes both the essential role of *history* in the evolution of meaning (opposing itself to the notion of meaning as timelessly valid) and the *material* basis of our experience (human action, in contradistinction to the preordained determinations of a spiritual or non-human realm). Adorno's philosophy is, obviously enough, situated within this broad tradition. Adorno, to be exact, identifies negative dialectics as a variety of materialism rather than historical materialism, as the latter is the name he associates with orthodox Marxism. (From what we have seen, Adorno's philosophy cannot be confused with the forms of materialism that emerged during the Enlightenment and of which twentieth-century physicalism is a descendent.)

From within historical materialism Adorno offers a complex reconceptualization of metaphysics and transcendence. And what he establishes is overtly directed against the flattening of intellectual experience which, he argues, is produced by positivist philosophy (which for Adorno encompasses any theorization which extends the methods and foundational concepts of science – e.g. causality – outside the space of physical nature). Indeed, in this regard Adorno strongly supported the position set out by Max Horkheimer who in his essay, 'The Latest Attack on Metaphysics' (1937) saw in logical positivism's endeavour to demolish metaphysical speculation an effort to discredit all speculation. No reflection that went beyond appearances could thereafter be legitimated. In examining Adorno's social theory we saw why he believes we need to adopt a speculative attitude to gain access to the social totality. As we shall see, transcendence in its reconceptualized sense will refer to our ability to think against what is given. Transcending 'givenness' does not mean for Adorno thinking above, beyond, or outside materiality. It is to a space within materiality that his notion of transcendence directs itself.

The conception of experience that Adorno develops, as we saw, emphasizes the need for philosophy to come to terms with particularity, the very opposite of what metaphysics, Adorno alleges, has apparently always regarded as the proper business of philosophy. The sense of particularity here is not what sense-data theorists hold to be the primitive components of experience and nor is it that of types that are differentiated from our tokens. By particulars Adorno has in mind human beings especially, whose distinctive identities cannot be encapsulated under universals: i.e. concepts or categories. According to Adorno, articulating that particularity should be a central task of philosophy:

> The matters of true philosophical interest at this point in history are those in which Hegel, agreeing with tradition, expressed his disinterest. They are non-conceptuality, individuality, and particularity – things which ever since Plato used to be dismissed as transitory and insignificant, and which Hegel labeled 'lazy Existenz'.
>
> (ND 8)

The point here, as ever, is not simply epistemological: it refers primarily to the status of particularity in a world conditioned by reification with all the destructiveness towards particularity that that has produced. And what is surprising in all of this is that it is metaphysics which enables us ultimately to take an interest in particularity, in the nonidentical. To make that turn, however, we must revise the traditional metaphysical concern with only what is general and universal. With that reorientation towards the nonidentical particular it becomes a negative metaphysics. There is, Adorno writes, 'solidarity between such thinking and metaphysics at the time of its fall' (ND 408), that is, at a time when metaphysics appears to warrant no place in philosophy. This solidarity – the relationship of nonidentity to metaphysics – produces the thesis of immanent transcendence. This is no paradox, as we shall see (in the final section of this chapter): it is a thesis developed through an innovative rereading, reconstruction and modification of the classical terms of the metaphysical tradition, often, in fact, against that tradition.

2. Against metaphysics

Adorno's reconceptualization of metaphysics is radical: it draws on no existing model from the philosophical tradition. In fact, Adorno devotes considerable time to a comprehensive repudiation of the central tendencies of metaphysics. It may be fair to say that a great deal of the reaction against metaphysics in contemporary philosophy is not always based on an especially rich understanding of the specific claims of metaphysical philosophers. This is not at all true of Adorno. We have his 1965 lecture series, *Metaphysics: Concepts and Problems*, and it shows us his efforts to analyse deeply many of the major metaphysical concepts of Western philosophy from the Greeks through to rationalism and idealism. Texts such as Plato's *Parmenides* and *Theaetetus* and Aristotle's *Metaphysics* especially, as well as the canonical works of the German Idealists are considered in some detail. This lecture course forms the background for the analysis of metaphysics that would be presented in a more compressed and allusive form in *Negative Dialectics*, the core text for the analysis of Adorno's relation to metaphysics.

To begin, it is clear enough that Adorno is a critic of – what he understands to be – all extant systems of metaphysics. His philosophical standpoint, informed by historical and materialist principles, cannot accept the fundamental theses of a philosophical enterprise which seems to him to represent a closed, static and systematic framing of reality:

> … metaphysical systems in the precise sense are doctrines according to which concepts form a kind of objective, constitutive support on which what is naively called 'the objective world', that is, scattered, individual, existing things, is founded and finally depends.
>
> (MCP 8)

We can group Adorno's criticisms under four main lines of concern: (1) metaphysics is committed to the fundamental invariance of the world (anti-historical); (2) metaphysics develops a constricted conception of subjectivity, leading to what Adorno describes as 'peephole' metaphysics; (3) metaphysics seeks an extra-worldly transcendent source of meaning-cum-consolation or reconciliation and is therefore ideological (anti-materialist); (4) Adorno develops specific criticisms of the idealist notion of universal history that operates with a metaphysically supported belief in the inevitability of progress. Let us look at each of these concerns in turn.

(1) *Invariance.* Metaphysics, Adorno alleges, 'is nothing more than a doctrine of invariants' (ND 96). It identifies patterns within reality which it then hypostatizes to the status of independent essences as though those essences existed – or subsisted – more fundamentally outside the conditions of historical reality. This type of criticism has an obvious Nietzschean background in its suspicion of metaphysics as the tendency to abstract from living processes. And indeed Adorno refers – with rare approval – to Nietzsche as the 'irreconcilable adversary of our theological heritage in metaphysics' (ND 169). Adorno's charge, in short, is that metaphysical conceptions with supra-temporal forms, categories or *a priori* structures dualistically separate philosophy from the realm of experience, that is, from the space of subject-object mediation. As 'invariance' metaphysics stands in opposition to an historical materialism that understands the key organizing principles of our experience to be produced by ideas developed within the array of social forms that human beings have themselves created.

Adorno regards the tendency towards invariance as a form of reification: it fits or reduces reality into rigid structures. Is there not a danger of anachronism here, though? Invariant structures in Greek metaphysics (though one may dispute this characterization) are hardly to be attributed to the consciousness determining business of capitalism. And nor could Adorno for reasons from within his own theory claim the presence of reification, in his sense, in, say, Athenian society. A transhistorical notion of reification would actually undermine Adorno's critical-theoretical effort to analyse the alleged destruction experience through the historically specific pathologies of capitalism.

Although he never explicitly states it Adorno's own interest in forming a philosophical assessment of metaphysics is largely an answer to the existentialist metaphysics of Martin Heidegger's fundamental ontology. He takes Heidegger's position to embody contemporary rationality in spite of its seemingly anti-modernist objectives. Existentialist metaphysics is analysed by Adorno as a product of a reified consciousness, a consciousness which cannot operate responsively to the world. Instead it reaches towards 'Being'. This is a complex charge which comes down to the idea that 'Being' is not part of the process of experience. Adorno alleges of Heidegger:

> Weary of the subjective jail of cognition, he becomes convinced that what is transcendent to subjectivity is immediate for subjectivity, without being conceptually stained by subjectivity.
>
> (ND 79)

'Being' is a reified concept supposedly because it is non-mediated: it is simply given. It is, Adorno claims, an invariant which is not part of the transformative dynamic of the subject-object relation. This notion of 'Being' therefore, according to Adorno, reflects the consciousness of the age:

> The reified consciousness is a moment in the totality of the reified world. Their ontological need is the metaphysics of that consciousness ... The form of invariance as such is the projection of what has congealed in the reified consciousness.
>
> (ND 95)

What sort of mistake does Adorno believe to be at issue here? Is it (a) the hypostatization of dimensions of experience or (b) the violation of history, in that invariance is transhistorical? Clearly both, which Adorno considers as of a piece:

> Transcendence, both beyond [a] thinking and [b] beyond facts, is derived by this ontology from the undialectical expression and hypostasis of dialectical structures ...
>
> (ND 108n)

Should critical theory take any special interest in the mistake identified in (a)? We might ask, for instance, whether the charge of
hypostatization is, in a way, beside the point or at the very least too
broad a complaint. Are there not metaphysical ideas which
although certainly committed to invariance do not impinge on
social reality? Take, for example, Kant's transcendentalism. In that
theory the *a priori* categories of the understanding are invariant
components of any epistemic experience. (The allegation of
abstraction is as old as the theory itself.) Their scope, however, is
limited to the form of spatio-temporal objects. Could one not be
both a transcendental idealist about our experience of objects
(entailing all *a priori* rules) and a historical materialist about the
normative forces of our social world? The answer must surely
be yes, but what, I think, drives Adorno's rejection of the invariance thesis, even in transcendental idealism, is its disinterest in
transformative experience. Transcendental concepts, for instance,
offer explanations which leave experience at the social level
untouched and that, within Adorno's philosophy, is precisely to
seek the explanation in the wrong place.

(2) *Peephole metaphysics.* Modern philosophy continued with the
classical metaphysical project of attempting to identify the supposedly fundamental structures and elements of reality. The theories
developed by, for example, Spinoza, Leibniz and even Hegel can be
understood as part of a tradition which reaches back at least as
far as the Pre-Socratics. There is a significant strand of modern
metaphysics that is also marked, however, by the innovative concern with subjectivity, a concern which takes metaphysics in a quite
new and different direction of analysis. This distinctive analysis
contends, in essence, that subjectivity (or consciousness or the
'I' functions) has a constitutive role in experience; in other words,
that the world as we find it is always already shaped by our constitutive activities (giving it 'concepts' or 'laws'). If this assumption
is correct then investigation of the nature of subjectivity can help us
to understand the world itself since the world can never be

anything more or less than what can be infused in it through the
subject's contribution. When the analysis turns away from the
empirical world and towards the capacities of subjectivity to produce that world we effectively generate the notion of a metaphysical
subject. The subject which is now understood to have the critical
role in the structuring of reality as we experience it cannot be part
of the empirical world. Were it part of the empirical world it would
belong to the very domain it allegedly structures.

Adorno characterizes the theory of the metaphysical subject with
an unusual term: 'peephole metaphysics' (ND 139) (*Guckkastenme-
taphysik*). The argument is that the metaphysical subject is, in
the end, an invariant with a seemingly fixed relation towards
the world. It is the founding, pre-existing agency of experienceable
reality. As that which gives structure to the world or experience
it is not determined by the conditions of experience. In that case it
can only – in Adorno's metaphor – 'peep' at the world which
supposedly does not in any sense constitute it. Adorno writes: 'The
subject – a mere limited moment – was locked up in its own self
by that metaphysics, imprisoned for all eternity to punish it for its
deification' (ND 139). In other words, the metaphysical subject is a
self-standing, ontologically separate sphere of the world which it
understands to be essentially distinct from itself.

What we have seen, in the notions of mediation and nonidentity, points us directly to the source of Adorno's rejection
of this metaphysical thesis. First of all, for the thesis to hold good
the metaphysical subject must be intelligible in separation from
the conditions to which it relates if experience is to arise. In this
sense it is 'unmediated' and therefore in no sense constituted
through the subject-object relation. Secondly, it excludes nonidentity in that it is, again, a fully self-constituted – i.e. self-
identical – something. The irony of this metaphysical conception of
the subject is that its 'deification' weakens subjectivity in according
it a fixed essence which can relate outwardly only through its own
determinate laws (ND 350). The contrasting notion of the

subject – Adorno's – is as agency dynamically contributing and responding to the world.

(3) *Extra-worldly meaning.* Perhaps the most ambitious version of metaphysics is that which although secular in orientation continued to be marked in its preferred forms of explanation by its theological heritage. It says more than that the *structure of experience* is *a priori* or irreducible to the conditions of materiality. Its claim rather is that the *sources of meaning* are not reducible to the material word, that there is something outside what we actually experience which gives it its purpose. Adorno, influenced by the Marx of *The German Ideology*, takes the Hegelian notion of spirit or *Geist* as the primary modern example of this thesis. Hegel's infamous notion of the 'cunning of reason' is in all but name an agency independent of the material world. In *Negative Dialectics* Adorno subjects the Hegelian notion of *Geist* to criticism in a manner familiar to the historical materialist critique of idealism. Its essential mistake, according to Adorno, is that it seeks in *Geist* what can only be explained through the labours of human beings. As Adorno puts it: 'The world spirit is; but it is not a spirit' (ND 304).

Adorno criticizes Heidegger also for mislocating the sources of meaning. He alleges that Heidegger's fundamental ontology aims to give the sheen of dignity to a distorted social world by positing a somehow reassuring 'meaning of Being'. This overarching meaning, should we encounter it, reconciles us with our condition. This is a quite difficult criticism to level definitively at Heidegger because of the variety of ways in which Heidegger's philosophy grounds itself in an ontology of being-in-the-world: it appears to be solidly materialist. However, the critique is not without a degree of purchase. To speak about the meaning of Being as Heidegger's – we should say – attenuated metaphysical philosophy does is to miss the historical materialist conditions which, according to historical materialism, shape existence through and through. The problematic society cannot be translated into a metaphysical problem, therefore. In such a world a philosophy which would seek to give transcendent meaning to life (ND 376) or indeed death (ND 369) must be suspect from a critical-theoretical perspective. Adorno claims that Heidegger's metaphysics:

> ... degenerates into a kind of propaganda for death, elevating it to something meaningful, and thus, in the end, preparing people to receive the death intended for them by their societies and states as joyfully as possible.
>
> (MCP 131)

What metaphysics of this type actually does, Adorno claims, is to translate the problems of our social reality into a metaphysical question. This, however, has the effect of taking us from a materialist perspective – in which we recognize that the world as we experience it is the product of human action – to one in which our condition seems like a kind of fate. There are ways in which Heidegger might be extricated from this charge. But there are parts of his philosophy to which it also sticks. And it is these parts which provoke Adorno's critique. In *Being and Time* Heidegger identifies existentialia or categories of human existence, such as fallenness and thrownness, which seem to circumscribe, in theologically resonant terminology, the human condition. This, Adorno argues, is ultimately an ideology – i.e. an unacknowledged normatively infused view of the world – in that its analyses tie human beings to a specific set of embedding conditions. It does not seek to accommodate the idea that human beings can fundamentally alter the world in which they live. And it therefore lends itself to an endorsement of the ways things are as somehow metaphysically grounded. As Adorno writes: 'Anyone who traces deformation to metaphysical processes is a purveyor of ideology' (ND 284). There is a very significant entailment in this criticism, one which points towards Adorno's reconceptualization of metaphysics. The point is that metaphysics has a social content: even when it looks towards invariance or transcendent meaning it is setting out a view of the world.

(4) *History and metaphysics*. To the contemporary mind the very notion of universal history is self-evidently absurd. This is the notion – for which both Kant and Hegel argued – that essential human history is a single process of progress. This process is realized, and history thereby ended, when a civilized and democratic social order has been achieved. The long and arduous path towards that goal, in which Hegel perceived a dialectic of failure and advance, encompasses the various civilizations that have appeared and fallen as well as the radical intellectual revolutions that make up the headlines of Western history. The staggering episodes of cruelty and violence carried out along the path are simply moments that history has had to undergo: it has been an educative process. By placing those episodes within a larger context it is no longer possible to make any conventional moral judgment of them. We can shudder but not denounce. Wars and other acts of ideologically driven violence were, after all, necessary in order that history might advance ever nearer to its full realization. Progress is, within the notion of universal history, a process that history, not individuals, undergoes. Individuals across great periods of time are disconnected and participate in no collective, global social project. The 'advances' each civilization makes are nevertheless not lost, because those advances do not rest with those civilizations. They are carried forward by history. It is because universal history operates above the motives of human agents that it is metaphysical. It is not driven by the intentional projects of individuals but by *Geist* (as Hegel identified it), a collective mind that persists and develops across history.

Adorno criticizes this notion on the basis of its claims that history is both continuous and teleological or, in other words, that history is conceived as an unbroken process, moving towards an end. As a philosopher of nonidentity it is clear that Adorno could not endorse a narrative that relativizes human suffering. The construction of universal history excludes the kinds of considerations of suffering that would bring the whole notion of progress into doubt. He writes:

> If Benjamin said that history had hitherto been written from the standpoint of the victor, and needed to be written from that of the vanquished, we might add that knowledge must indeed present the fatally rectilinear succession of victory and defeat, but should also address itself to those things which were not embraced by this dynamic, which fell by the wayside – what might be called the waste products and blind spots that have escaped the dialectic.
>
> (MM §98, 151)

A reasonable reaction to the thesis of continuity would be to reject it by pointing instead to the myriad of discontinuities that mark recorded human history: phases of history that appear to have led to little else. Adorno is not, however, satisfied with the purely discontinuous interpretation of history. It excludes in principle both that there may sometimes be historical patterns that can be objectively identified and that we can gain some insight into the process of social evolution by connecting one phase of history with another. (For instance, Adorno and other members of the Frankfurt School were generally agreed that there is a history of capitalism, in which its development from the early mercantile phase to its current totalistic and consciousness distorting form can be witnessed.) Adorno's own notion of the social totality requires us to accept the operation of processes that are in some way continuous and indeed outside immediate perception.

Adorno, then, is opposed both to the metaphysical thesis of continuity and to the naïve perception of its discontinuity and yet he holds both that there are historical processes that are in some respect continuous and that reflections on the nonidentical moments of history highlight its discontinuity. The complexity of Adorno's conception of history arises from his efforts to position himself within a synthesis of these competing options. He declares: 'discontinuity and universal history must be conceived together' (ND 319). What Adorno understands by discontinuity is that events cannot be made intelligible simply by placing them within an historical narrative. That approach not only does violence to the specifics of the event, it also does not realize how the event itself can alter the future direction of history. He writes: 'History is not an equation, an analytic judgment. To think of it this way is to exclude from the very outset the possibility of anything qualitatively different' (P 61). Qualitative differences are produced within specific historical contexts. Those differences are found not only in events, however, but also in the fact that across history there are, what he refers to as, 'structural disparities' (INH 122). The differences between historical forms of life would suggest that they cannot be related to each other as on a continuum of some kind. To invoke the notion of the discontinuity of history, then, is to capture 'life perennially disrupted' (HF 91). This directly repudiates the metaphysical perception of history as a process of unfolding, in which what is latent from the beginning is developed and eventually fully realized.

It is more difficult to see how Adorno accommodates the notion of universal history within his complex conception. In spite of his obvious difference with the Hegelian metaphysics of history he states the following: 'If you wish to say anything at all about the theory of history in general, you must enter into a discussion of the construction of universal history' (HF 81). It might appear that Adorno enters into that discussion simply to reverse the main assumption of universal history. In view of Adorno's claims about the distinctive historical developments of the twentieth century – the rise and domination of reifying rationality, the increasing closure of the social totality, and its unparalleled murderousness – he might have replaced universal history's notion of progress with that of decline. Indeed, he appears to have taken precisely that decision in the remark: 'No universal history leads from savagery to humanitarianism, but there is one leading from the slingshot to the atom bomb' (ND 320). But an obvious worry arises here: does a narrative of decline not at least imitate the metaphysics of universal history, explaining it as a process seemingly outside the control of human beings and determined to go in only one direction? And it does not appear that Adorno's explanation of the continuity of history itself acknowledges any disruptive events. Hegel was charged with fabricating a linear process of continuous history, yet Adorno himself writes: 'the unity that cements the discontinuous, chaotically splintered moments and phases of history' is 'the unity of the control of nature, progressing to rule over men, and finally to that over men's inner nature' (ND 320).

Adorno's position is not, however, a metaphysical one: the processes that unfold in the history of domination are not inevitable and they should not, for that reason, be construed to be irreversible. The ideas that lead to the increasing reach of the social totality are human in origin and can be shown, through criticism, to be in some way confused because they ultimately work against the interests of individuals. In this context, we might think of the notion of continuity in Adorno's complex theory as an effort to draw attention to the processes that operate underneath the appearances of a disconnected social reality.

3. A metaphysics of nonidentity

The materialist critique appears to leave us with no grounds on which to persist with metaphysics. The key concepts of metaphysics, as Adorno presents them, are, after all, based on exactly those philosophical principles which his own version of historical materialism rejects. Yet Adorno's most important philosophical work, *Negative Dialectics*, culminates with the section 'Meditations on Metaphysics', a reflection on the possibility of a renewed metaphysics. The considerable critical analyses that precede this section – the key contentions of which we have just examined – prove to be preparatory. Through those analyses Adorno carefully peels away what he regards as the misdirection of metaphysics throughout the philosophical tradition (with special reference, as we saw, to Hegel and Heidegger). Adorno's critique emerges, then, as anything but a final judgment on the very notion of metaphysics. What he tries to establish, ultimately, is the truth in metaphysics. For Adorno this truth is not to be found in any of its traditional objects, the array of transtemporal non-material objects which metaphysics at various times has sought to verify. Nor is it the search for transcendent meaning. Rather, its truth lies in our desire for a kind of thinking which transcends sheer givenness. Adorno finds that the current condition of rationality inhibits the realization of that desire, a difficulty that he formulates in this way:

> Kant's epistemological question, 'How is metaphysics still possible?' yields to a question from the philosophy of history: 'Is it still possible to have a metaphysical experience?' That experience was never located so far beyond the temporal as the academic use of the word metaphysics suggests.
>
> (ND 372)

Adorno's reconception of the metaphysical enterprise presents quite a challenge to the reader in that he employs terminology in ways that are plainly at odds with their classical connotations. This is the product of his efforts to rescue certain terms from their allegedly reified forms. Through those efforts he develops a post-metaphysical version of the metaphysical project. That means, in actuality, reframing the core metaphysical notion of transcendence − of going beyond what is immediately given − within a materialist philosophy. In contrast to what traditional metaphysics seeks to explain through that notion, Adorno proposes that we can think against the given without reaching for a realm lying outside the historical-material sphere. Adorno puts it this way: 'the intra-mundane and historic is relevant to what traditional metaphysics distinguished as transcendence' (ND 361).

The very idea of immanent or intramundane transcendence looks, however, like a contradiction in terms. One way into Adorno's thought is through a comment he offers on Kant's notion of noumenality: 'Kant on his part in defining the thing in itself as the intelligible being had indeed conceived transcendence as nonidentical' (ND 406). It is nonidentical in that it is never directly given, yet it somehow stands behind the things as they appear, an ever present image of what cannot be reduced to the intentions or concepts of the subject. It is therefore, in a sense, logically immanent to the experience. It needs to be noted, though, that the Kantian notion of the thing-in-itself does not serve rigorously for what Adorno wants to explain as his materialist metaphysics. The thing-in-itself cannot be encountered in experience and in that way cannot be part of the subject-object dynamic which underpins the claims of nonidentity. It is a philosophical conception of what is not directly given and therefore not experience of any kind of transcendence.

Despite this complicated enlistment of Kant, the passage itself points towards the connection between Adorno's notion of metaphysics and his theory of experience. As we saw, Adorno thinks of experience as containing the potential for responsivity, as the process in which subjectivity goes beyond itself, a process of nonidentity. This means, no less, that nonidentity is a fundamental characteristic of full experience: it is the experience of the subject transcending its preconceptions. Nonidentical thinking, as Adorno conceives it, transcends reification but it is not an encounter with absolute otherness. Its metaphysical character contains no reference to something that lies in principle outside the domain of our experience. The objective of negative dialectics is, after all, to provide us with ways of reflecting on the limitations of our experience of objects. As we have seen, Adorno argues that the prevailing canons of reason narrow thinking itself to unreflective conceptual activity, that is, to categorization. Adorno's revised metaphysics validates the space in which we can think outside those narrow limits and thereby come to know the object as a particular and not as an instance of something general.

This reframing of metaphysics substantially alters the account of the role of the subject in the business of metaphysics. The transcendent notion of metaphysics places objectivity in the metaphysical phenomena themselves: our task is supposedly to get to these phenomena through forms of philosophical discovery which we might describe as 'doing metaphysics'. In the materialist version of metaphysical thinking proposed by Adorno, however, there is the subjective dimension which is the agency of the subject responding reflectively to the particularity of the object, a particularity which transcends the variety of ways in which the subject tries to encapsulate it through its concepts. Adorno writes: 'The interpretative eye which sees more in a phenomenon than it is – and solely because of what it is – secularizes metaphysics' (ND 29). An implication of the interpretative character of metaphysics is that it becomes open to 'fallibility and relativity' (ND 374). And this is precisely what, for Adorno, rationality consists in: the ongoing effort to respond, in contrast to working with a set of limiting schemata which we apply to a straightforward reality. Metaphysics – metaphysical thinking – is thereby an exercise of intellectual freedom: 'Subjectively liberated experience and metaphysical experience', according to Adorno, 'converge in humanity' (ND 397).

In light of this immanentization or materialization of metaphysics, it is striking that Adorno ultimately associates the notion of metaphysical thinking qua nonidentical thinking with the very idea of the 'absolute'. This is actually a key element of his reconception of metaphysics. He formulates the connection between the absolute and nonidentity in the following way: 'the absolute, as it hovers before metaphysics, would be the nonidentical that refuses to emerge until the compulsion of identity has dissolved' (ND 406). This seems a stretch too far: how can nonidentity be conceived alongside the absolute given the latter's connection with the speculative theological-philosophical tradition as the name of 'the unconditioned' (Kant's definition of the absolute), which is understood to be certain, foundational, and above all materiality? This is the 'unconditioned' which modern philosophy has largely rejected on the basis that it lies outside the conditions of experience or the frameworks of any possible theoretical knowledge. Adorno, in fact, points to the inconsistency of modern philosophy's critical standpoint: 'it is precisely through its denial of objectively valid cognition of the absolute', he writes, 'that the critique of reason *makes an absolute judgment*' (ND 382, emphasis added). That is, it closes off completely the possibilities of experiences that do not conform to specified conditions. It concludes that philosophy falls into error as soon as it reaches beyond those conditions. In so far as this critique is directed towards an ideal or spiritual order or pure concepts subsisting independently, it is supported by Adorno. The meaning of the absolute is not, however, exhausted by what Heidegger called its onto-theological conceptualizations.

The absolute for Adorno signifies a desire for something which is not co-extensive with immediate given experience. The alternative to what is immediately given will not be found in spirit or the heavens. Again, we look to the experience of nonidentity, of relating to the particularities of things and thereby transcending the schemas and frameworks that narrow our engagements with objects. For that reason Adorno claims that no 'absolute can be expressed otherwise than in topics and categories of immanence' (ND 407). Within that immanence is the possibility of self-transcendence in which a subject relinquishes the authority it has arrogated when it claimed to 'identify' the object through its descriptive or categorial practices. Instead, the pursuit of the object – a particularity with its own distinctive identity – drives the subject beyond the point from which it begins its pursuit.

Adorno's criticism of the metaphysics of meaning, which we saw in the previous section, is motivated by his perceptions of its ideological character. We need to revisit that complaint because Adorno acknowledges that any effort to 'find meaning' faces the risk of falling into ideology. But what other than the effort to gain a perspective on historical and empirical reality – an effort which seems to respond to a need to understand its 'meaning' – prompts speculative thought, including, not least, the variety Adorno himself defends? On this very issue philosophy, Adorno claims, faces a constitutive challenge:

> ... on the one hand, any construction of a meaning, however constituted, is forbidden to us, but that, on the other, the task of philosophy is precisely to understand, not simply to reflect, what happens to be, or to copy it ... This has placed philosophy in a true quandary.
>
> (MCP 114)

Adorno's way through this quandary distinguishes his position from that which motivates, let us call it, an affirmative metaphysics of meaning. At the centre of that difference is the relation to history that each of these options seeks to develop. According to Adorno, the affirmative metaphysics of meaning is an effort to reconcile us with history, that is, to submit ourselves to the order of things. It does so, however, without understanding that meaning is socially and histori-cally mediated. It does not recognize the social-historical sources which have broken our sense of the coherence of the world. It is, as we have seen, Heidegger who exemplifies this effort. He pursues, Adorno claims, the meaning of Being while eschewing a normative critique of the society in which individuals find themselves:

> If it is the case that no metaphysical thought was ever created which has not been a constellation of elements of experience, then, in the present instance, the seminal experiences of metaphysics are simply diminished by a habit of thought which sublimates them into metaphysical pain and splits them off from the real pain which gave rise to them.
>
> (JA 38)

In this non-critical attitude it is ultimately a failure: it does not change the conditions which lead us to search for meaning: 'Metaphysics ends in a miserable consolation: after all, one still remains what one is' (JA 116). This tendency is entirely discredited by history. Adorno writes: 'Our metaphysical faculty is paralyzed because actual events have shattered the basis on which speculative metaphysical thought could be reconciled with experience' (ND 362). Central to Adorno's sense of the shattering effect of 'actual events' is the catastrophe of Auschwitz, after which genuine experience seems almost to be impossible. A metaphysics of meaning starts with this reality and attempts to give it a metaphysical significance. In so doing it fails to confront history in any sense.

Reacting against the affirmative metaphysics of meaning leads Adorno towards the space of an historically sensitive immanence. That is, the objects of the world are the content of metaphysical thinking, but what is of significance in them is what traditional metaphysics does not see: the damage the world has inflicted on them. Adorno writes: 'This is the transmutation of metaphysics into history. It secularizes metaphysics in the secular category pure and simple, the category of decay' (ND 360).

As history is dominated by the malevolent phenomenon of Auschwitz metaphysics must turn towards the 'somatic, unmeaningful stratum of life ... the stage of suffering' (ND 365). To seek to transcend this, in the traditional sense, or to give meaning to a world in which Auschwitz could happen would be to ignore it. Sensitive then to what lies outside immediacy metaphysics in the era of Auschwitz is no longer oriented towards spirit but to the material. He writes: 'The course of history forces materialism upon metaphysics, traditionally the direct antithesis of materialism' (ND 365). Its materialization involves metaphysical thinking in rescuing what lies outside the usual narratives of theory. Its objective is to reach those moments which metaphysical abstractions ignore. It is the effort to express the suffering, a reality which seems to be of such little concern to philosophy. As Adorno explains: 'The need to lend a voice to suffering is a condition of all truth. For suffering is objectivity that weighs upon the subject ... ' (ND 18). Reified consciousness, however, cannot recognize 'substance and quality, activity and suffering, being and existence' (DE 3). To engage with suffering is to think nonidentically against a reified system that no longer understands its own reification. A social totality in which individuals conform to norms that frustrate their need for happiness persists because individuals do not realize that the totality is the very reason for the absence of that happiness. It is, Adorno claims, 'part of the mechanism of domination to forbid recognition of the suffering it produces' (MM §38, 63). To take that suffering seriously is to think outside that mechanism and thereby to move closer to what it – systematically – keeps from view. It is a process of resisting the 'effacement of memory' (CM 92) so that the victims and the disfigurements of history are not forgotten.

For Adorno, then, metaphysical thinking is not a formal effort to transcend one's conventional ways of relating to particular objects just for the sake of that transcendence. It is a response to violence which has been blindly produced by commitments to identity and exclusion. It is that thinking that metaphysics should resist not only in politics but in all our engagements with what we presuppose is other than us. Through engagement with forgotten particularity alone metaphysical experience, Adorno holds, can be realized.

Summary

Adorno argues that metaphysics underpins the very possibility of nonidentity thinking. This notion is developed through a radical rereading of the metaphysical enterprise. Adorno, in common with much of contemporary philosophy, rejects all existing versions of metaphysics (as he understands them). Nevertheless, he attempts, from within the perspective of historical materialism, to retrieve notions of transcendence and the absolute and to explain their truth within his own philosophy of nonidentity.

He offers a number of criticisms of existing models of metaphysics, concentrating in particular on the theories of Hegel and Heidegger.

(1) He claims that metaphysics is anti-historical in its efforts to identify the invariant structures of the world. (2) Metaphysics – in its idealist variety – develops a conception of the subject in which the subject becomes separate from the world. That subject, he metaphorically claims, can gain access to the world only through a 'peephole'. (3) The turn to metaphysics to find extra-worldly or transcendent sources of meaning that might console us in the face of a meaningless world is criticized by Adorno on the basis that this in turn deflects attention from the problematic world. It is in this respect ideological. (4) The metaphysical notion of history, expressed by Hegel pre-eminently as universal history, is rejected by Adorno because that notion falsely represents history as continuity. Adorno offers an alternative, a complex notion of history as a unity of discontinuity – historical developments are not simply evolutions of each other – and continuity – a non-random pattern of historical development is evident in the increasing hold of the social totality over individuals. He does not attempt to reverse the idealist thesis of progress by proposing a narrative of inevitable decline.

Metaphysics must, nevertheless, be defended, Adorno argues, as it is a space of thinking which is not reducible to sheer givenness. But it needs to be reformulated and separated from the kinds of commitments which Adorno criticizes in traditional metaphysics. The result is a metaphysics which is still willing to speak about transcendence, but to refer to transcendence as an intramundane or immanent space. What nonidentity thinking aims at is the particularity of the object. That particularity lies beyond conceptuality – it is analogous to the absolute of traditional metaphysics in this regard only – but is nevertheless within the space of historical-material reality. To reach it, thinking, according to Adorno, must transcend its narrow conceptualizations (and thereby transcend itself). The subject in metaphysics engages interpretatively rather than cate-gorically with the object. Our capacity for (immanent) metaphysics allows us to think about the particular moments of history that have suffered through identity thinking (and politics) and reification.

Further reading

Jarvis, S. (1998) *Adorno: A Critical Introduction*, Cambridge: Polity Press, chapter 8.
Wellmer, A. (1998) *Endgames: The Irreconcilable Nature of Modernity*, trans. D. Midgley, Cambridge MA / London: MIT Press, chapter 7.
Zuidervaart, L. (2007) *Social Philosophy after Adorno*, Cambridge: Cambridge University Press, chapter 2.

Five

Freedom and morality

Adorno develops his conception of freedom through a critical engagement with the idea of autonomy. Within the philosophical tradition, autonomy has become the most prestigious idea of freedom as it identifies (and thereby celebrates) a higher human capacity to be self-directed in accordance with reasons. It effectively underpins modernity's claims that human beings have the right to bring about rational transformation of their lives and the societies in which they live. Autonomous agents reject any normative recommendation that they cannot endorse through their own 'canon of rationality' (Scanlon 1972: 215).

It was Kant, building on an insight of Rousseau, who brought together the notions of freedom and reason under the concept of autonomy. He argued that the exercise of reason is integral to the freedom of moral actions. In his strongest formulations Kant even seems to say that the individual is free in the sense that does justice to the dignity of the human being only when acting under reason. This means that 'pathological' acts – of passion or of sentiment – are relegated to the lower levels of human motivation (heteronomy), though they are nevertheless also freely chosen. The rational agent is one who can act without pathological motivations and on the grounds of, what Kant calls, pure practical reason. Autonomy in this philosophical sense entails the operation of the reflective capacities of the agent since it is only through reflection and deliberation that an individual can come to possess reasons for action.

Adorno, among many others, offers a number of criticisms of the philosophical theory – of Kant's especially – of autonomy. But he is also a sharp critic of the actual form that autonomy has taken on in contemporary society. He argues that autonomy has developed an ideological character: it is not genuine freedom. Rather it has become the circumscribed freedom of the individual that allows the system – bourgeois capitalism – to function and persist. As a requirement of the system, Adorno holds, autonomy in this form both works against and distorts the deepest interests of the individual. The individual is repressed, in the name of the socially dominant conception of reason, and does not enjoy spontaneous and responsive interactions with others.

Yet Adorno also has a positive account of the possibilities of autonomy in which he separates it out from the ideologically distorted form it has taken. The exercise of autonomy can be the distinctive normative behaviour of emancipated individuality. The autonomous person, ideally, has the power to reject and resist standing societal norms. Gaining that power is, he proposes, the task of education. As we shall see, this conception of autonomy's potential contrasts sharply, for Adorno, with the reality of autonomy within an ideologically infused social totality.

As part of his examination of autonomy as an attitude of resistance to conventional norms Adorno turns to a critical consideration of morality. He puts forward the thesis of a 'new categorical imperative'. It is offered as a response to the moral derangement of a world which could create Auschwitz. It is an effort to reinvigorate our moral 'impulses' which, Adorno holds, have been weakened by modernity's efforts to locate morality in acts of intellection.

We will begin the analysis by examining Adorno's account of the emergence of the notion of autonomy during the period of the Enlightenment. His critique of the ideological character of the conception of autonomy that developed during that phase of Western history will then be set out. The next section will deal with his account of the repressive nature of autonomy. What Adorno gains from these criticisms is an identifiable space in which a new conception of genuinely rational and free moral agency must be developed. Adorno's recommended model of autonomy – autonomy as resistance – and his conception of morality – the new categorical imperative – will be considered separately.

1. Freedom and the dialectic of Enlightenment

Adorno recognizes that it was during the Enlightenment period of Western history that the notion of autonomy first appeared in the form it bears in contemporary society. During this period societies began to reconstruct themselves on what they took to be post-feudal, rational and constitutional bases. Under these arrangements the individual threw off the status of 'subject' to become a citizen with prescribed freedoms. In *Dialectic of Enlightenment* Adorno and Horkheimer write: 'We have no doubt – and herein lies our *petitio principii* – that freedom in society is inseparable from enlightenment thinking' (DE xvi). They follow the conventional view that the Enlightenment generated the conditions in which human beings were no longer to be guided by a would-be natural order. Political authority, in its feudal era, was justified on the grounds of natural – i.e. divinely ordained – law, and individuals were bound to that authority. Enlightenment societies, based on democratic principles, however, evolved the notion of autonomous agents who could determine for themselves what the authority of the state should be and how it would be exercised. Social freedom in this historical sense, then, refers to the freedom to be a self-determining person in an organized community.

But there is, according to Adorno and Horkheimer, a further dimension which complicates the Enlightenment's role in the development of freedom. Here they articulate a radical criticism that brings the achievement of the Enlightenment as a whole into question. They allege that the Enlightenment evolved into a self-perpetuating rationalistic system which fatally compromised the potential of autonomy. This evolution is the *dialectic of enlightenment*, the tendency of enlightenment thought – release from magical or superstitious authority – to become anti-enlightenment: anti-enlightenment in that it becomes a new form of apparently natural authority.

Adorno and Horkheimer claim that the use of reason in Enlightenment's revolutionary phase was critical. It provided human beings with intellectual tools and strategies with which to reject the putatively natural authority that had been employed to protect power and knowledge. But the critical enterprise of the Enlightenment appeared to end almost as soon as it had effectively undermined that form of authority. This is because reason itself was compromised. In their efforts to bring reason into some kind of order – to avoid any regression – Enlightenment intellectuals, according to Adorno and Horkheimer, believed it was necessary to give it a discipline of correct procedure. They produced science as a model of this discipline. But this was bound to destroy the creative and emancipatory energy of the Enlightenment. Impressed by the power and success of scientific methods and scientific criteria in their original domain, the theorists of the Enlightenment never considered whether science could serve as the foundation of rationality elsewhere. Adorno and Horkheimer claim that 'on their way toward modern science human beings have discarded meaning' (DE 3). The scientific model became authoritative in settling questions of how rational beings should think and act. Reason in this new form acquired an authority that could not be contested: it did not (unlike critical reason) contain the space for reflection on its own value. There was no effective means of self-critique since any effort at critique could only be seriously entertained if it played by the rules of the very form of reason it might seek to criticize. Reason could not see beyond its existing form. It is this historical 'dialectic' – through which Enlightenment reason becomes unquestionable – that Adorno and Horkheimer call the 'self-destruction of enlightenment' (DE xiv). The development of modern societies was accelerated by the use of this form of reason. It offered clear advantages in the organization of newly industrialized societies as its abstract, scientific methodology (strongly influencing social science) facilitated the coordination of emerging democratic systems.

Adorno and Horkheimer are guided on the history of rationalization by Max Weber. In *Economy and Society* Weber described purposive or instrumental rationality (*Zweckrationalität*) as 'determined by expectations as to the behavior of objects in the environment and of other human beings; these expectations are used as "conditions" or "means" for the attainment of the actor's own rationally pursued and calculated ends' (Weber 1978: 24). It was the increasing extension of this variety of reason to social processes that gave rise to the distinctive character of modern rationalization. Purpose rationality gained ascendancy over what Weber called value rationality (*Wertrationalität*), which he claimed was 'determined by a conscious belief in the value for its own sake of some ethical, aesthetic, religious, or other form of behavior, independently of its prospects of success' (Weber 1978: 24–25).

The varying forms that authority has taken in the course of the dialectic of enlightenment suggest to Adorno and Horkheimer that reason 'is historical' (ND 26). What is accepted as a good justification or a winning claim is an historical variable. In the current socio-historical environment individuals are regarded as rational if they act according to considerations of self, profit, personal advantage; they are merely emotional if sympathy and sentiment guide them. We can refer back to the earlier discussion of the social totality for Adorno's explanation of how the form of reason distinctive to the era of capitalism prevailed. As we saw, capitalism – which developed rapidly during the period of the Enlightenment – operates with abstract notions of equivalence and exchange. They determine the normative processes of society. They proved successful because they were complementary to the Enlightenment's 'scientific' conception of reason. Adorno and Horkheimer do not declare whether this conception of reason gave rise to modern capitalism or whether the pathologies of capitalism predisposed us to some form of abstract reason. The accounts they offer of the development of both can hardly be disentangled.

This picture of the socio-historical reality of reason has, for Adorno, implications for how we might theorize autonomy. When individuals seek freely to organize their lives they operate with some implicit conception of what would be reasonable. In taking ourselves as rational actors, in possession of rational justifications for what we do, we operate with an understanding of what we can justify in our decisions and actions. It is therefore a matter of the deepest significance to be able to take a critical perspective on the form of reason that prevails. Adorno's contention is that the form of reason that allows society to reproduce itself is the one that individuals will use in their own seemingly autonomous actions. And this is because – as again we saw in the discussion of the social totality – of the socialization process. Adorno understands this process, however, to have – under the conditions of organized industrial society at least – a tendency to produce social conformism. In effect, individuals order their lives in ways that their society understands to be rational, i.e. instrumental, calculative rationality. Considerations that, for example, stem from value rationality (as Weber had described it) have no authority in this environment. But this narrowing of rationality, Adorno argues, stands in direct opposition to the ideal of autonomy. The power to determine one's actions in an independent way – the ideal – is compromised by the use of a particular form of rationality in the exercise of that power. Acting under reason in this regard is integrational rather than emancipating. Yet it was on the assumption that human beings have a capacity for emancipation from their natural and social environments that the very notion of autonomy was developed.

2. Autonomy as ideology

Adorno maintains that the expansion of the capitalist mode of production required autonomy – innovative, adventurous, and independent producers and merchants – but it also would end up framing the limits of that autonomy. As he puts it: 'The individual was free as an economically active bourgeois subject, free to the extent to which the economic system required him to be autonomous' (ND 262). To propose autonomy as an ideal, therefore, is to celebrate naïvely the historically evolved and integrated actor of contemporary society. Understanding the autonomous individual as purely self-directing mistakes the degree to which the individual is *mediated by society*. We are not, as the ideal of autonomy would have us believe, abstracted actors whose norms are unmarked by specific socio-historical contexts. We should not imagine that in acting autonomously we have some-how managed to step outside or transcend social influence. It is a critical matter, Adorno claims, that we come to 'see through the autonomy of subjectivity' and gain 'awareness of its own mediated nature' (ND 39).

The fact of mediation means, for Adorno, that the question of autonomy cannot be adequately addressed without consideration of its social dimension. As he contends, 'society determines individuals to be what they are, even by their immanent genesis' (ND 219, translation adjusted). The social determinism to which Adorno refers here is historical, a characterization of the formative influence of society on the individual in capitalist societies. It does not hold that the individual must necessarily in every situation be shaped by social influence. As we recall from the discussion of the social totality, Adorno states that a 'liberated mankind would by no means be a totality' (IPD 12). In the current historical environment, however, the totality is all pervasive. Activities which appear to be individually motivated and rationally justifiable – apparently free – accord, in ways that individuals do not perceive, with the needs of the totality. We enjoy freedoms that are consistent with those needs, and equally experience unfreedom when our desires are at odds with the normative order of the social totality. As Adorno explains: 'freedom and unfreedom are not primary phenomena, but derivatives of a totality that at any given time exercises dominion over the individual' (HF 207).

The notion of autonomy, then, cannot be properly considered in abstraction from the totality. Autonomy has actually become, Adorno argues, a *function* of the capitalist system which shapes the totality:

> The process of evolving individual independence [i.e. autonomy] is a function of the exchange society and terminates in the individual's abolition by integration. What produced freedom will recoil into unfreedom.
>
> (ND 262)

He claims, on the basis of its functionality, that 'bourgeois freedom' is closer than is generally recognized to the freedom experienced in the highly centralized and authoritarian societies of the (former) Eastern Bloc. While acknowledging the distinctive form of coercion required for the preservation of a totalitarian state, he identifies the tendency of Western and Communist social organization to reduce freedom to what preserves the totality and its processes over the interests of the individual. He writes:

> … a direct progress towards freedom cannot be discerned. Objectively, such progress is impossible because of the increasingly dense texture of society in both East and West; the growing concentration of the economy, the executive and the bureaucracy has advanced to such an extent that people are reduced more and more to the status of functions. What freedom remains is superficial, part of the cherished private life, and lacks sub-stance as far as people's ability to determine their own lives is concerned.
>
> (HF 5)

Functional freedom is ultimately the freedom that the system defines for us. Adorno develops a concrete account of this functionality in his discussion of *social roles*. In contemporary society a key element in the process of socialization is the acquisition of a role. Adorno claims that the identity of the individual is determined and socially validated through the role that individual takes on. But, Adorno argues, the connection between role and individuality is obviously contrary to a fundamental principle of freedom, namely the absence of a constraining identity. He writes: 'The liberated ego, no longer locked up in its identity, would no longer be condemned to play roles either … society would lose the horror of shaping the individuals throughout' (ND 278–79). In reality, then, social roles are identical with socio-economic roles and are determined by a social totality over which the individual has no power.

The critique of social roles is of central significance to the critical theory of society. The persistence of current social arrangements is attributed by Adorno to the grip roles have over our identity. The very experience of selfhood – of being somebody in the world – is mediated through the roles one possesses. Yet these roles are required for the perpetuation of society. They are so compelling, it seems, that we adopt them even as they work against our deeper needs and more comprehensive sense of ourselves. Adorno writes, in this regard, of 'a contradiction like the one between the definition which an individual knows as his own and his "role", the definition forced upon him by society when he would make his living … ' (ND 152).

Even if individuals do experience this contradiction they generally fail to realize that the role is wrong, that it is a constraint. Individuals, 'in the modern sense' (ND 218), perceive that, as individuals, they seem to have some freedom to act 'against society and other individuals' (ND 261), i.e. to pursue their own ends (ND 261). Furthermore, the range of individuals' free actions seems to go beyond what is defined as their social roles: actions are not restricted, apparently, by the social role. But this, Adorno claims, is 'delusive' (ND 262). It is delusive because the individual is essentially 'an economically active bourgeois subject, free to the extent to which the economic system required him to be active in order to function' (ND 262). There is room for creativity within the prescribed role so long as it does not bring the role into question. With that constraint, Adorno concludes, 'autonomy is thus potentially negated at the source' (ND 262). What we really might be – the identity we could recognize as the produce of our efforts to determine ourselves freely – is replaced by an identity that renders us as functions of society. It is, Adorno writes, 'a loss of identity for the sake of abstract identity' (ND 279).

Adorno's main contention, then, is that the very idea of autonomy has become the theoretical expression of just the version of free individuality that is required by and *perpetuates bourgeois society*. Autonomy is complicitous in a social totality we must criticize and reject. In essence, therefore, autonomy is, for Adorno, an *ideological* notion. By reading the notion of autonomy as a social phenomenon Adorno attempts to undermine the view that it is somehow essential or transcendental (that is, universal and given in the same form to all human beings). It is, rather, a 'category of freedom' that 'has been created in the unfree individual's image' (ND 275). In the tragedy of modernity the very ideal of freedom that we valorize is precisely the kind of freedom which preserves us as functionaries of an ordered society.

It is because the question of freedom is fundamentally a social one that Adorno thinks he is justified in not considering it by means of the familiar preoccupations of modern philosophy. He explicitly rejects the philosophical dilemma of the choices between free-will and determinism. The question of freedom has to be, rather, that of whether society can impede or enhance the conditions in which we are able to act autonomously or otherwise. It is not an analysis of the legal constraints under which individuals must act. For Adorno, freedom relates instead to the issue of how social norms facilitate or exclude a meaningful sense of personal responsibility and self-determination. It is for that reason 'naïve', he claims, to ask the perennial philosophical question of whether 'are you responsible or not responsible' because freedom 'in the sense of moral responsibility can only exist in a free society' (HF 203). Adorno does not explain what conditions would need to be in place for such a genuinely free society of responsible individuals to be possible. And given the moral outrage he expresses against agents of the Nazi regime (as we shall see below) it is not always clear that social integration, for him, actually absolves individuals of their moral responsibility.

3. Autonomy as repression

Any theory which, like Adorno's, proposes that human beings habitually act contrary to their better interests raises this obvious question: why are we unable to recognize the detrimental effects of the norms under which we act? Why do we aspire to the ideal of autonomy even though, according to Adorno, autonomy narrows our freedom to the interests of the social totality? Some of Freud's ideas about the structure of the self are enlisted by Adorno to help answer just these kinds of questions. He uses the language of psychoanalysis when he describes autonomy as freedom achieved through 'repression'. It is, he says, 'rule over one's inner nature' (ND 256). This repression ('inner rule') allows individuals to adapt, contrary to their impulses, to the exigencies of their environment. The environment which concerns Adorno is, obviously enough, the social totality, and adapting to it enables effective function within its specific prescribed procedures and conventions. For Adorno, repressive freedom is by no means an inevitable or natural development of those groups of human beings who have moved from some state of nature to ordered society or civilization. Rather, it is his claim – from within the perspective of critical theory – that our particular civilization, our specific societal norms, have been achieved and are sustained through repression. In *Dialectic of Enlightenment* Adorno and Horkheimer offered an account of this repressive process through the story of Odysseus who chose to have himself bound to the mast of his ship in order to resist the alluring song of the sirens. This act of denial symbolizes the act of repression through which humanity 'had to inflict terrible injuries on itself' (DE 26).

What exactly has been repressed? Adorno, appropriating Freud's schema, speaks of repression as 'the ego's rule over the id' (ND 273). The proposition, then, is that the ego asserts itself by the repression of the id. What Adorno builds on that proposition is a critical perspective on the notion that what we essentially are is reasoning selves who can determine ourselves through our intellectual processes alone. We must also think of ourselves as creatures of the drives to which the id refers. The repression of those drives centralizes the ego. Psychoanalysis is of value in the critique of the ego that supposedly stands at the centre of autonomous agency because, Adorno writes, it 'reminds the ego of the shakiness of its definitions compared to those of the id, and thus of its tenuous and ephemeral nature' (ND 352). As a critique of the constructed subject Freud's theory – in this respect at least – surpasses, Adorno thinks, one of the twentieth century's most influential repudiations of the modern conception of subjectivity: 'The things which the anti-metaphysician Freud taught us about the id come closer to a metaphysical critique of the subject than Heidegger's metaphysics' (ND 281). And it does so not by dismissing the ego as an unfortunate philosophical construction – as Heidegger does – but by showing how it has appeared as part of the evolutionary process of civilization. In this respect it properly acknowledges the role of history in the evolution of subjectivity. Hence, to criticize ego-centric philosophy is to criticize a construction whose origins lie beyond philosophy.

Adorno develops a suggestive new account of freedom by addressing the nature of those drives the ego represses. There is, he argues, a freedom impulse, associated with what Freud had called the 'id'. This impulse is the source of our sense of freedom: freedom, he writes, 'feeds upon the memory of the archaic impulse' but it is not 'yet steered by any solid "I"' (or 'ego', 'Ich') (ND 221). While Adorno never quite says that we can have a pure experience of this impulse he identifies it as a layer of meaningful human motivation that lies below concepts, prior to the ego. In that respect it precedes reasoning and justification. He states the idea in this way:

'a certain archaic element is required for there to be such things as free impulses, or spontaneous modes of behaviour that are not triggered by reasons'; it is not 'behaviour in *accordance with reason*' (HF 213). This is certainly a radical thesis, and that is reflected in the odd terminology Adorno uses to capture it. He speaks of the impulse as the '*Hinzutretende*', translated variously as the 'addendum', 'supplement' or 'additional factor' that cannot be captured under the rationalistic explanations of action. The '*Hinzutretende*' is the impulse for spontaneous action. It should be noted at this point that Adorno's various formulations of the impulses as prior to any conceptual experience do appear to accord the impulses the status of immediacy, that is, as outside mediation. Yet for Adorno it is generally the case that claims to immediacy are suspect.

The blindness of modern thought to the impulsive dimension of freedom is, Adorno believes, exemplified in Kant whose theory of autonomy represents 'a strong ego in rational control of all its impulses' (ND 294). The Kantian ideal of autonomy effectively downgrades the impulses. It reconceives the experience of freedom as based, rather, on reason to which the impulses are subordinated. Our most valuable experiences of freedom, for modernity, are those which can be explained in terms of universalizable reasons. In this model the 'impulse' for freedom is construed as a property of the rational 'ego' or 'I'. But this, Adorno claims, is a distorting notion of freedom. Not only is (a) freedom narrowly identified with the ego (never with the body) but (b) the very notion of an impulse – what is not identifiable with the ego – is denigrated and marginalized. The motivations to act that comes from the impulses are associated, in this model, with mere inferior nature and thus, ironically, with unfreedom (as nature and reason/freedom are allegedly opposed). In Kant's theory, for instance, the impulses are pathological, not rational. Against that theory Adorno writes:

> Without an anamnesis of the untamed impulse that precedes the ego – an impulse later banished to the zone of unfree

bondage to nature – it would be impossible to derive the idea
of freedom …

(ND 221–22)

When the impulses are in that way construed, as mere nature, freedom, according to Adorno, takes on a 'perverted form' (ND 222).
Freedom as a power of, for instance, law-giving rationality, not of
impulse, constrains freedom under a rationalistic principle of action.

From the perspective of modern conceptions of freedom it
appears as though Adorno is attempting to replace rational agency
(autonomy) with some primitive natural freedom (impulse). Adorno
is certainly seeking to be provocative. But, more importantly, he is
offering a profoundly challenging thesis – directed against the
German Idealist tradition in particular – that *freedom cannot be derived
from reason*. He rejects the modern belief that it is 'only as rational
creatures that human beings' can 'raise themselves just one little bit
above nature, and that men are only free because they are thinking
beings, *res cogitans*' (HF 227). Adorno argues that the rationalist
theory of freedom fails to make sense of the totality of human
motivations. It acknowledges that we have drives that are 'prior to
the ego', yet these drives are also – as, again, exemplified by the
Kantian notion of autonomy – 'subjected to the centralizing
authority of consciousness' (HF 213). That account of freedom
means, though, that we are free when those drives are suppressed
by our higher, truly free, rational selves. In this act of self-mastery –
which Adorno finds at work in the autonomy model of freedom – the
supposedly irrational and erratic is kept in check. It is a notion of
freedom that, according to Adorno's interpretations, actually
requires human beings to be at odds with themselves.

Adorno's comments about this act of self-mastery are not of
course concerned exclusively with a philosophical account of freedom.
That problematic philosophical account of freedom reflects, he holds,
the one concretely experienced by modern repressed individuals. The
modern self is a 'strong ego as a firm identity' (ND 241). Modern

individuals are expected by others and by themselves to take total possession of their decisions and actions. Their actions should be subject to the control of their rational selves. But this effort at self-possession cannot, Adorno claims, succeed. The impulses will break through and trouble the purity of the ego's identity. This break-through of the impulses is an experience that the self, which understands itself as the master of its own experience, will struggle to recognize as its own. As Adorno notes, these impulses are sometimes understood by us as 'not me'. In the language of psychoanalysis, those impulses which are experienced as contrary to the will of the ego – neuroses – are encountered by the self as alien precisely because it is the ego which has come to be identified as the core of our personal identity: 'This truth content of neuroses is that the I has its unfreedom demonstrated to it, within itself, by something alien to it – the feeling that "this isn't me at all"' (ND 222).

Against Adorno it might be argued that the impulses are hardly likely to contribute to any kind of rational social order. And critical theory surely has no interest in replacing current societal norms with chaos. The impulses are commonly represented as drives which, like the id, threaten to overwhelm the conscious control of the agent, leading to actions which are incompatible with any social norms. Repression, Freud had claimed, is necessary because the libidinal expressions of the id would constantly disrupt any possibility of organized society. However, Adorno gives Freud's thesis a socio-critical significance by arguing that the libido becomes problematic – apparently contrary to reason and wild – *only in the context of repression*. For Adorno it is an 'insight of psychoanalysis ... that civilization's repressive mechanism transforms the libido into aggression against civilization' (ND 337), that is, that the repression of the id situates it beyond the reach of civilization and therefore in some way in opposition to it. What this thought invites us to consider is the idea that the destructive characteristics of the id are contingent upon a context of repression. The absence of a particular kind of ego – the repressive ego – would not simply release the id. Thinking dialectically about the ego and the id means appreciating the effects of the relation on each element of the relationship. This may then allow us to conceive of the impulses – in so far as they are associated by Adorno with the id – as containing a currently constricted potential.

Yet even if we can broadly appreciate why the impulses need not be understood as essentially destructive it is difficult to know how they, the impulses, can be intelligibly presented as compatible with any notion of autonomy. The question of this compatibility arises because, as we shall see more clearly in the following section, Adorno does not reject the notion of autonomy in principle. He develops a notion of freedom that integrally involves rational, reflective processes. His argument is with the repressive conception of autonomy. But is a non-repressive – in Adorno's terms – theory possible? That is, is there any coherent conception of autonomy which does not require the agent to repress the impulses and, instead, give priority to reasoned action?

Adorno provides us with a thought which, potentially at least, is the basis for a non-rationalistic, impulse inclusive notion of autonomy. The thought is that reason itself might be understood, contrary to the conventional rationalistic line, as compatible with the impulses. Adorno holds that the notion that the impulses stand in opposition to reason has its origins in the modern dualistic conception of the human being. This dualism, as already noted, gives us the options of freedom as a feature of our intellectual being or, as the only alternative, unfreedom in tying us to impulsive nature and pathological determinations. This notion of freedom elevates the self beyond the space of causality and therefore outside of corporality or the body. Rejecting the dualism upon which this notion of freedom is based also means that our explanation of freedom has to take account of its material location. Adorno claims, in fact, that the impulses are the bodily location of freedom. The rationalistic account sees the 'will' – our faculty of freedom – as occupying a space of reasons in principle separate from the space of causes, i.e. nature.

Adorno, by contrast, seeks to resituate the will – the basis of freedom – within the body. He writes:

> A will without physical impulses, impulses that survive, weakened, in imagination, would not be a will. At the same time, however, the will settles down as the centralizing unit of impulses, as the authority that tames them and potentially negates them. This necessitates a dialectical definition of the will.
>
> (ND 241)

A dialectical notion of the will, which does not oppose mind to body, has implications for reason: it undermines the notion that how we *reasonably choose* is an activity exclusive to the mind. In a daring and programmatic passage Adorno writes:

> Both body and mind are abstractions of their experience. Their radical difference is posited, reflecting the mind's historically gained 'self-consciousness' and its rejection of what it denies for its own identity's sake. All mental things are modified physical impulses, and such modification is their qualitative recoil into what not merely 'is'.
>
> (ND 202)

Reasons, as 'mental things', can also be included under the description of 'modified physical impulses'. While there are a great many questions to be raised about this naturalization of reason it is clear what Adorno's intention is: to reposition reason by rejecting the claims for its supra-natural basis: 'the transcendentally pure I would be incapable of impulses' (ND 215). And that, again programmatically, points to the possibility of reason and nature (impulse) reconciled.

Adorno supports this reconciliation by offering an evolutionary account of reason. Reason, he claims, is a process through which human beings have achieved independence from the natural environment. The notion of reason as a transcendental property does not realize that reason is, in fact, a distinctive mode of our natural self-preservational relationship to our environment:

> The prehistory of reason, that it is a moment of nature and yet something else, has become the immanent definition of reason. It is natural as the psychological force split off for purposes of self-preservation.
>
> (ND 289)

The psychoanalytic theory reappears here: the exigencies of self-preservation require the deferral of pleasure. When there is this forgetfulness about the natural basis of reason it – reason – comes to be construed as independent of us, as having an authority which transcends our natural being and our array of natural needs. These needs are placed outside reason: 'once split off and contrasted with nature, it also becomes nature's otherness' (ND 289). Conceived as opposition to nature reason acts against the impulses: 'reason has its origin in the suppression of impulse and of impulses of the will' (HF 256). A critical awareness of reason's natural foundation – in contrast to the notion of reason as existing above nature – suggests for Adorno the possibility of a reconciliation between reason and non-repressive of autonomy.

Adorno was not alone in the effort to develop a critical theoretical version of psychoanalytic psychology, i.e. a version which sees the phenomenon of 'repression' or the current characterization of the 'id' as historically and normatively contingent. His one time colleague Herbert Marcuse attempted to explicate the notion of non-repressive freedom without rendering that freedom irreconcilable with reason. Marcuse develops Freud's thought that the basic instincts are destructive in that 'they strive for a gratification which culture cannot grant' (Marcuse 1956: 11). They are destructive in the sense that they are not constructive, and they cannot be gratified in that the reality in which human beings live is one in which there is scarcity: we do not live in a paradise where all our needs are granted. But in regarding repression as necessary Freud seems to be committed to what we might term an 'economic inevitabilism' in which a society organized more or less along the lines of current Western societies is what is logically produced by the civilizing process. The generation of civilization in this form is achieved through the repression of the pleasure principle. The id drives, whose relation to the world is mediated by the ego, are eventually dominated by the ego in the face of a reality ever more antagonistic to the needs of the id. The ego has the task of (Marcuse quotes Freud):

> ... representing the external world for the id, and so of saving it; for the id blindly striving to justify its instincts in complete disregard of the superior strength of outside forces, could not otherwise escape annihilation.
>
> (Marcuse 1956: 30)

What Marcuse proposes is that against Freud the development of the reality/performance principle from the pleasure principle is not inexorable since it arises as a response to scarcity/*Ananke/Lebensnot*. Scarcity, however, is an exogenous factor 'not inherent in the "nature" of the instincts' (Marcuse 1956: 132). It is therefore a practical problem of under-production rather than a fact of nature. Nevertheless, contemporary society continues to perpetuate scarcity since it does not gear itself towards the satisfaction of needs, as the persistence of poverty seems to suggest. Rather, it involves competition among its members who vie for resources and goods. In this world, individuals develop what Marcuse calls 'surplus-repression' in order to survive within a hostile social environment. Importantly, in Marcuse's discussion, the idea that pleasure might sometimes be healthily deferred is not denied. His critical thesis is that contemporary society forces us to repress pleasure most of the time. The conception of repression in Marcuse has, then, two levels: (i) modification of the instincts that is consistent with any kind of ordered community of individuals and (ii) surplus-repression in which our actions are motivated by a desire to survive in a society which does not seek to satisfy our needs for once and for all. Even moments of apparent release from surplus-repression bear the marks of self-control and structured action. Marcuse claims, for instance, that the libido 'is diverted for socially useful performances', that is, towards reproduction (Marcuse 1956: 45). The implications of the removal of surplus repression would be virtually utopian, but Marcuse sees it as a realizable possibility were the means of production to be reorganized in order to resolve the underlying problem of scarcity. Adorno expresses himself more cautiously about the utopian prospects of a critique of organized freedom. Yet Marcuse, through his two-layer conception of repression, provides what Adorno did not: an explicit explanation of the possibility of a non-repressive form of rational freedom which accommodates what is currently marginalized as the 'impulses'.

At the beginning of this section the question was raised of why individuals act with apparent freedom under norms that critical theory, at least, understands to be against the best interests of human beings. From the material we have examined above we can see the general answer Adorno provides. The modern denigration of the impulses – 'libidinal' energies and spontaneous drives – is part of the construction of the image of human beings as 'egos' who should be able effectively to control themselves through reason. Rational self-control becomes the prevailing understanding of freedom. But it is false because it is repressive. Social norms – which oblige behaviour of a particular kind – place a demand on individuals that makes repression central to the reality of being a modern individual. Individuals cannot easily cast off constraining norms because they themselves are built on constraint. This is the 'normal man' (Sándor Ferenczi) who, Adorno writes, 'actively and passively lends himself to every social repression' (ND 273). This 'normal man', built on the ego, operates with the repressive notion of freedom: 'the repressing agent, the compulsive mechanism, is one with the I, the organon of freedom' (ND 223). Adorno's alternative idea of spontaneous reason is, we might say, an imaginative philosophical proposal. Modern individuals could not act in that way without, somehow, surrendering a great deal of what they – egocentric individuals – have understood themselves to be.

4. Autonomy as resistance

In view of Adorno's criticisms of autonomy it would seem that we could have no reason to continue to base our ideals of freedom on the apparently ideological notion of the autonomous agent. Yet it is a notable feature of Adorno's work that as a public intellectual in post-war Germany he was energetically engaged in advocacy for the necessity of personal autonomy. In particular, he argued that the decisions made by millions of Germans during the period of the Third Reich could largely be explained by the absence of autonomous consciousness. The task of education, he proposed, was to develop a form of critical self-reflection – which he refers to as autonomy – that would ensure that the blind behaviour of the past would never recur. In this context he presents autonomy as a valuable innovation of modernity, albeit one that was never realized. He writes, for example:

> The objective end of humanism is only another expression for the same thing. It signifies that the individual as individual, in representing the species of man, has lost the autonomy through which he might realize the species.
>
> (MM §17, 38)

The ideal of autonomy, Adorno argues, continues nevertheless to be relevant to the contemporary challenge of social renewal. In his discussions of education, in particular, he maintains (as we shall see), though without ever quite giving philosophical substance to it, that the developmental goal of a rational society is a community of autonomous individuals. And what is striking about Adorno's presentation of the need for education for autonomy – which we shall now examine – is that it is articulated in separation from his concerns about autonomy's ideological and repressive character.

In an essay of 1959, 'Theory of Pseudo-Culture (*Halbbildung*)' Adorno identifies '*Bildung*' – the humanistic formation of the educated individual – as fundamental to any society in which autonomous individuality is to flourish. In such a society the individual would be self-directed yet somehow not directed (selfishly) against society. That self-directedness would mark out the individual as a rational, rather than instinctual being. He writes:

> *Bildung* was supposed to benefit the free individual – an individual grounded in his own consciousness but developing within society, sublimating his instincts purely as his own spirit (*Geist*). It is implicitly the prerequisite of an autonomous society – the more enlightened the individual, the more enlightened society as a whole.
>
> (TPC 19, translation adjusted)

Bildung does not place the individual above society: it enables, as Adorno elaborates, 'the individual to preserve himself as a rational person in a rational society, as a free person in a free society' (TPC 19). For Adorno, in that essay at least, the conditions of contemporary society – with the requirements of functional freedom and the stupefying effect of popular culture – work against the potential of individuals to realize themselves through *Bildung*. We are left, rather, with a disfigured and unproductive version of it, '*Halbbildung*' (literally, half-education or half-formation). Education which gives individuals some knowledge of the 'facts' of cultural history or superficial acquaintance with its main ideas, but which does not actually cultivate them, is *Halbbildung*. Adorno finds this in the current educational system and among the various entertainment providers – radio and publishing – that attempt to make culture into something which can be acquired without any personal transformation. The analysis of the possibility of autonomy in this 1959 essay is pessimistic. But the uncomplicated appreciation of autonomy must nevertheless be noted. Adorno does not regard autonomy as a fantasy or philosophical construction, but as an objective relevant to the kinds of beings we are and whose realization is obstructed by the practices of contemporary society.

Adorno returned to this notion in the essay, 'Education After Auschwitz' (1966). He charts a number of features of German society which he believes set the conditions for the realization and implementation of the Nazi's genocidal policies. He considers the role of *authority* in German life as one explanation for the blind rule-following that was required for enforcement of the laws of the state. And he explores the attendant issue of the common desire to 'fit in' by *following the rules*. Also discussed are the dangers of a community that closes itself through *social bonds*, based on sentiment. Those who are connected through these bonds may form hostile perceptions of outside groups who are, their assumption goes, spiritually incapable of true social belonging. Adorno expresses worries about a contrived 'aggressive' (CM 192) and 'evil' (CM 203) nationalism. Opposing all of these tendencies, he claims, is the potential of autonomy:

> The single genuine power standing against the principle of Auschwitz is autonomy, if I might use the Kantian expression: the power of reflection, of self-determination, of not cooperating.
>
> (CM 195)

He recommends a new programme of education geared towards the development of a capacity for the exercise of this power. And it has to meet a concrete challenge. 'The premier demand upon all education', Adorno writes, 'is that Auschwitz not happen again' (CM 191). He adds: 'Every debate about the ideals of education is trivial and inconsequential compared to this single ideal: never again Auschwitz' (CM 191). Education for autonomy should enable individuals to recognize the dangers of the assumptions and practices which lead to a collective and generalized hatred of a group identified as not truly part of the communal 'whole'.

To invoke autonomy in this context gives it a specific historical character: it involves, primarily, taking an oppositional attitude to those norms which carried non-reflective, non-self-critical individuals into the collective blindness and brutality of the Holocaust. In a radio discussion with Hellmut Becker, broadcast in the month of his death, Adorno considers the question of intellectual maturity, Mündigkeit. In that discussion he makes it equivalent to autonomy. He laments a contemporary lack of 'regard to autonomy, and therefore to maturity' (EMR 24).

Kant announced, in 'What is Enlightenment?' (1784) the Enlightenment – an intellectual revolution which included among its achievements Kant's own theory of autonomy – as the first stages of humanity's realized maturity: 'Enlightenment is man's emergence from his self-incurred immaturity (Unmündigkeit). Immaturity is the inability to use one's understanding without the guidance of another' (Kant 1991: 54). Kant perceives this Unmündigkeit as a moral failing which can nevertheless be overcome with courage. 'Sapere Aude!', dare to know, he declares. Elsewhere Kant develops a pedagogy for moral education which effectively acknowledges that autonomy is an achievement, rather than the default position of human beings (Kant 2011).

Adorno specifies that education for Mündigkeit is one of 'education for protest and for resistance' (EMR 31). He provides some concrete exercises which might be used to develop the capacities for resistance. Children would be exposed to various forms of allegedly manipulative media – commercial movies, mood setting music broadcast on radio, magazines, pop music – and the teacher would help them to see through the 'hypocrisy', delusion, emotional exploitation and inauthenticity at the core of these media (EMR 31). Through this process, Adorno claims, 'all we try to do is simply to open people's minds to the fact that they are constantly being deceived' (EMR 31).

We can see from Adorno's observations that what education must work towards, for him, cannot after all be Bildung. Bildung, in the classical sense, is an ideal which is unrealistic in the present. Society has 'deprived it of a foundation' (TPC 38). Bildung allowed, as we saw above, 'the individual to preserve himself as a rational person in a rational society, as a free person in a free society', but a society characterized as deception is not conducive to the development of a rational person. Education is therefore to be directed towards the development of critical consciousness in which individuals learn to resist various forms of manipulation. Instruction in substantive ideals about humanity or morality is not specified as part of the curriculum. Autonomy is, as Adorno presents it, a negative behaviour: a capacity to resist collective political and cultural norms.

The exercise of autonomy, in this context, looks like the practice of a critical-theory minded individual. What Adorno describes as autonomy – resistance – is, in fact, very close to the philosophical attitude he explicitly recommends. In 'Why Still Philosophy' Adorno sets out the hostile conditions in which philosophy must operate. Here, as ever, he sees philosophy endangered by recent trends in philosophy, by two in particular. The first is Heideggerian philosophy with its 'intimidation not to think anything that is not pure' and the second is positivist philosophy with its 'scientistic intimidation not to think anything that is not "connected" to the corpus of findings recognized as scientifically valid' (CM 13). Ontology allegedly raises itself above history and withdraws from the essential philosophical enterprise of critique (CM 7–8), while positivism commits itself to the authority and objectivity of science. In contrast philosophy – in this respect closely resembling Adorno's notion of autonomy – must insist on critique:

> If philosophy is still necessary, it is so only in the way it has been from time immemorial: as critique, as resistance to the expanding heteronomy, even if only as thought's powerless attempt to remain its own master ...
>
> (CM 10)

He goes on to argue that this is achieved through immanent critique: critique means 'to convict of untruth, by their own criteria' those models of thought which threaten philosophy (CM 10). Without this 'resistance against the common practices of today and what they serve' (CM 6) philosophy as a critical enterprise ceases: the 'autonomy of reason' vanishes (CM 9). (In fact, Adorno's philosophy, as we have seen, self-evidently offers a number of theses which are not purely critical, but also constructive.)

The model of autonomy as resistance is made necessary by historical developments. Adorno cannot, as we have seen, reinvoke the Kantian notion of autonomy as the self-legislation of the self-determining rational agent and nor is autonomy as *Bildung* realizable. The 'reasons' available to the individual in an irrational society provide no basis for genuine self-determination. Further, because of the historical situation of late capitalist society we cannot expect individuals simply to know what to do through pure and undistorted reason. The prevailing norms – the prevailing philosophies too – have nothing to do with an emancipated world. Resistance, however, is not a matter of blank rejectionism: the individual asserts autonomy through critique of specific forms of manipulation. Adorno's discussion of freedom does not end with negativity, that is, with resistance alone. In his considerations of the possibility of morality, to which we now turn, he offers an account of a free moral agency which might regain a capacity to contribute to rebuilding a moral community.

5. Morality

In *Negative Dialectics* there is considerable focus on what Adorno regards as the problems of moral philosophy. He works to reveal these problems through criticisms of Kant's moral theory. He takes this approach because he believes, as he announced in a lecture, that the concept of morality has been 'developed above all and with the greatest incisiveness in Kantian philosophy' (PMP 15). By examining

Kant's central claims we can, Adorno thinks, gain access to the particular way that morality has evolved and adapted to the distinctive conditions of modernity.

But there is a further dimension to Adorno's engagement with the idea of morality. He develops a *new categorical imperative* in order to provide us with some way of stimulating our capacity for moral responsiveness. It attempts to redress what Adorno sometimes speaks of as 'bourgeois coldness' (MM §6, 26; MM §46, 74), an absence of feeling necessitated by the terms of survival within current socio-historical arrangements (ND 363). This categorical imperative is not, as we shall see, a reflective instrument in which the individual withdraws from 'pathological' motivations in order to act only under a pure moral law. On the contrary, as Adorno puts it: 'the new imperative gives us a bodily sensation of the moral addendum – bodily, because it is now the practical abhorrence of the unbearable' (ND 365). The basis of this claim will be clarified as we move to Adorno's criticisms of the alleged gap between intellectualism and action that is characteristic of modernity.

Much of what Adorno has to say about the nature of moral action is closely aligned with the conception of autonomy he recommends. He frequently associates moral action with resistance, though they appear to refer to separable perspectives. Autonomy is negative. It is the power of the individual to take a critical view of rules that individual is expected to be guided by: it is 'resistance to heteronomy ... the countless forms of morality that are imposed from outside' (PMP 170). Morality, by contrast, relates to what we ought to do. Yet identifying those 'oughts' has become problematic. Traditional moral precepts could not withstand the normative forces that overwhelmed the Germany of the Third Reich. Adorno proposes that it is only by way of a radical reconception of what we take to be a moral norm that we can move towards a genuinely moral condition.

The original Kantian version of the categorical imperative brings a formal element to morality. It asks us to consider whether our

maxims for action could be coherently universalized. It enables us
to identify unconditional – categorical – principles of morality. In
one of several articulations of the categorical imperative Kant states:
'act only in accordance with that maxim through which you can at
the same time will that it become a universal law' (Kant 1997:
31 [IV: 421]). Adorno understands his alternative version of the
categorical imperative to be driven by a substantive reaction to
concrete suffering. He writes:

> A new categorical imperative has been imposed by Hitler upon
> unfree mankind: to arrange their thoughts and actions so that
> Auschwitz will not repeat itself, so that nothing similar will
> happen.
>
> (ND 365)

This presence of the image of Auschwitz in the process of moral
decision means that Adorno's categorical imperative is not a for-
malistic device. Formalism is moral thinking guided by some criterion
of correctness: the internal consistency of the moral judgment or
the pre-establishment of moral principles designed to cover all
moral contingencies. While Adorno certainly prefers formalism in
ethics – with its context-independent stipulations of universalism
and categorical obligation – over the 'bloody colors' (ND 236) of
ethnic politics it nevertheless falls short of genuine moral responsiveness. Its 'painful abstractness' (ND 272) means, for Adorno,
that it departs from the particular experience of moral situations.

Adorno does not direct us on how exactly the new categorical
imperative is to be fulfilled nor what precise demands it places on us.
It is not difficult, however, to expand on his position by considering
the imperative alongside the central contention of his entire philosophy. The new categorical imperative is an unconditional
demand that we act against identity thinking. As we have already seen
in a number of contexts, identity thinking is accused of marginalizing
and imperilling particularity by seeking only what is general or

universal. The genocidal reconfiguration of Europe is, for Adorno, the apotheosis of identity thinking. What was not compatible with the generalized identity of German society was expelled as an enemy to that identity. It was an instance of what Adorno describes as 'the equation of the dissimilar ... with the opponent' (MM §85, 132). The very presence of people with a Jewish background was construed by this form of thought as a danger to the very idea of Germany and thereby (somehow) to its greatness. Adorno, with Horkheimer, explains it in this way: 'For the fascists the Jews are not a minority but the antirace, the negative principle as such; on their extermination the world's happiness depends' (DE 137).

In its insistence that we act without commitments to identity thinking the new categorical imperative involves vigilance against not only anti-Semitism but all forms of social essentialism. Adorno considers racism and nationalism to be the definitive cases of identity thinking. But we would today add a number of further ones – such as sexism, ageism and sectarianism – which have allocated disadvantaging spaces to various 'out groups'. Acting with consciousness of any tendency we might have to assume that social delineations are natural – rather than historical and, sometimes, functional – is effectively the demand the new categorical imperative places on us.

In Adorno's few comments on the new categorical imperative there is no recommendation that we turn to any existing moral values. Why does he not simply remind us of our well-established injunctions against murder, torture, prejudice and dispossession? The answer is obvious: these injunctions had no power over those who initiated, supported or tacitly agreed with the anti-Semitic policies of Nazi Germany. Adorno's view is that conventional morality is, ultimately, interpreted through the needs of the social totality: it has become the set of instructions that allows for the coordination of individuals within the system. It has its function within the whole. (On just this problem we have seen Adorno's concerns about the ideological form of autonomy: it turns out not to be genuine freedom but rather freedom functionally related to the needs of a capitalist system.) Hence, Adorno's remark on the impossibility of a moral life in a society not designed for the emancipation and flourishing of individual human beings: 'wrong life cannot be lived rightly' (MM §18, 39). Our 'wrong' or 'false' communities contain no values from which we might simply select in order to develop a moral resilience to the evils of Auschwitz. The norms that bind society together serve merely to perpetuate a society that does not contribute to the fulfilment of the individual: 'life itself is so deformed and distorted that no one is able to live the good life in it or to fulfil his destiny as a human being' (PMP 167).

But it appears that for Adorno the traditional injunctions are not wrong: they have simply become optional, partial or degraded. They are instructions without reference to all of humanity, allowing, as Auschwitz has shown, exceptions to be made on the basis of some alleged political necessity. It is in response to that deficiency that the new categorical imperative is conceived. For Adorno it is not a conceptual activity through which moral precepts are to be generated out of nothing. It infuses our intuitions about what we should do with historical experience. It tries to make categorical – not contingent or hypothetical – our human revulsion against violence. Its objective is to give our intuitive reactions of horror to what is wrong a new vitality.

Specifically against the intellectualism of Kantianism – with its 'abstract rigorism' (PMP 168) – Adorno argues that the new categorical imperative has a 'bodily' location. It is through the body that we experience what is morally objectionable. Auschwitz was wrong not for its formal violation of the moral law but because of the suffering it inflicted. A sympathetic – bodily – response to that suffering is urged by the new categorical imperative. It is 'now the practical abhorrence of the unbearable physical agony to which individuals are exposed' (ND 365).

Adorno also calls this bodily reaction an 'impulse'. It is not clear what connection he wishes to make, if any, between the freedom impulse and the impulse to react against suffering. He holds that the impulse is a fundamental moral disposition with the potential to react spontaneously to situations of human suffering. This is obviously disputable. And he claims that the existence of the moral impulse speaks against the notion of morality as the outcome of reflection:

> The impulse – naked physical fear, and the sense of solidarity with what Brecht called 'tormentable bodies' – is immanent in moral conduct and would be denied in attempts at ruthless rationalization. What is most urgent would become contemplative again, mocking its own urgency.
>
> (ND 286)

Through a consideration of the figure of Hamlet Adorno explores the idea that moral action is originally determined by contemplation. He argues that Hamlet's famous flaw, his procrastination, is a powerful artistic representation of the modern separation of thought and action, of theory and practice:

> ... it is at the outset of the self-emancipating modern subject's self-reflection, in *Hamlet*, that we find the divergence of insight and action paradigmatically laid down. The more the subject turns into a being-for-itself, the greater the distance it places between itself and the unbroken accord with a given order, the less will its action and its consciousness be one.
>
> (ND 228)

The Hamlet figure, as a being-for-itself, is immobilized by the separation for him of knowledge and action. This separation has been produced by the modern conception of the moral dimension as control of one's impulses (repression, as we have seen). The pre-modern condition – Adorno asserts – comprehended reason and action as a fundamental unity. The unity was broken down, by modern reason, into separate elements. A consequence of this separation is the problematization of the very idea of action. Adorno claims: 'people suffer from their knowledge [like Hamlet] because they discover that no direct path leads from knowledge to practice' (PMP 112–13).

We moderns are left with the disposition of Hamlet: we are able to think abstract moral principles and their contraries. And we are thereby quite uncertain about acting at all. Adorno claims that for action to occur it needs 'a third thing, namely that injection of irrationality, of something no longer reducible to reason ... ' (PMP 113). It is within this framework that Hamlet's hesitation can be explained:

> ... for Hamlet to be able to put into practice the moral and political ideas he has formed, he must perforce regress; he must return to an earlier archaic stage – the stage of immediate expression, that is to say, of hitting out ... Hamlet, then, must in a sense have acted in accordance with some such archaic desires in order to obtain his revenge. Revenge, for its part, is likewise an archaic phenomenon that is not really compatible with a rational, bourgeois order of things.
>
> (HF 234–35)

Adorno seems to believe that the impulsiveness that Hamlet lacked is an essential feature of any moral act. That is evident in his discussion of the July 1944 assassination attempt on Hitler. Adorno reports the reply he received from one of the plotters when he asked him why he had acted against Hitler when the consequences of failure were so obviously grave. The reply was that it seemed like the right thing to do, regardless. Adorno comments:

> I would say that this is the true primal phenomenon of moral behaviour. It occurs when the element of impulse joins with the element of consciousness to bring about a spontaneous act.
>
> (HF 240)

Certainly the moral consciousness of the plotters was not like that
of Hamlet for whom detached morality could not find 'immediate
expression' in action.

There is an obviously troubling feature of what Adorno here
commends to us. It replaces an intellectualism, whose deficiencies
are well expressed, with impulsiveness. And it seems to say that an
impulse quickly settles questions of morality. This is confirmed by a
comment he makes about the Nuremberg trials:

> If the men charged with torturing, along with their overseers,
> had been shot on the spot, this would have been more moral
> than putting a few on trial … Once a judicial machinery must
> be mobilized against them, with codes of procedure, black
> robes, and understanding defence lawyers, justice – incapable
> in any case of imposing sanctions that would fit the crimes – is
> falsified already.
>
> (ND 287)

This appears very much like a version of 'wild justice', somehow
encouraging people of conviction to dispense with life without any
scruples about matters of justification or consideration of their effects
on the broader legal order. And it is at odds with a common perception
that the Nuremberg trials, however flawed, were important contributions to the development of a legal framework for dealing with
major human rights transgressions. In fact, Adorno in *Minima Moralia*
concedes something like this point. He claims that the very nature of
morality may leave us with a divided perspective: we both want to
act within just institutions but can also believe, at the very same
time, that acting justly may sometimes mean acting against those
institutions. Reporting his own personal standpoint he writes:

> To the question of what is to be done with defeated Germany,
> I could say only two things in reply. Firstly: at no price, on no
> conditions, would I wish to be an executioner, or to supply

legitimations for executioners. Secondly: I should not wish, least of all with legal machinery, to stay the hand of anyone who was avenging past misdeeds. This is a thoroughly unsatisfactory, contradictory answer, one that makes a mockery of both principle and practice. But perhaps the fault lies with the question and not only in me.

(MM §33, 56)

Adorno – in this passage at least – is prepared to think of morality as antinomical, that is, of supporting two mutually exclusive accounts of what it is (governed by principles, lived through impulse). But this perhaps should serve as a warning against the tidy interpretative conclusion that Adorno is attempting to develop a systematic moral theory based on impulse, that is, a theory which can anticipate the correct response in advance of experience. By acknowledging the antinomy Adorno frankly distances himself from a central objective of traditional theory: comprehensive explanation. In this light Adorno's discussions of the impulse undermine, though without trying to replace, the rationalist account of human motivation. (Complicating this further, we might observe that at the time that Adorno suggested the antinomy of moral action he had yet to develop his notion of the impulse. *Minima Moralia* appeared in 1951, and Adorno began to formulate the idea of the impulse in lecture courses of at least ten years later in preparation for *Negative Dialectics*).

Adorno draws out a further implication of moral action no longer generated by the intellect. He believes – and this is also a consequence of his unwillingness to play along with tradition – that what he is proposing undermines the certainty for which abstract moral reasoning reaches. Against the modern tradition he writes: 'There is no moral certainty' (ND 242). This uncertainty, in fact, is a feature of the moral life, not a state of loss. For Adorno this means that any effort to deny moral uncertainty in action would be a violation of morality itself. The assumption of certainty, he writes, 'would be immoral, would falsely relieve the individual of anything that might be called morality' (ND 242–43). In other words, the activity of applying moral judgments to a situation as though they were a perfect fit is not an activity of genuine moral practice. It is, rather, identity thinking which attempts to control experience by the deployment of rules that have authority in advance of what we contingently face in reality. What Adorno says here is obviously consistent with his general notion of the dialectic of experience, yet what is lacking in Hamlet, and what is commendable about those who reacted impulsively against Hitler, is 'certainty'.

As I noted at the beginning of this chapter, Adorno did not set out to offer a systematic moral theory. The various commitments entailed in his notions of autonomy as resistance, the new categorical imperative, and the moral impulse at every point defy the idea that moral experience can be framed by rational principles. A systematic theory, however, does just that: it operates outside the space of moral situations and establishes what are supposed to be our norms on purely conceptual grounds. It offers a misleading account of what Adorno believes is more fundamentally at work in the genuine moral agent: an impulsive responsivity. To conduct morality through the conclusions of conceptual reflections can therefore only undermine it. Adorno expresses that danger in this way: 'We criticize morality by criticizing the extension of the logic of consistency to the conduct of men; this is where the stringent logic of consistency becomes an organ of unfreedom' (ND 285–86). Against the tradition Adorno positions his moral theory as an anti-theory. It certainly theorizes the nature and possibilities of morality, but it consciously refuses to rewrite our moral nature or to deduce a normative framework. And it rejects any notion of morality as a kind of argument in which reflection primarily determines its course. Speaking of the new categorical imperative, Adorno claims it would be an 'outrage' to deal with it 'discursively' (ND 365). Its reason is 'bodily' rather than 'formal'. It is the moral reason which underpins responsivity to the reality of suffering, a responsivity that, as we have seen Adorno argue, cannot be superseded by or translated into pure practical reason.

Summary

Adorno claims that the modern concept of autonomy has evolved within the dialectic of enlightenment. Human autonomy was a means of achieving emancipation from nature and authority. But as rational freedom it was influenced by the model of rationality that had brought success to scientific endeavours. Eventually, according to Adorno, the very notion of what it is to be a rational agent was marked by that model, and the modern individual was restricted in the exercises of reason to the kinds of calculative decisions that are distinctive to instrumental engagements with the environment. This development ultimately worked against the exercises of critical reason directed towards emancipation.

Autonomy, Adorno argues, is a form of freedom compatible with capitalist modes of behaviour. Individuals understand themselves to be free, but freedom is circumscribed by the needs of the social totality. This is evident in the ways in which social roles – effectively socio-economic – form the identity of the individual. The exercise of autonomy in this context therefore perpetuates the norms of bourgeois capitalist society.

Adorno interprets autonomy as repression. He makes use of psychoanalytic concepts to develop an account of the modern autonomous individual as the product of the ego's domination of the id. This repression produces agents who conceive themselves as purely rational actors. However, this is a distortion of our potential for action. Adorno holds that free action is, what he calls, impulse (though impulse is now repressed). Freedom is bodily, not the product of the ego. Adorno suggests an integrated account of mental and bodily aspects of experience. Herbert Marcuse's critical theoretical reading of psychoanalysis addresses the question of how a non-repressive form of rational freedom might be possible without the loss of any recognizable form of subjectivity.

The notion of autonomy is also given a positive account by Adorno. In this context autonomy must be pursued as a practice of resistance.

He develops a conception of education as geared towards the achievement of a capacity for critical self-reflection, a capacity that underpins the possibility of autonomy as resistance. Self-reflection would enable individuals to identify tendencies, either in society or in their own commitments, to prejudiced beliefs. The absence of that capacity provides the conditions in which Auschwitz could happen. Autonomy, Adorno also specifies, requires a kind of maturity. The mature autonomous agent will not be susceptible to the various forms of deception that mark contemporary life.

If moral agency is to regain its power to act against what is abhorrent its traditional models will need to be revised. Adorno proposes a new categorical imperative which, unlike the Kantian one, explicitly contains an image of what is wrong and what must be avoided. It is not formal. The notion of the impulse is at work in this conception of the categorical imperative. Adorno explores the loss of a capacity to act caused by the elevation of contemplation above the moral impulse. Hamlet is a paradigmatic figure of modernity in this regard. Adorno's notion of impulsive moral action appears to propose the opposite: spontaneous and decisive actions. However, Adorno also sets out an antinomy of the relationship between morality and just institutions, and that antinomy suggests that he is unwilling to provide a comprehensive theory of moral motivation.

Further reading

Bernstein, J. M. (2001) *Adorno: Disenchantment and Ethics*, Cambridge: Cambridge University Press, esp. chapter 8.

Finlayson, J. G. (2002) 'Adorno on the Ethical and the Ineffable', *European Journal of Philosophy*, Vol. 10, No. 1.

Freyenhagen, F. (2008) 'Moral Philosophy', in D. Cook (ed.) *Adorno: Key Concepts*, Stocksfield: Acumen.

Schweppenhäuser, G. (2004) 'Adorno's Negative Moral Philosophy', in T. Huhn (ed.) *The Cambridge Companion to Adorno*, Cambridge: Cambridge University Press.

Six
Aesthetics

Adorno is the unrivalled philosopher of aesthetic modernism. His reflective engagement with the artworks of his times was intense. As the author of books and numerous papers on twentieth-century composers he brought philosophical and musicological considerations to bear as well as a perspective gained from his own experience of composition. The critical approach Adorno took to music was often no less polemical than his interpretations of philosophy, both seeking to defend what he considered to be 'authentic' musical developments and to identify destructive directions within modernism itself. The works he most valued could be characterized as resolutely anti-totalistic, avoiding at all times what he conceived as forced reconciliations expressed through insistent harmonies. His interest in music, we should note, was not strictly confined to the contemporary scene.

Adorno's analyses of literature, although taking up a significantly smaller part of his collected works than those on music, are, nevertheless, of perhaps greater importance to his philosophical project of critical theory. Particular authors allowed him to articulate more exactly than through 'pure' theory alone what he understood as the truth about the social totality. Baudelaire, Kafka and Beckett were of pre-eminent significance to Adorno in this very regard. Adorno's many writings on a vast array of issues in modernism have made lasting impacts in the fields of literary studies and music theory. His strengths did not extend to offering an equally complex appreciation of the visual arts.

Towering over all of his already exceptionally innovative philosophical studies of art is the book that lay unfinished at the time of his death, *Aesthetic Theory*. Adorno's editors – his wife Gretel Adorno and Rolf Tiedemann – posit that Adorno was motivated to move beyond a disparate approach to writing on art (in essays and short monographs, usually devoted to a single artist) towards the challenge of the great book – which *Aesthetic Theory* certainly is – in order to integrate

> ... his ideas on aesthetics and to develop as a theory what until then he had notated in his many writings on music and literature. These ideas had often been taken to be, if not downright rhapsodic, then mere flashes of insight.
>
> (AT 362, editors' afterword)

Although this is not quite fair to the previous efforts it does encapsulate what *Aesthetic Theory* itself was trying to achieve: an analytical study in which the central elements of the theory of art and aesthetic experience were explored at a level of detail that was quite unprecedented in his work.

His editors tell us that the following maxim by Friedrich Schlegel was to have been the epigram for *Aesthetic Theory*: 'What is called the philosophy of art usually lacks one of two things: either the philosophy or the art' (AT 366, editors' afterword). Even through the inevitable imperfections of its unfinished state it is possible to judge that Adorno did not leave himself vulnerable to Schlegel's two-pronged admonition. The artists and artworks he discusses are not convenient examples of an antecedently established theory. And nor does Adorno lose his analysis in the particularity of the artworks he is considering. Numerous visits to the work of artists of the highest significance for him (in fact, he had intended to dedicate *Aesthetic Theory* to Beckett) stand alongside his dialectical appraisals of the aesthetic theories of Kant, Hegel and Benjamin.

What is not to be found in *Aesthetic Theory*, and this is not a consequence of its incompleteness, is a system. Adorno's many theses, concepts, proposals and interpretations add up, effectively, to his most comprehensive conception of aesthetics. But the relationship between the elements of his work is not deductive: those elements emerge in the manner – described in Chapter 1 – of an essayistic composition. Adorno understood himself to be responding to the *object*: the phenomenon of art and its various theories, an object that could not be systematized without distortion. *Aesthetic Theory* is Adorno's central work on aesthetics and therefore the book we must try to come to terms with if we are to grasp his overall conception of aesthetics. At the same time, it is a book that because of its robustly non-systematic form cannot truly be analysed without a loss of its original intricacy. Notwithstanding, we should not be deterred from the task of bringing to light Adorno's extraordinary contribution to aesthetics, even if no small amount of what *Aesthetic Theory* says and means must be left aside for the sake of expedience.

This chapter will mainly consider the two themes that dominate *Aesthetic Theory*: *mimesis* and the *autonomy of art*. As we shall see, the issues that Adorno considers within these themes constantly intersect. The interest he brings to bear on his understanding of mimesis and the autonomy of art is that of the critical potential of art and aesthetic experience. This interest penetrates every analysis he offers and effectively underpins an associative relationship between his constant flow of arguments and concepts.

1. Mimesis

The most elusive notion in all of Adorno's philosophy is that of mimesis. It appears in *Dialectic of Enlightenment* as part of Adorno and Horkheimer's speculative anthropology. In *Negative Dialectics* mimesis is carried, little more than suggestively, into Adorno's conception of experience: it names the rudimentary basis of the subject-object dynamic, but it is not another name for the subject-object relationship.

It is the pre-conceptual human desire to imitate and to seek affinity with an other, underpinning, what we saw in Adorno's discussion of morality, 'the sense of solidarity with what Brecht called "tormentable bodies"' (ND 286). In a non-reified realization of the subject-object relationship, this desire is pursued through the activities of conceptualization and judgment and through the correction of the content of those activities when contradictions emerge. It is in *Aesthetic Theory* that mimesis becomes a central theoretical principle. In that work Adorno endeavours to articulate a distinctly critical-theoretical account of the mimetic basis of art. Art is mimetic not only in its content – that is, in how what it says is in some way imitative of reality – but also in the aesthetic activities of performance and experience: the full range of the aesthetic realm is mimetic.

Although Adorno frequently contrasts the mimetic activity of aesthetic experience with reification it would be a mistake to think that he is doing so in order to recommend that we free ourselves from the distortions of the social totality by adopting a more generally aesthetic mode of behaviour. Aesthetic mimesis is rather a diagnostic concept. It serves as a reference point in Adorno's theory for non-reified human behaviour. It assumes a particular form in aesthetic activity, but even in that form it points towards something that is absent from the everyday experience of life within the social totality. Aesthetic experience possesses, he claims, 'the mimetic vestige, the plenipotentiary of an undamaged life in the midst of mutilated life' (AT 117), providing us with a glimpse of our mimetic potential. It is in this respect 'the unimpaired corrective of reified consciousness' (AT 330). In the experience of aesthetic mimesis – imitative creativity – there is 'the happiness of producing the world once over' (AT 339), that has almost entirely been eliminated by the reifying rationality of the social totality. Mimesis, then, is a dimension of human behaviour whose origins precede the development of the aesthetic realm, while somehow surviving only as a 'vestige' in an aesthetic form.

Aesthetic Theory contains, without methodical treatment, numerous references to mimesis or mimetic capacities, though no concentrated account of them. It would be easy to agree with Fredric Jameson's often quoted remark that mimesis is 'a foundational concept never defined nor argued but always alluded to, by name, as though it had preexisted all the texts' (Jameson 1990: 64). But it is possible to piece together what Adorno understands by this notion across its various contexts. And it is vital to do so. Without appreciating how mimesis relates to experience we would not only fail to understand Adorno's considerations of the aesthetic, we would also miss a vital part of the story he wants to tell about the nature of experience in general: that subjects have a capacity to orient themselves non-instrumentally towards objects and that an understanding of that orientation gains us a critical perspective on the current condition of experience.[1]

In the following sections I shall first turn to Adorno's earlier − i.e. pre-aesthetic theory − anthropological discussions of mimesis in order to see why he considered it a fundamental mode of human behaviour. His conceptions, in *Aesthetic Theory*, of the relationship between mimesis and imitation in art and between mimesis and aesthetic experience will then be examined before I explore the perhaps pivotal question of the rationality of mimesis.

2. Mimesis and the dialectic of Enlightenment

Adorno's earliest conception of mimesis is found in *Dialectic of Enlightenment* as part of his and Horkheimer's reconstruction of the pre-history of civilization. Mimesis is understood there as an original imitative capacity through which human beings once sought to apprehend the outer world. That mimetic apprehension was a process of human beings somehow likening themselves, through imitation, to mysterious parts of nature. As an example, they write: 'The magician imitates demons; to frighten or placate them he makes intimidating or appeasing gestures' (DE 6). The relationship between the subject and the object, in this context, is one of 'kinship' (DE 7), even in cases, as the example shows, when the individual is in confrontation with the forces of nature. The magician makes himself like the very demons he fears in order to place himself nearer to them. This mimetic orientation towards objects involves the individual in acts of adjustment towards the object. That adjustment is conducted through actions, behaviour and gestures.

Adorno and Horkheimer conceive of mimesis as a condition of objective human apprehension not exclusive to earlier human beings. The external orientation towards objects in our knowledge gaining activities is, for them, grounded in our basic mimetic capacity. However, that capacity is not adequately exercised when knowledge becomes – as it does in modernity – a matter of con-structivism: that is, when the subject seeks to generate knowledge through systems it establishes prior to engagement with objects. Constructivism is, they argue, a reversal of mimesis. It may well seek to apprehend the world but it does so by making the world fit with its systems. Writing of the notion that the world is most adequately grasped through mathematical conceptualizations they claim: 'mathematics made thought into a thing – a tool, to use its own term. Through this mimesis ... thought makes the world resemble itself ... ' (DE 19).

In mimetic behaviour the subject loses itself in an 'object of desire' (DE 27). The self driven by an affective interest in the world expands beyond itself. Constructivism, in stark contrast, is without the affective dimension. In *Negative Dialectics* Adorno would go on to characterize constructivism, in the shape of idealism, as a preda-torial 'devouring' rage against the world (ND 22–23). Adorno and Horkheimer's account of mimesis identifies a dimension of human engagement with the world not considered by the conventional explanation that human interest in the surrounding environment was originally motivated by practical concerns alone. Mimesis is a desire driven, transformative opportunity for the individual. Habermas describes it well:

> Imitation [or mimesis] designates a relation between persons in which the one accommodates to the other, identifies with the other, empathizes with the other. There is an allusion here to a relation in which the surrender of the one to the example of the other does not mean a loss of self but a gain and an enrichment.
>
> (Habermas 1984: 390)

This 'imitative' process is suggestive of Adorno's account of non-identical experience, which involves subjects adjusting, as we saw it argued, 'to a moment which they themselves are not' (ND 138). Adorno and Horkheimer contend that the dialectic of enlightenment eventually replaced the original mimetic immersion with conceptual structures that obviated the affective dimension. It thereby delimited the scope of the subject's capacity to know an object: 'Along with mimetic magic' enlightenment 'tabooed the knowledge which really apprehends the object' (DE 10).[2] Adorno and Horkheimer describe the original environmental relation as 'purely natural existence' (DE 24). However, it was precisely this natural immediacy which enlightenment sought to overcome. It succeeded, first through myth, in which human beings explained the processes of life through the actions of the gods, and then through systems of reason that would supersede the theocentric mediation of experience: 'the myths which fell victim to the Enlightenment were themselves its products' (DE 5). Adorno and Horkheimer posit that the pure, natural phase of human existence would come to represent a frightening image of humanity to those civilized orders that valorized the efforts of human beings to elevate themselves from mimetic relations to nature and to achieve a distanced, instrumental relationship towards it. Mimetic comportment, Adorno and Horkheimer claim,

> ... held the terror that the self would be changed back into the mere nature from which it had extricated itself with unspeakable exertions and which for that reason filled it with unspeakable dread.
>
> (DE 24)

Reason would have to prevent a reversion to that natural existence: it imposed the discipline of self-control. And what receded was the thought that subjects might not relate to objects primarily through systems of concepts or that their interest in objects might not be motivated by purely instrumental needs.

3. Mimesis, imitation and aesthetic theory

The possibilities of mimesis may, for Adorno, be distorted by the tendencies of modern rationality, but it is preserved, seemingly without distortion, in aesthetic activity. In *Aesthetic Theory* Adorno connects mimetic behaviour directly with the practices of art. He writes: 'Art is a refuge for mimetic comportment. In art the subject exposes itself, at various levels of autonomy, to its other, separated from it and yet not altogether separated ... ' (AT 53). The question of why art came to have this role has no satisfactory answer, as Tom Huhn points out (Huhn 2004b: 10). In fact, Adorno does not appear to consider the historical process that has underpinned the continuity between original mimetic comportment – operative in 'purely natural existence' – and the aesthetic domain. Adorno develops his theory of this domain through an analysis of modern art especially, though art, unlike purely natural existence, is an activity demarcated by certain norms, institutions, traditions, practices and media. Adorno nevertheless holds implicitly to a continuity between original mimesis and aesthetic mimesis. Aesthetic mimesis allows us to see the potential of non-rationalized human behaviour. Yet if we do not know why art is the refuge for mimetic comportment we cannot simply accept the claim of continuity between the two instantiations of mimesis. And that problematizes Adorno's efforts to extract some fact about the potential of human behaviour – a diagnostic concept – from the evidence provided by aesthetic mimesis precisely as a continuity with original mimesis. However, this worry does not have to bring Adorno's aesthetic theory to a standstill. The question of what art's mimetic dimension consists of – continuous or not – can still be asked. And, indeed, Adorno provides a complex set of analyses in answer to this question.

The effort to explain art as a mimetic activity is not, of course, unprecedented. The earliest and perhaps most influential philosophical discussion of this issue can be found in Plato and Aristotle who between them offer strikingly different conceptions of art's mimetic dimension. In trying to understand Adorno's sense of aesthetic mimesis some ground can actually be gained by a consideration of the ancient debate, even though Adorno himself barely mentions it.

In Plato's infamous denigration of art the term mimesis names the simple copying or imitation of material reality. According to Plato's metaphysics material reality is mere appearance of the ideal world of forms. It is a kind of imitation of the ideal. Art, which copies material reality, cannot be true since it is the 'imitation of appearance'. Indeed, it is imitation (the artwork) of an imitation (appearance of the ideal). In contrast, philosophy is oriented towards truth, as it is directly concerned through concepts with ultimate and ideal 'reality' itself (Plato 2000: 317 [598b]). Aristotle takes a quite different view of art, partly as a result of his rejection of Plato's metaphysics of appearance and reality.[3] He offers a profound reconception of what it means for art to have an imitative character, eschewing entirely the idea that it is mere copying. In the *Poetics* he claims that mimesis or imitation is a natural human capacity, one which informs the very processes of learning. He also holds that our appreciation of art is appreciation of its mimetic qualities. Yet these mimetic qualities are in no sense the artwork's representational accuracy. As Aristotle points out, we do in fact admire artworks that do not imitate any object (mythic or fictional beings) or perhaps imitate objects that we have never seen (and against which we therefore do not measure the artwork's verisimilitude). But in what way is an artwork imitative if it does not seek representational accuracy? Here we see the innovativeness of Aristotle's theory. In his conception of the art of tragedy the artwork imitates (a) 'nature itself, the universal immanent process of self-unfolding, the internal principle that produces and manifests itself in natural beings' (Bredin and Santoro-Brienza 2000: 38) and (b) action or praxis understood as 'a single spiritual event, a coherent set of existential experiences, a mental project, one single order of events, one *mythos* and one fundamental plot' (Bredin and Santoro-Brienza 2000: 39). Aristotle reconceives mimesis, then, as the effort to imitate processes. And the artwork itself must somehow embody, as tragedy actually does, the processual structure it imitates.

Adorno's conception of aesthetic mimesis is surprisingly close to Aristotle's, surprising given that Adorno's position emerges through reflections on modernist artworks in particular. For Aristotle and Adorno the aesthetic process is mimetic, though not representationally imitative (Plato could see in it only the latter and hence his deprecations of it). Adorno's rejection of representation as a genuinely aesthetic quality leads him to a sharp repudiation of photography as an art form. He criticizes Benjamin's thesis of 'copyrealism', describing as 'barbaric' 'a view of art that takes photography as its model' (AT 56). This assessment may be disputable. It is useful to us, though, in that it allows us to see Adorno's view of the dividing line between properly aesthetic imitation and what he takes to be mere representation. The non-representational principle of mimesis frames Adorno's ideas of how social reality is to be treated aesthetically. Art fails, he argues, if it attempts to express that reality through social realism, which he thinks of simply as representation and therefore as not genuinely aesthetic. This repudiation of representationalism applies no less forcefully to virtuous politically charged realist works that endeavour to represent empirical social reality as it is – its politics, its inequities and its evils – in order to educate their audiences. Adorno regards this work as 'crude propaganda' (AT 243) or, in the case of socialist realism, 'simply childish' (AT 250). Art must not either, Adorno holds, present images of a better life, one that would be free of reification. As representations they are without the mimetic dimension that is constitutive of art. More importantly, they also threaten to beguile us by offering images of a reconciled social reality in the absence of the conditions that would allow reconciliation. He figuratively invokes for art the theological notion of 'the prohibition on graven images' (AT 22; AT 104), that is, on representations of a better world. Adorno writes: 'For the sake of happiness, happiness is renounced' (AT 13).

What Adorno considers to be authentic art, then, does not attempt to name social processes. Yet Adorno is convinced that authentic art does succeed in effectively conveying the distinctive conditions of late capitalism, the period of the irrational social totality. His demanding claim is that authentic art expresses (mimesis) the destruction of experience in late capitalism without naming it (non-representationalism). It achieves this by enabling us to have experience of experience that has become irrational. Outside the space of the aesthetic, Adorno effectively says, there is simply withered experience. But authentic art provides us with an entirely different relation to that experience: it is no longer undergone without a sense that there is something wrong. The irrational norms of the social processes that govern us, and which are occluded in conventional life, become apparent. Crucially, they are not named: they are experienced. As Adorno writes:

> The opposition of artworks to domination is mimesis of domina-
> tion. They must assimilate themselves to the comportment of
> domination in order to produce something qualitatively distinct
> from the world of domination.
>
> (AT 289)

Through these artworks we gain a heightened experiential appreciation of a reified world in which we are normally uncritically immersed. Adorno's description of Kafka's work as a 'mimesis of reification' (AT 230) might be used to designate Adorno's own historically reconceived notion of mimesis.

4. Kafka and the mimesis of reification

Adorno considers Baudelaire's poetry an important instance of this
'mimesis of reification'. From the following passage we can see
how, through Baudelaire, Adorno understands the mimetic character
of modernist artworks:

> Baudelaire neither railed against nor portrayed reification; he
> protested against it in the experience of its archetypes, and
> the medium of this experience is the poetic form … The power
> of his work is that it syncopates the overwhelming objectivity of
> the commodity character.
>
> (AT 21)

Baudelaire's poetry expresses reification and commodification without
representing them. There is no recourse to realism. Adorno does not
ascribe a critical social intention to Baudelaire. But he finds a
mimetic character in Baudelaire's poetry through which the essential
norms of social reality are experienced. And this is because Baudelaire
is mimetically responsive to the world and all its distorting forms
of life. As Adorno also claims:

> Baudelaire proved to be correct: Emphatic modern art does not
> thrive in Elysian fields beyond the commodity but is, rather,
> strengthened by way of the experience of the commodity
> world …
>
> (AT 298)

Through its mimesis of the conditions of social reality Baudelaire's
poetry stands in implicit opposition to it: his poetry brings to
experience the problematic conditions of that reality – thereby
complicating our relationship with it. Prior to *Aesthetic Theory*
Adorno had developed a reading of Beckett's *Endgame* that, in certain
respects, anticipates the very idea of a mimesis of reification. The
play, he claims, situates itself within the 'complete reification of

the world' (NL I 245), though it is without reference to reification. As Adorno puts it, 'the name of the catastrophe is to be spoken only in silence' (NL I 249). The play's characters may appear as clowns with ridiculous purposes, but they are, Adorno believes, simply intensifications of the 'normal personality' (NL I 257). Nevertheless the play does not itself fall into meaninglessness. It successfully expresses, what Adorno calls (contrary to the existentialist reading), the 'final history of the subject' (NL I 271) – the destruction of human autonomy – through its specific aesthetic form: 'organized meaninglessness' (NL I 242).

However, it is Adorno's appraisal of Kafka that illustrates most extensively his notion of modernist mimesis. His main study of Kafka is the long and complex essay 'Notes on Kafka' (1953), which he republished in the collection *Prisms* (1955). But numerous references to Kafka are found throughout *Aesthetic Theory* and in the four part collection of essays, *Notes to Literature*. We can also see how deeply Adorno had been considering Kafka's work from the very beginning of his professional career from his correspondence with Benjamin (on the subject of Benjamin's essay, 'Franz Kafka').[4] Adorno claims that historical 'processes' are found as 'ciphers' in Kafka's work (P 252). This might seem to say that Adorno takes Kafka to be a social commentator who sought to say something about history. Although Adorno is aware of Kafka's political standpoints he does not take them to be determinative of the content of Kafka's fiction. Kafka *qua* writer was engaged in a purely aesthetic activity which nevertheless unintentionally but necessarily achieves a mimesis of social reality. As Adorno writes:

Kafka's works protected themselves against the deadly aesthetic error of equating the philosophy that an author pumps into a work with its metaphysical substance. Were this so, the work of art would be stillborn; it would exhaust itself in what it says and would not unfold itself in time.

(P 247)

Adorno's reading of Kafka, then, is not an effort to find an implicit
theory or illustrated examples of philosophical insights in the texts.
Adorno does not 'read off' a Kafkaesque philosophy from the literary work. He adopts Benjamin's description of Kafka's works as
'damaged parables' (AT 126): damaged in that they constantly suggest
complexes of metaphors, metaphors that cannot be unlocked. The key
to the interpretation of Kafka's work, Adorno says, 'has been stolen'
(P 246). Each work invites decoding yet 'none will permit it'
(P 246). When Adorno speaks about Kafka he is not attempting,
then, to tell us what the works are really all about: the hidden
meanings that he can bring to our attention. He treats them as works
of art with their own irreducible integrity. The philosophical claims
he makes about Kafka's work relate to the forms they distinctively
bear within the historical conditions of modernity.

   Adorno characterizes Kafka's works as mimetic expressions of
reified life, as, indeed, 'a cryptogram of a decaying capitalist social
order' (Corngold 2002: 27). In spite of their apparent indifference
to social reality the form of those works – their logic – reveals the
form of social reality. And they do so without any attempt at
realism. If 'social realists', Adorno notes,

> ... took reality seriously enough they would eventually realize
> what Lukács condemned when during the days of his imprison-
> ment in Romania he is reported to have said that he had finally
> realized that Kafka was a realist writer.
>
> (AT 322)

The 'realism' of Kafka's work lies is its effective expression of the
distinctive conditions of late capitalism, the period of the irrational
social totality. Kafka never names the social totality, yet, as Adorno
writes, no

> ... world could be more homogeneous than the stifling one which
> [Kafka] compresses to a totality by means of petty-bourgeois

dread; it is logically air-tight and empty of meaning like every system.

(P 256)

The totality encompasses all behaviour and all interaction. It thereby renders its own justifiability opaque in that individuals constituted through it do not conceive it as unreasonable, unnecessary or unnatural. Kafka's work is set within this totality, and it mimetically adopts the form of that totalized world. The logic of the totality, however, is false, as are the conventions of the worlds set out in Kafka's novels. What gives those worlds their coherence is not their truth, but their sustained falseness. Adorno writes:

> Kafka, in whose work monopoly capitalism appears only distantly, codifies in the dregs of the administered world what becomes of people under the total social spell more faithfully and powerfully than do any novels about corrupt industrial trusts.

(AT 230)

And he does so simply by expressing society's form: closed, unjustifiable, yet determining the lives of everyone within it. In the 'mimesis' of social processes 'a universal which has been repressed by sound common sense' becomes apparent (P 249): the universal and all-pervasive social totality. Kafka's works are negative not in any explicit 'negation' of social reality, but rather in the sense that they express patterns of irrationality and unsettle the unthinking relationship we have with societal norms.

Adorno does not consider the form of experience enabled by Kafka's works of less significance to the business of illuminating the essential character of society than philosophical critique. His works puncture the illusion of a neutral social totality with no determining power and that is supposedly merely a form of social organization which pragmatically facilitates self-preservation. Kafka demystifies social experience in a purely negative way, that is, he does not indicate anything about a new world, free of reification. No utopia is offered in image. Adorno identifies this approach as Kafka's literalness. His works 'take everything literally; cover up nothing with concepts invoked from above' (P 247). However, this literalness has a productive negativity. It is what Adorno generally refers to as determinate negation. Kafka, Adorno claims, can define society 'all the more precisely in its negative' (P 256). A determinate negation is knowledge bearing. This knowledge – in this context – has emancipatory potential in that it gives us a view of what our deepest beliefs (about society and ourselves as individuals in it) actually commit us to doing. Conceiving of our impulsive identification with society as a neurosis Adorno says of Kafka:

> Instead of curing neurosis, he seeks in it itself the healing force, that of knowledge: the wounds with which, society brands the individual are seen by the latter as ciphers of the social untruth, as the negative of truth.
>
> (P 252)

By admitting no concepts 'from above' Kafka's engagement with society is immanent. His consistent immanence gives exact – literal – expression to the nature of the social totality. Kafka's work, according to Adorno,

> … must renounce any claim to transcending myth, it makes the social web of delusion knowable in myth through the how, through language. In his writing, absurdity is as self-evident as it has actually become in society.
>
> (AT 230–31)

Kafka's works confirm that there are no apparent norms beyond the institutions and conventions of the totality. The existing conventions predominate and, in the absence of any consciousness of alternatives, take on the character of inevitability. It is the 'closed

complex of immanence' (P 265). Kafka's purely immanent
approach, then, disturbs the settled experiences of everydayness
without referring to anything outside those experiences.

5. Mimesis and aesthetic experience

Mimesis, as I have noted, is co-extensive with the aesthetic
domain. Although Adorno's primary analyses deal with the mimetic
expression of social reality in artworks he also considers the
mimetic comportment that is characteristic of creativity, performance
and aesthetic experience. The experience of engaging in musical
composition might seem quite different from that of the captivated
visitor to a museum, and the experience of the dancer is surely
difficult to align with that of the poet. Each of these activities
belongs nevertheless within the domain of the aesthetic. I shall consider them in detail below, but even a brief initial characterization
allows us to appreciate Adorno's position. It is not sufficient to
conceive of the *creative process* as a matter of putting a plan into effect.
For instance, the materials of art – e.g. words, notes, colours – drive
the process in ways the artist does not anticipate. Certain aesthetic
media live through *performance*, in which a fixed text – a drama, a
choreography, a musical score – is interpreted, but never mastered, in
order to realize the work. And there is also the aesthetic *experience* of
the viewer, listener or audience, characterized by a specific kind of
absorption.

Mimesis and creativity. Creativity has been explained in many different
ways throughout the history of philosophy. Once understood as a
power given to certain individuals by external forces it took on a distinctly modern conception in Kant's *Critique of Judgment.* Adorno directs
some criticisms against Kant's idea of aesthetic genius as a means to
articulate more keenly his idea of the mimetic character of creativity.
According to Kant aesthetic production, unlike the productivity
of nature, is 'production through freedom' as it is 'a capacity
for choice that grounds its actions in reason' and is thereby free

(Kant 2001: §43, 182). Beautiful arts, he specifies, 'must necessarily be considered as arts of genius' (Kant 2001: §46, 186). He understands genius as 'a talent for producing that for which no determinate rule can be given' and that cannot be learned 'in accordance with some rule' (Kant 2001: §46, 186). How a creative idea might come to the aesthetic genius – the artist – is, Kant claims, a mystery to the artist too. That means, he thinks, that the artist 'cannot teach' creativity 'to anyone else either' (Kant 2001: §47, 188). (The opacity of an aesthetic genius' ideas renders them, according to Kant, inferior to those of the scientific genius whose concepts are rationally communicable. Adorno comments: in Kant 'the aesthetic is subordinated to the primacy of discursive logic' (AT 164).) The creative process is not, though, an indeterminate productivity. It is undertaken within the space of the established norms of art. These norms appear to delimit the content of the genius' aesthetic conceptions. Kant maintains that an 'academic constraint of all rules' is required for the formation of a work of fine art, and a condition of that rule-following is a talent that has been 'academically trained' (Kant 2001: §47, 189).

While Adorno shares with Kant the notion of the opacity of the creative process he strongly rejects Kant's thesis of the genius as the agent of creativity. He puts his objection in this way: 'the concept of genius is false because works are not creations and humans are not creators' (AT 170). What Adorno is specifically criticizing in this difficult remark is the idea of genius operating with a spontaneity that involves no reactivity. He alleges 'that Kant restricted geniality exclusively to the subject, indifferent to its ego-alienness' and creativity is thereby attributed, 'with idealistic hubris', he claims, to 'the productive artist' (AT 171). What this idealistic model misses, however, is that in aesthetic production the subject's agency is evident in its responsiveness to the material it tries to work its way through, rather than as an absolute creator. To attribute creativity to genius, in the Kantian sense, is to extract the artist from the process of production which involves working through material, rather than operating as a pure spirit of invention.

This claim seems to resonate with Adorno's theory of experience in placing the subject in a certain kind of reciprocally constitutive relationship with the object. His rejection of the Kantian idea of aesthetic genius as the single pole of creativity is aimed, as is his theory of experience, against the priority of subjectivity. Is there not, however, a significant difference between the sense in which mimesis is being used here and a central plank of Adorno's theory of experience? The object of the creative process – what the artist seeks to produce – might seem to be a reality only within the creative process itself. Unlike the object that has priority – another person, a thing, or even idea – it appears to have no existence that precedes the efforts of the creative agent. How are we to think of aesthetic mimesis as possessing the qualities of mutuality and empathy that Habermas ascribes to mimetic behaviour? Adorno does not develop an account of the difference between the objects of aesthetic and non-aesthetic experiences. To establish a cleft between these two fields of experience would be, however, a mistake. Certainly, the 'object' of the artist is not that of non-aesthetic experience. But it is false to think that it exists solely within the moments of the creative process. Adorno's characterization of the historical development of music, for instance, frames it as a series of challenges that confronted innovative composers. They were presented, by their predecessors, with materials that could no longer be accepted as appropriate: the previous forms of music had run their course or had broken down. Faced with this the composer sought new directions, taking music beyond the problematic models, yet partly through the materials of those models. This is a dialectical evolution. (For example, Adorno interprets Beethoven's struggles in the *Missa Solemnis* as deriving from the resistance of the liturgical mass to Beethoven's progressive creativity. The mass is, in this respect, material with properties and limitations and therefore not a mere reality of the creative process.[5])

Mimetic creativity entails a relinquishment of subjective control, but it is not a matter of passivity. The subject is involved in a series of decisions thrown up within the creative process itself as the problematic legacies of the artist's recent tradition. This process requires freedom, an absence of strict rule-following and of, indeed what Adorno says of Kantian autonomy, 'a strong ego in rational control of all its impulses' (ND 294). In *Aesthetic Theory* he writes similarly:

> Only the autonomous self is able to turn critically against itself and break through its illusory imprisonment. This is not conceivable as long as the mimetic element is repressed by a rigid aesthetic superego ...
>
> (AT 117)

From among the modernists Adorno usually identifies Schoenberg's expressionistic work as exemplary 'untrammelled, mimetic creation' (P 151). Schoenberg, Adorno claims, had the 'ability to follow the breath of music unafraid ... and that meant developing its substance according to its intrinsic processes ... ' (P 152). Schoenberg is also, for Adorno, the 'dialectical composer', dialectical as he sought to develop the material from within the tradition.[6] But dialectics is not logic: it does not lay down a definite direction. To think of the mimetic dimension of creativity as dialectical, then, is to conceive of creativity as responsiveness to the material the artist is attempting to produce, thereby remaining open to the possibilities of the material over which the artist does not have complete control.

Among the most controversial of all of Adorno's writings – comprising a small number of essays – are those on jazz. His repudiation of improvisation as a mimetic behaviour is fiercely resisted by Adorno's many critics who see jazz improvisation as a notable innovation within twentieth-century Western music. In an essay of 1953, 'Perennial Fashion – Jazz' he tackles the claim – appearing to treat it as a rival to his theory of the mimetic dimension exclusive to modernism – that jazz might contain an emancipatory potential. He notes that jazz is often presented as music originating from 'untrammelled nature' (P 22) and 'untrammelled subjectivity'

(P 126). In Adorno the term 'untrammelled' (*ungebändigt*) generally designates the freedom that is exercised through the mimetic impulse. In *Negative Dialectics*, as we saw in the previous chapter, he writes: 'Without an anamnesis of the untrammelled impulse that precedes the ego … it would be impossible to derive the idea of freedom' (ND 221–22). Adorno, however, forcefully rejects the notion that jazz is, in effect, mimetic composition. Strikingly to the contrary, it is a commodity, he argues, manufactured with 'machine-like precision' (P 123) according to a winning formula. And its productions involve the 'rigorous exclusion of every unregimented impulse' (P 122). The improvisations that appear to a naïve audience as genuine spontaneity 'conform largely to norms and recur constantly' (P 123). Jazz, thus understood, is devoid of the mimetic qualities characteristic of authentic art.

Adorno's judgment has certainly not gone unchallenged. The frequent allegation that it is founded on elitist attitudes is, of course, philosophically meaningless. However, he is correctly accused of writing on the subject without clarifying how broadly he thought it covered jazz in its full range. Adorno's uncompromising conclusions were, in fact, built on an analysis of only the quite uncelebrated form of jazz with which he was acquainted: 'big band/orchestra dance music' (Leppert 2002: 349).[7] Such music, though, was in its time designated as jazz. In so far as his criticisms of jazz are criticisms of that particular form his hostile assessment of its commodity-like properties need not be so contentious at all. It seems that Adorno was indirectly aware that the jazz of the big bands was a commodification of authentic African-American forms. He did not choose to write about the latter, though, and we can therefore form no conclusions about whether he would have perceived in it a mimetic dimension.

Mimesis and Performance. The mimetic plays a role in the performance of artworks too. The artist who effectively performs a text – for example, a musical score, a drama, a poem to be recited – clearly does not do so by following instructions or by passively playing, acting or reading them through. The performing artist engages with the text, interpreting it without imposing on it, sensitive to its complexity. The performance is a process of 'aesthetic forming' which does no 'violence' to the text (AT 294), Adorno claims. Sensitivity and responsiveness are required by any effective performance, qualities that are directly attributable to our mimetic capacities.

But how does performance meet with one of the stipulations of Adorno's notion of mimesis, namely, that of following 'mimetic impulses without planning' (AT 44)? Indeed, as a sometime composer and performer himself Adorno would have appreciated the enormous degree of planning that precedes any musical recital: decisions are made on every aspect of a score as an over-arching interpretation of the piece is developed. This is obviously true too for drama and dance. The performance seems to be the expression of these culminative decisions. The important point, however, is not to think of performance as the mechanical enactment of a plan but as the mimetic conduct of the performer in action. The mimetic is witnessed, according to Adorno, in the performer's openness to the unanticipated moment as an interpretation is played or acted out. Even when a performer has prepared thoroughly by thinking through every part of the text to be performed the performance will be mimetic only if that analysis is not rigidly imposed (AT 292). Furthermore, the decisions that are reached are themselves mimetic. Adorno claims that the 'musician who understands the score follows its most intimate impulse and yet in a certain sense he does not know what he plays' (AT 125). The musician necessarily approaches the performance with preconceptions, but to perform mimetically means not allowing those preconceptions to delimit the response to the material during the performance. The material has a dynamic of its own that the performer does not control, but seems only to follow.

This thesis of an uncontrollable dimension of mimetic performance is the basis of Adorno's central criticism of the classical music industry. He quotes the view of Eduard Steuermann (his old piano professor) that the industry's ideal of performance is 'the barbarism of perfection' (FCM 301). And although he does not explicitly attribute this 'barbarism' to non-mimeticism he does consider it to be the 'reification of music'. The music is presented

> ... as already complete from the first note. The performance sounds like its own phonograph record. The dynamic is so predetermined that there are no longer any tensions at all.
>
> (FCM 301)

We can infer from this that the mimetic performer – by contrast – is open to the possibilities of the work. The performer enacts the work without a definitive conception of where it will go, abandoning, what Adorno calls, 'iron discipline' (FCM 301).

Mimesis and aesthetic receptivity. The experience occasioned by art-works is the form of mimetic comportment given most considera-tion in Adorno's *Aesthetic Theory*. In the case of the experience of artworks – our aesthetic receptivity to and absorption in them – all of the fundamental aspects of mimesis are clearly visible: the responsivity to an other, the active adjustment to it, the abandonment of planning, transcending the limiting sphere of a self-mastering autonomy and the emancipation of selfhood that is achieved through the interaction with an other. Although Adorno does not actually specify that it is aesthetic receptivity that is the paradigmatic mode of mimetic behaviour, it is the mode most in evidence when he employs mimesis as a critical category. The form of behaviour that Adorno discovers through his analysis of aesthetic receptivity is a direct contrast with the reified behaviour of the social totality. As Axel Honneth notes,

> It is precisely the inability to imitate strangers and thus to give up one's own, particular standpoint that marks the distance of prevalent instrumental reason from its original potential ...
>
> (Honneth 2009: 66)

This potential is preserved, according to Adorno, in art.

Adorno is not the first philosopher to characterize aesthetic experience as a kind of absorption in which the ego or self no longer relates to its objects instrumentally. What is original about Adorno's contribution, though, is that he attempts to explain this capacity for absorption as a fundamental mimetic mode. We have already discussed the theory of that mode in some detail. Interestingly, Adorno does not defend the thesis purely theoretically. He also provides a phenomenology of aesthetic receptivity. He identifies a moment in which we make the transition from non-mimetic experience to aesthetic receptivity as a moment of shock (Erschütterung). It is, for him, a shock precisely in its radical departure from what we take to be our normal experience:

> The shock aroused by important works is not employed to trigger personal, otherwise repressed emotions. Rather, this shock is the moment in which recipients forget themselves and disappear into the work; it is the moment of being shaken. The recipients lose their footing ...

(AT 244)

The experience of the 'loss of footing' is not an injury of selfhood. Again, it is a release from the restricted self of autonomy after which agents find themselves experiencing in a fulfilling way, thanks to their own activity, what they cannot anticipate and what they have not constructed. It is that moment of shock, Adorno writes, that 'rescues subjectivity ... by the negation of subjectivity. The subject, convulsed by art, has real experiences' and, consequently, 'true happiness' (AT 269). No longer guided by the norms of the reified society the subject 'breaks through the spell of obstinate self-preservation' (AT 346). Of course the individual may not thematize this shock as Adorno does, as a thrilling disengagement from the requirements of socially effective selfhood. His contention, however, is that it is precisely its catastrophic break from what the individual is supposed to be that underpins the continuing value of aesthetic experience.

6. The rationality of mimesis

If mimesis can be deployed as a critical category against irrational society, it must itself be contrastively a form of rational behaviour. And that indeed is what Adorno claims. But we might think that the qualities Adorno ascribes to mimesis – adjustment towards the object, accommodation, absorption – designate empathetic though not rational ways of relating to objects. However, it is precisely this dualism of socially effective rationality and the kinds of reaction we experience in our aesthetic activities that Adorno encourages us to reconsider. Adorno, as we have seen, describes reified consciousness as irrational: it applies limiting judgments to objects and cannot respond to countervailing evidence that the object may be more than what those judgments allow. Irrationality is characterized, therefore, by an inability to respond in the face of conflicting evidence: it is a resistance to the dialectic of experience. But from the perspective of reified experience it is aesthetic comportment that is irrational because it follows no method nor does it limit itself to agreed boundaries of what an object is supposed to be. In aesthetic experience the object is the end of the experience, whereas in socially effective rationality – instrumental rationality – the object is the means, and it is used in order to allow the agent to achieve some end that is indifferent to the object. As Adorno writes: 'What marks aesthetic comportment as irrational according to the criteria of dominant rationality is that art denounces the particular essence of a *ratio* that pursues means rather than ends' (AT 330). The claim, then, is that any mode of engagement with objects that is closed to their possibilities cannot be considered to be genuinely knowledge oriented as it is a confusion of knowledge with manipulation. In contrast, Adorno claims that art, as a mimetic activity, is rational in this responsive sense: 'The survival of mimesis, the nonconceptual affinity of the subjectivity produced with its unposited other, defines art as a form of knowledge and to that extent as "rational"' (AT 54). In a remarkable passage Adorno goes so far to claim that those without an aesthetic sensibility – those who are therefore without the vestige of mimesis – are susceptible to reification: ' ... in the *Dialectic of Enlightenment*, strict positivism crosses over into the feeble-mindedness of the artistically insensible, the successfully castrated' (AT 331).

The lesson we are to take from this is not, however, spelled out by Adorno. If it is in aesthetic experience that mimesis – 'our special, imitation-based capacity for reason', as Honneth puts it (Honneth 2009: 61) – is preserved should we seek to transform all experience into aesthetic experience? If this is what Adorno is suggesting it is a programme of immense difficulty. What kinds of decision making can a practical agent engage in aesthetically? As Habermas expresses this concern:

> ... the aestheticizing, or the scienticizing, or the moralizing of particular domains of life ... give rise to effects for which expressivist countercultures, technocratically carried out reforms, or fundamentalist movements can serve as drastic examples.
>
> (Habermas 1990: 340)

In short, the complexity of the lifeworld, with its diverse norms and practices, would have to be narrowed to the model of aesthetic experience, rich though it nevertheless is. Adorno, however, speaks of 'aesthetic rationality' as a distinctive form of rationality, not as a synonym for rationality *tout court*. And we might infer from this his acknowledgement that it is not to be extended to all aspects of the lifeworld *because it is* 'aesthetic' and not a higher rationality or true rationality. Furthermore, *Aesthetic Theory* does not, at any point, actually recommend the aestheticization of behaviour. To understand why Adorno has so much to say about aesthetic mimesis without prescribing it as an alternative to reification we must return to a suggestion made earlier in this chapter, namely, that for Adorno the mimetic comportment that is characteristic of art is to be adopted by theory as a diagnostic concept. An appreciation of aesthetic experience allows us to see conventional experience not as natural but as a particular form. Aesthetic experience stands in contrast with that form too, though not necessarily as an exemplar. Artworks and the experiences they enable are, for Adorno, 'the determinate negation of the existing order of the world' (AT 89). They bring into question the virtually ceaseless processes of the social totality. As determinate negations they do not stand as alternatives, waiting to replace what they negate. The analysis of the mimetic comportment of art furnishes an account of the subject's capacities that reified society does not perceive nor can afford to recognize if the model of instrumentality – the socially effective model – is to persist. It endures as the dominant form of rationality unless a critical perspective from which to criticize it can be gained.

7. The autonomy of art

Adorno argues that authentic works of art in modernity have a certain kind of autonomous relationship to the life-processes of society. To describe art as autonomous is not to attribute to it a reality outside history or society. As Adorno writes: 'The Hegelian vision of the possible death of art accords with the fact that art is a product of history' (AT 3). And nor does the autonomy of art mean, for Adorno, the indifference of art towards the societies in which it appears. The complexity of Adorno's thesis consists in its claim for a very specific relationship of art to society: it is autonomous from the processes of reification that, according to the critical tradition to which he belongs, disfigures the social world. At the same time autonomous art draws its content from society. Adorno believes that the philosophical image – from Leibniz – of the monad captures this dual character of independence from reflection of social processes:

> That artworks as windowless monads 'represent' what they themselves are not can scarcely be understood except in that their own dynamic … not only is of the same essence as the dialectic external to them but resembles it without imitating it.
> (AT 5)

As we have just seen in the discussion of mimesis, art expresses the conventional forms of rationality that 'irrationally' structure social reality. Yet, art is not a product of society, like any other. Its autonomous position is often explained contrastively by Adorno: in conventional non-aesthetic expression reified life is represented in reified ways (e.g. reified communication is produced by reified social processes). Autonomous art, however, breaks with those conventions or modes of expressions. It does not thereby *positively* reproduce the norms of society. As we saw in Adorno's evaluation of two exemplary cases – Baudelaire and Kafka – art expresses those norms in a way that gives heightened perception to them. It reproduces them *negatively*. Negative reproduction is possible because autonomous art has the capacity to determine itself through its own modes of expression, working independently of the available, heteronomous forms of representation (which are offered para-digmatically, as we shall see, by the 'culture industry'). There are two complementary senses of the autonomy of art in Adorno's theory, both of which are ascribed by him to every authentic work of art: the autonomy of self-determining production and the autonomy of aesthetic experience generated by authentic works.

Adorno does not maintain that art has always been autonomous, though the period in which it supposedly became autonomous is not exactly clear. He broadly associates the emergence of art's autonomy with an historical development he calls 'the emancipation of spirit' (AT 200). This emancipation refers to the achievement of human beings in gaining a critical perspective on the given socio-historical norms that governed them. Emancipation in this context was not the actualization of freedom. It was a realization that the prevailing norms were not 'universal', in a Hegelian sense, in that they were not coextensive with new ideals of the flourishing of all. Societies during this time of 'emancipation' began to lose confidence in traditional sources of authority and initiated the project of modern democracy based on the collective powers of individuals. This political reality informed art: the content of art, indeed the very activity of art, would in some way follow that same emancipatory evolution. Adorno writes: art's 'autonomy, its growing independence from society, was a function of the bourgeois consciousness of freedom ... ' (AT 225). The form that this emancipated sensibility took in aesthetic creativity was the production of works no longer concerned with socially affirming content (i.e. the glorification of religion or power). If Beethoven's work is an example of art in the new era of bourgeois freedom – as Adorno often claims (e.g. AT 221) – then we might think that art at that time seemed to have little to do with society at all. Now as we know from the previous chapter, Adorno is suspicious of the very notion of autonomy associated with bourgeois freedom. He argues that the ideal, perhaps problematic from the start, eventually became a moment of the social totality. Autonomy was reduced to the freedom of the agents to perform roles over which they had no control and which they naïvely perceived as second nature. But what happened to the emancipation of art during the growing destruction of autonomy? We can surmise Adorno's answer: art, somehow, retained its autonomy. And with the growing totalization of society it became less and less an activity that was harmonious with that society. Art became, as Adorno puts it, 'the social antithesis of society' (AT 8).

This way of conceiving art's relation to society accords it some kind of oppositional status: it is what society is not. In a section below we shall see Adorno's efforts to frame this oppositional relationship as criticism. Interestingly, though, Adorno's thesis of the autonomy of art is a modification of Hegel's non-oppositional notion of autonomous art's truth-bearing capacity. Hegel theorized that art could realize itself as art – not as an instrument of anything else – only once it pursued a purely aesthetic agenda. Art, he writes, 'cuts itself free from ... servitude in order to raise itself, in free independence, to the truth in which it fulfils itself independently and conformably with its own ends alone' (Hegel 1975: 7). Although this idea of the purification of art could be found among several other philosophers of the time, Hegel added to it a radical new claim. Art expresses the historical 'spiritual' conditions under which it is created. By virtue of its very autonomy – or freedom – art thereby achieves the capacity to present the truth. In its freedom art actually becomes, what Hegel describes as, a deposit for the 'richest inner intuitions and ideas' that a nation possesses (Hegel 1975: 7). Unfree art, by contrast, gives aesthetic form to conventional views of historical reality: it seeks to represent power or ideology. It is constrained, in its creativity, by that agenda. Hegel's innovative thesis, then, is that the less artists try to portray their socio-historical reality the more they actually communicate of its essential intellectual/ spiritual commitments. This revelatory power of art places it, Hegel believes, 'in the same sphere as religion and philosophy' (Hegel 1975: 7). However, art is revelatory in its own specific way in that it, unlike the other two, is a sensuous discipline. It gives material form to the space of ideas. Hegel describes it as 'the first reconciling middle term between pure thought and what is merely external, sensuous, and transient, between nature and finite reality and the infinite freedom of conceptual thinking' (Hegel 1975: 8).

8. The culture industry and heteronomy

Adorno, as noted above, tends to specify the characteristics of autonomous art contrastively. It is set against heteronomous production. Extreme cases of heteronomous 'art' are generated by what Adorno refers to as 'the culture industry'. The very term polemically designates a form of activity geared towards the industrial production of mere commodities. The commodities of the commercially oriented culture industry are understood by Adorno as manipulative devices, devoid of any genuine aesthetic trait. Their content is determined and valued by the role they are to serve: they have therefore a distinctive *external* purpose. In the essay, 'The Culture Industry Reconsidered' Adorno describes heteronomous art in the following way: 'The cultural commodities of the industry are governed ... by the principle of their realization as value, and not by their own specified content and harmonious formation' (CIR 232). Autonomous artworks, however, are determined by the efforts of the artist to pursue, on purely aesthetic considerations – i.e. considerations that are *internal* to the process – the creation of an artwork. As Adorno puts it: 'The work's *terminus ad quem*, however, has its locus exclusively in itself, not externally' (AT 217).

This difference between internal and external considerations is highlighted in the respective uses of 'technique' by autonomous and non-autonomous (particularly cultural industry works) processes. It is through technique that the artist/producer develops complexity within the work: e.g. colour, inventive form, decoration. In authentic art, technique, according to Adorno, 'is concerned with the internal organization of the object itself, with its inner logic' (CIR 234). In heteronomous works technique is employed to elicit particular responses, planned out in advance of any composition, from those who are to consume those works. Typically, such works are for this very reason manipulative. They seek to push their audiences towards experiences that are not aesthetic (e.g. commerce, political allegiance, social conformism). Speaking of the alignment of the culture industry with advertising, Adorno and Horkheimer write that it is 'a procedure for manipulating human beings ... everything is directed at overpowering the customer ... ' (DE 133). The skills or techniques that have been developed throughout the history of art are appropriated and turned towards external purposes.

What are we to think of genuine works of art that come to be used by the culture industry (in, for instance, soundtracks, advertising jingles, as decoration of a commodity, or 'adapted' for a film script (DE 96))? Is their aesthetic value transformed simply because they are used in ways not intended by their creators? Adorno holds that the appropriation of autonomous art by the culture industry de-contextualizes the artwork. The translation of autonomous artworks into effects designed to generate a response external to the works' original

creative impulse destroys them: 'The autonomy of works of art ...
is tangentially eliminated by the culture industry', he writes
(CIR 232). A work of art manipulated into a heterogeneous role
must take its 'place among consumer goods' (DE 127). Once the
internal processes of the artwork art are reconceived externally – as
purposive – they lose their autonomous, self-determining character
as art.

There is another important sense in which the products of the
culture industry – popular culture – are not autonomous. They
bind their consumers to society as it is: there is no antithetical
relationship, therefore, between popular culture and society. Popular
culture may give pleasure in providing occasions of escape from a
reality deficient in happiness. But it is always an escape, Adorno and
Horkheimer argue, into a polished up version of the reality from
which they seek to escape: 'The culture industry presents that same
everyday world as paradise' (DE 113). This is satisfactory for individuals in a reified social world as alternatives to their current
conditions are imagined only through the very reification that inflicts
upon them the misery or boredom they would seek to escape: commodified amusement (e.g. cinema, popular music) 'is the prolongation
of work under late capitalism' (DE 109) in that the very processes
of mechanization that dominate the workplace also produce the
entertainments furnished by the culture industry. The mechanization
manifests itself in the repetitive, simplistic structures of popular 'hit
songs' (DE 132) and in the predictable, repetitive plots of Hollywood
movies (DE 109). These characteristics of popular art forms parallel
processes that the consumers of those products ordinarily experience
in their socially determined lives. The very social structures, then, that
inhibit the possibility of rational experience determine the forms of
experience that popular culture can offer. Popular culture, in contrast to autonomous art, therefore perpetuates society. It offers no
alternative to the basic norms of experience and nor does it express
those norms in ways which allow us to gain some perspective on
their irrationality (there is no mimesis of reification).

9. Autonomous art as social criticism

For Adorno the idea that art is self-determining has a vital significance for the particular concerns of critical theory. Art's antithetical relationship to society implies, for him, that art occupies a *critical* or *oppositional* relation to society: 'art becomes social by its opposition (*Gegenposition*) to society, and it occupies this position only as autonomous art' (AT 225), he writes. Its critical relationship is historically specific: it criticizes the society in which it is produced. As we saw in the discussion of the mimesis of reification, art cannot remain mimetic if it addresses social conditions realistically. Similarly, the autonomy of art is compromised by making art into overt social protest. Criticism, inherent in autonomous works, can be made explicit by interpretation. Autonomous works indicate to us – if we can read them – the current conditions of social reality. For that reason, these works can be, as Adorno says of the example of Beckett's *Endgame*, 'historico-philosophical sundials' (NL I 269).

The very notion that art is socially critical seems to attribute purpose to it. We have seen Adorno's differentiation of heteronomous and autonomous art made on the basis of his distinction between the external and internal purposes of art. It would seem, though, that if art is to offer social criticism then it too is guided by an external purpose, i.e. a purpose that is not purely aesthetic. Indeed, we know Adorno's low estimation of art that commits itself to political propaganda. The difficulty is that the ascription of a critical dimension to art seems to imply purposiveness, while the autonomy of art thesis means precisely that purpose is immanently oriented to the artwork itself, and not towards anything else. As Adorno puts the latter claim:

> That artworks, in accord with Kant's magnificently paradoxical formula, are 'purposeless', that they are separated from empirical reality and serve no aim that is useful for self-preservation and life, precludes calling art's meaning its purpose.

(AT 152)

However, Adorno thinks of art's critical relationship to society as a dimension of art *per se*. This relationship has nothing to do with the political or philosophical intentions of the artist. We are to think, rather, of art as being critical by virtue of its very status as art within its socio-historical reality. Adorno provides two general lines of thought on this inherently critical positionality of art towards society. (1) Art's specific intra-aesthetic motivations contrastively expose the deterministic life of purpose embodied in society. (2) The dynamic of an artwork diverges from the narrow logic of reified society.

(1) Art exposes the version of purposiveness that predominates in everyday life. Society is understood, by Adorno, as blind purposiveness, in which individuals gain meaning and significance only in so far as they accommodate themselves to the self-reproducing norms of society. Art, by contrast, does not have a socially functional purpose. Indeed, its anti-purposiveness is what allows the subject to experience 'happiness' (AT 389) during aesthetic experience. The very presence of art within purposive society undermines – determinately negates 'determinate society' (AT 226) – the social imperative that everything should be useful. What artworks offer, without intention, is 'the critique of the practical positing of purposes' (AT 288). Aesthetic experience seems like something worth having, yet it is without any sense of purpose as defined by the functional processes of society. (Weber's notion of value-rationality, which we saw in Chapter 5, supports the notion of action unmotivated by purposive-rationality.)

(2) Adorno specifies that the process of an autonomous work is 'objectively the counterimage of enchained forces' (AT 226). The enchained forces refer to what Adorno describes as the integrational effects of the social totality. Against the pressure of conformism, in which each process is to be made entirely predictable, we have the authentic work of art. 'Every authentic artwork is internally revolutionary', he writes (AT 228). And this revolutionary aspect is its innovation of aesthetic form. Through form an alternative to the grammar of experience to that offered by 'administered society' is

produced. As we saw, art, for Adorno, is a 'refuge for mimetic comportment'. This comportment, with its openness and flexibility is quite the contrary of the planned out operations of instrumental reason. Art's own rationality, then, 'criticizes rationality' (AT 55) through its own contrastive example of non-reified experience.

Adorno argues that the self-purposiveness of the work of art is semblance (*Schein*) and illusion (*Illusion*). These are not, obviously enough, quasi-Platonic denigrations of the artwork. They are characteristics of the kind of object the artwork is: it is neither literally internally-purposive and nor is it a genuine whole. Yet it bears the semblance, in aesthetic experience, of purpose and wholeness. Artworks, Adorno writes, 'not just the illusion they evoke, are the aesthetic semblance. The illusory quality of artworks is condensed in their claim to wholeness' (AT 101). But surely, one might counter, a work of art *is* a whole? Adorno rejects that notion on materialist, anti-idealist grounds. He cannot accept that artworks have a reality independent of history, the processes of their production and the conditions of their experienceabilty and interpretation. Were the reality of artworks anything more than semblance we would have to think of them as the proprietors of meanings and purposes. This would accord them an objectivity analogous to that of spiritual entities. Adorno's repudiation of that metaphysical notion leads him to insisting that there is nothing behind the artwork that appears to us. In 'artworks', he writes, 'appearance is that of essence' (AT 109). This is quite the contrary of Hegel's notion of art as, to use Adorno's description, the 'sensuous semblance of the idea' (AT 108). Hegel sees artworks as the outward form – a sensuous one – of the spiritual essence of their historical location. They bear truth as the sensuous representation of history. But does Adorno not also think that art – in some sense, at least – is truth bearing? He very clearly does, but in a way that needs to be distinguished from the idealist model. As Tom Huhn explains, Adorno thinks of the Hegelian notion of the truth content of art as an 'immanent possession' of the artwork, whereas Adorno himself sees it as a 'potentiality unlocked by philosophical reflection' (Huhn 1985: 188). It is through the intervention of philosophy that we can achieve, what Adorno calls, the 'redemption of semblance' (AT 109), the retrieval of the capacity of art to have a truth content which thereby allows it to be somehow more than mere appearance. Adorno's aesthetic theory might be summarized as the effort to find in aesthetic semblance art's critical potential.

10. The autonomy of art and the possibility of aesthetic experience

Adorno, as we have seen, argues both that art is a 'product of history' and that it is critically positioned against historical social conditions. Our experience of these artworks, he argues, must therefore also be historical. He defines authentic works of art as 'those that surrender themselves to the historical substance of their age without reservation' (AT 182). And the fullest possible reception of these artworks is similarly historical: 'Artworks may be all the more truly experienced the more their historical substance is that of the one who experiences it' (AT 183). The contrastive relations, which we have just considered, between art's non-purposiveness and social function, and between art's immanent, dynamic processes and the narrow logic of reified experience inform aesthetic experience itself. It is because of these contrasts that aesthetic experience contains an emancipatory dimension. Autonomy is a property of artworks that is relative to their historically conditioned social location: they are autonomous *against* those conditions. Art is therefore not conceived as revelatory of timeless truths, but of the truths of its own historical location. Through these various claims, Adorno places art within the realm of finitude. What that finitude implies is that the experience of an artwork can be lost: as historical conditions change the artwork will not continue to stand in critical or contrastive relation to society, to a society which, in effect, it no longer belongs. Artworks are 'archaic', according to Adorno, 'when they can no longer be experienced' (AT 349).

Adorno offers a complex set of thoughts on the notion of 'archaism' in art history. Among these thoughts is his longstanding criticism of a tendency in some modernist artists – the composer Igor Stravinsky's 'artistically produced regression' (PNM 116) in particular – to incorporate archaic, lost elements into their works. He sees this as a misunderstanding of what the archaic is. The historical developments that render a work 'archaic' place it at a distance from our possible aesthetic, though not intellectual appreciation. It cannot be retrieved as an authentic possibility as it is now without experienceable aesthetic significance. He writes: 'The concept of the archaic defines not so much a phase of art history as the condition of works that have gone dead' (AT 27). The mistake is to identify – what Adorno interprets as – the experience of loss or distance, with which archaic works present us, as inherent features of the work. That is nothing more, he contends, than a 'regression to the archaic fetishism' (AT 17). To turn, then, to the archaic for aesthetic materials is to detach aesthetic experience from the possibility of a critical relation to the present. Adorno cites Rimbaud's motto to capture this normative requirement: 'il faut être absolument moderne' (AT 192) (one must be absolutely modern).

The concept of the archaic enables us to see that aesthetic experience is an historical phenomenon, in which a contemporaneous artwork autonomously expressing social reality provides the historically situated individual with a critical experience of that reality. The loss of possible experience of works that are now archaic is an implication of Adorno's autonomy thesis. Adorno recognizes that it may be possible to retrieve something of the meaning of an archaic work through the appropriate historical analysis. In fact, Adorno holds that aesthetic experience and performance are always informed by analysis, that is, intellectual interpretation. In an essay on the analysis of music he writes: 'Works need analysis for their truth content to be revealed'.[8] This is the meaning of the claim that '[a]esthetic experience must overstep itself' (AT 349). The realm of the aesthetic is not isolated from the realm of the reflective. What he does not appear to say, however, is that a reflective relation to art is sufficient to generate the aesthetic experience of it. He must therefore deny that what might be considered aesthetic experience of the archaic is any such thing. It is pleasure or enjoyment of some kind – he refers witheringly to 'fun' (AT 39) and 'amusement' (AT 311) when speaking of non-aesthetic experiences of 'art' – carrying with it no possibility for emancipation which, as we have seen, is distinctive to the aesthetic experience made possible by autonomous works.

Summary

Aesthetic Theory is Adorno's attempt to bring together and to develop further the numerous concepts on the philosophy of art that he had only briefly stated in earlier books and essays. The work is his most comprehensive statement on aesthetics, but Adorno did not – consistent with his view of philosophical thought – prepare it as a systematic treatment of the concepts of art. The examination of his aesthetic theory offered in this chapter focused on its two dominant themes: mimesis and the autonomy of art.

Mimesis is, according to Adorno, a dimension of human behaviour which precedes the development of the aesthetic realm. It is a form of uninhibited interaction which has been damaged by reified life, though it is now preserved in aesthetic activity. For that reason aesthetic activity serves as a kind of critical contrast with the prevailing norms of experience.

Adorno, with Horkheimer, first explored the notion of mimesis in the speculative anthropology of *Dialectic of Enlightenment*. Human beings originally sought to relate to nature by likening themselves to it. This comportment stands in contrast with modern constructivist approaches to nature. Mimesis is the characteristic of non-distorted interactions between subjects and the rest of nature.

Although Adorno is not interested in the Greek discussions of mimesis certain parallels between his theory and that of Aristotle suggest themselves: art is mimetic not as representation or copying but in its expression of the processes of reality. The central claim in Adorno's notion of mimesis is that modernist artworks mimetically express the norms and processes of the social totality. The works of these modernists never 'name' the phenomenon of reification and nor do they offer images of a world that would be free of reification. But by fully immersing themselves in the world they express it as it actually is. This 'mimesis of reification' is found exemplarily in Baudelaire, Kafka and Beckett. Through innovative aesthetic form these artists permit the experience of experience that has become meaningless.

Mimetic behaviour, Adorno holds, is a characteristic of all aesthetic experiences. *Creativity* is mimetic in that it involves the artist in a process of interaction with aesthetic material. On that basis Adorno disagrees with Kant's notion of the artistic genius because that notion considers only the subject's role in creativity. Rather, the artist must respond to the material as it unfolds and also to the tradition within which the production is taking place. For Adorno, the composer Schoenberg exemplifies 'untrammelled' mimetic creativity. The question of whether Adorno should also have considered jazz improvisation in these terms remains open. *Performance* is mimetic in that the performer does not mechanically reproduce a text (for example, a score or drama). Even after thorough preparation the performer is never master of the text and will only perform well by remaining open to the unanticipated possibilities of the text. Aesthetic *receptivity* is the form of mimetic behaviour which is given most discussion by Adorno. It involves the subject in a kind of interaction with an object that allows the subject to liberate itself from its own hardened selfhood.

Adorno argues that mimesis contains its own rationality. It contrasts with instrumental rationality which is irrational because it closes us off from objects by permitting only purposive engagements with them. Adorno does not recommend that the solution to reification is to turn all experience into a variety of aesthetic experience. Mimetic experience serves Adorno as a diagnostic concept.

Authentic artworks, Adorno claims, stand in an autonomous relationship to the life processes of society. They do not exist outside or beyond social reality, but they do not follow the norms of reason that hold the social totality together. Historically, autonomous artworks began to emerge when art ceased to be geared towards social affirmation. In so far as art is autonomous it has an oppositional and historically determinate relationship to society.

According to Adorno, the culture industry exemplifies nonautonomous aesthetic productivity. It heteronomously creates commodities which manipulate consumers into reacting in ways that entrench social norms. The forms of its commodities are predictable and simple and therefore provide no contrastive experience to that of everyday life. As a consequence, no possibility of a critical perspective on the conditions of social reality is given by heteronomous works.

Autonomous art has a critical potential because it stands in opposition to social norms. This critical relationship has two dimensions. (1) The distinctive practices of purely aesthetic works are at odds with the prevailing norm of usefulness. (2) Autonomous works are revolutionary in their constant renewal of aesthetic form. This distinguishes them from the limited negotiations of the world permitted by reified consciousness.

The oppositionality of artworks underlines Adorno's claim that artworks are historical. An implication of this historical reality is that the fullest experience of artworks is available only to those who live within the same historical conditions as those in which the artwork was created. Adorno describes as archaic artworks which are no longer experientially available to us. He criticizes the 'regressive' efforts of Stravinsky to give aesthetic form to the loss of experience that is characteristic of the archaic.

Further reading

Bernstein, J. M. (1993) *The Fate of Art: Aesthetic Alienation from Kant to Derrida and Adorno*, Cambridge: Polity Press, chapters 4 and 5.

Huhn, T. (1985) 'Adorno's Aesthetics of Illusion', *The Journal of Aesthetics and Art Criticism*, Vol. 44, No. 2.

Menke, C. (1998) *The Sovereignty of Art: Aesthetic Negativity in Adorno and Derrida*, trans. N. Solomon, Cambridge MA /London: MIT Press, chapters 1, 3 and 5.

Paddison, M. (1993) *Adorno's Aesthetics of Music*, Cambridge: Cambridge University Press.

Zuidervaart, L. (1991) *Adorno's Aesthetic Theory: The Redemption of Illusion*, Cambridge MA / London: MIT Press, esp. chapters 2 and 8.

Seven
Adorno's philosophical legacy

Adorno wrote with authority not only on philosophy but on music, literature, sociology and cultural theory. He brought a consistently philosophical approach and characteristic style of analysis to all of the areas of intellectual enquiry that were of interest to him. Historically, however, appreciation of his work has largely been divided among those academic disciplines into which his studies seem for the most part to fall. A complete account of Adorno's intellectual legacy would require an assessment of his contribution to those separate disciplines. A study which has concentrated mainly on Adorno's central philosophical claims and arguments ought to confine itself to a consideration of the evolving interpretation of his place in contemporary philosophy.

The publication of Adorno's first book in 1933 marked the appearance of a new and brilliant philosopher. But it was during the mid 1950s that he entered the most important phase of his work.[1] Giving formulation to his implicit conception of the dialectical structure of experience became Adorno's major preoccupation. This conception was developed through his reading of the problems he found in the accounts of the subject-object relationship in the various philosophical works he considered significant. Adorno was thereby setting out both a distinctive account of experience and a powerful form of philosophical criticism. His work became progressively more complex and far reaching as he sought to identify, with potentially devastating implications for philosophy, the relationship between philosophical conceptions of experience and reason and our epistemic, interpersonal, moral and aesthetic practices. His constant dedication to this project is evident in, especially, *Negative Dialectics* (1966), *Critical Models* (two volumes, 1963 and 1969) and the unfinished *Aesthetic Theory*. Yet it is the earlier *Dialectic of Enlightenment* (completed first in 1944) that would turn out to be the most crucial work of all – initially at least – in shaping perceptions of Adorno's philosophical legacy.

As noted earlier, the student activists of the 1960s expected Adorno to share their understanding of the practical potential of the ferocious critique of capitalism and the administered world offered in *Dialectic of Enlightenment*. But Adorno could see no form of transition between the ideas of that book, or indeed his more cautiously articulated post-war works, and political action. It is not that Adorno was unpolitical. He was, for instance, very publicly opposed to what he saw as the anti-democratic Emergency Acts of 1968, passed by the Government of West Germany (Berman 2002: 129). And his preference was to address the problems of the state through democratic methods. The student movement, however, sought to bring every institution of the state – including the practices of the university – into question. In their choice of methods – protests and sit-ins – they found themselves in confrontation with the authorities, a path Adorno was not prepared to take. Hans-Jürgen Krahl, a former student of Adorno and a leading member of the student movement, roundly criticized Adorno's 'private absti-nence from praxis' (Krahl 1974: 165). He claimed that for Adorno the notion of praxis had become a purely abstract business, com-pletely disconnected from the challenges of the very 'social change' whose necessity Adorno's own diagnoses of modernity seemed to imply (Krahl 1974: 166). In the first pages of *Negative Dialectics* Adorno had nevertheless defended a distinctly theoretical stance, not for theory's sake, but because of the dangers of a praxis which did not fully explore its own commitments (a worry which also informed, as we have seen, Adorno's considerations of autonomy as resistance). For the activists this attitude did not merely locate Adorno outside politics but, rather, in opposition to it.

The apparently anti-political nature of Adorno's philosophy would become, for some time, the defining characteristic of his work. It was not, however, the excoriations of this characteristic by Adorno's radical critics that would be decisive in allocating him a particular place in the history of contemporary German philosophy. The role of inscribing the apparent limitations of Adorno's philosophy into the record of critical theory was assumed by Jürgen Habermas. This could not have been easily anticipated. Habermas had been an assistant of Adorno's at Frankfurt, and his first substantial contribution to critical theory – *The Structural Transformation of the Public Sphere* (1962)[2] – resonated with Adorno's conception of society. He was also an intellectual ally to Adorno during the 'positivist dispute'. Furthermore, like Adorno he had been forcefully attacked by the student movement for a perceived lack of political urgency.[3] In the year of Adorno's death, with his stare fixed on the student radicals, he offered a nuanced appraisal of Adorno's philosophical commitments and style. He chastised those 'impatient practitioners' who had vulgarly and mistakenly read the critique of Enlightenment reason as a generalized theory of society (Habermas 1983: 109).

Nevertheless, by that time Habermas had already effectively concluded that Adorno's critical theory was incapable of realizing the more sober political ideal that both he and Adorno fundamentally shared: the possibility of a rational society. Such a society would be sustained by open-minded, self-critical individuals seeking to develop universally – i.e. not tribally – valid principles. A society normatively strengthened in this way could be expected to be resistant to the forms of social life which were once hospitable to Fascism. But Habermas believed that Adorno's philosophy could not provide an account of the variety of rationality that would underpin a rational society. A conception of reason that was neither instrumental (and therefore unusable) nor exotically mimetic (and therefore irrelevant) – the only alternatives allegedly at Adorno's disposal – would have to be found from within existing social practices if the achievement of a rational society was to be maintained as an ideal of critical theory.

In a paper published in 1979 Axel Honneth noted that Habermas, at that point, had not made explicit 'his own criticism of critical theory' (Honneth 1979: 45). That would, though, come only a few years later. Nevertheless, it was clear even then that the new direction in which Habermas was attempting to point critical theory served as a systematic solution to the impasses of *Dialectic of Enlightenment* in particular. Honneth understood Habermas' various conceptual innovations as being prompted by the need to address the 'methodological bareness in Adorno's work' (Honneth 1979: 45). Anxious to 'go beyond the defensive posture' of Adorno's negativism and to reorient critical theory towards 'the present historical context' (Honneth 1979: 46) Habermas strove to develop a critical theory which could effectively engage the ideological blindness of society with the hope that that engagement might lead to actual social transformation. If that outcome was conceivable then Adorno's claim that reification had become total was, at best, hyperbolic.

Habermas' major methodological innovation was to abandon dialectics – with its distinctive notions of conceptuality and consciousness – and to seek within the resources of linguistic theory a new conception of reason. What Adorno had theorized as the space of the 'nonidentical' Habermas, Honneth noted, began to read as the space of 'suppressed meanings' (Honneth 1979: 48). It would be through rational communication that those meanings could eventually be released. Against the reification thesis Habermas sought to give critical significance to 'the communicative rationality of internal socialization' (Honneth 1979: 53). The very idea of an inherent communicative rationality was supported by arguments derived – via Karl-Otto Apel – from the Kantian transcendental tradition. Habermas was endeavouring to take critical theory away from the apparently 'hermetic mode of description' offered by Adorno – a theory of society devoid of emancipatory potential – and towards a critical theory expressly designed to 'mediate politics' (Honneth 1979: 60).

Habermas' reconception of the methodology and potential efficacy of critical theory quickly gained significant influence. In some quarters Adorno's philosophy was consigned to obsolescence. At least as early as 1976 the history of the Frankfurt School was being set out as a series of evolving stages. *Dialectic of Enlightenment* was the main work of the second phase (Connerton 1976: 27). Marcuse, rather than Adorno, because of his 'renewed search for a "negative"' – i.e. practical forces of resistance in the absence of mass social movements – was the third phase (Connerton 1976: 28). Habermas, thanks to the political orientation of the theory of communicative action, occupied the culminating fourth phase (Connerton 1976: 30).[4] The pre-eminence of Habermas' position was gained without Habermas himself having offered any direct criticisms of his predecessors. During the 1980s, however, he decided it was time to spell out his worries about Adorno's philosophy, and he did so in surprisingly trenchant terms. In *Theory of Communicative Action* (1984) Habermas outlined the historical trajectory of critical theory. Habermas' own work, it seemed, stood at the endpoint of that tradition. He wrote: 'I want to maintain that the program of early critical theory foundered not on this or that contingent circumstance, but from the exhaustion of the paradigm of the philosophy of consciousness' (Habermas 1984: 386). The effort to explain interaction on the basis of mimesis was a hopeless one. The 'rational core' it vainly claimed could be given theoretical grounding only if we moved, as Habermas had, to 'the paradigm of linguistic philosophy' (Habermas 1984: 390). And in *The Philosophical Discourse of Modernity* (1990) Habermas placed Adorno and Horkheimer, together with Nietzsche, within the paradoxical project of 'totalizing critique' (Habermas 1990: 126–27). The notion of nonidentity was also, for Habermas, a philosophical paradox (Habermas 1990: 129). Adorno's aesthetic theory was decried as the 'surrender of cognitive competency to art' (Habermas 1990: 68).

Not everyone within the circles of German social theory was prepared to leave Adorno's philosophy to history, though. Albrecht Wellmer, a former assistant to Habermas, was a dissenting voice. In 1986 he wrote of 'the abiding relevance' of Adorno's 'ways of thinking that cannot be straightforwardly subsumed within a form of Critical Theory that has been revised in light of language philosophy' (Wellmer 1998: 258). The distinctive qualities of nonidentical philosophy were being neglected rather than superseded by the enthusiasm for Habermas' 'language pragmatics' (Wellmer 1998: 259). Later Wellmer would pointedly describe nonidentity thinking as 'a vulnerable type of thinking, not one that clings to the guardrail of preconceived concepts and a cast-iron methodology' (Wellmer 2007: 137).[5] And, in striking contrast to Habermas, he was prepared to defend, cautiously no doubt, Adorno's critique of reason (Wellmer 1991).

The progressive narrative about the development of critical theory began, in practice, to unravel. Habermas' intellectual revolution had been perhaps too violent in its disavowal of so much that preceded it. Since the late 1980s Axel Honneth has been developing a version of critical theory which draws from the Hegelian rather than the Kantian tradition that had informed Habermas' discourse ethics. Prior to this phase of his work Honneth's general assessment of the possibilities of Adorno's critical theory was broadly in line with that of Habermas.[6] But in the course of providing theoretical grounding to the notion of recognition, which he argues is the basis of social-emancipatory practice, Honneth has adopted from Adorno several notions that had seemed, in light of Habermas' forceful criticisms, to be faulty beyond repair. Adorno's difficult notion of the impulse, elaborated through psychoanalytic theory, and the theoretically interconnected idea of mimesis (or imitation) are at work in Honneth's

conceptions of recognition and reification.[7] And again, flatly contrary to Habermas, he develops the case for negative dialectics as
itself – and as Adorno believed – an act of justice (Honneth 2009).
Whereas Habermas, as we noted, dismissed the very notion of a
totalizing critique Honneth has defended it, rather, as a disclosing
critique not paradoxical in its very conception (Honneth 2007).
The receding influence of the paradigm of language has opened up
an opportunity for a renewed and productive involvement by critical
theory with Adorno's work.

***

Numerous comparisons have been drawn between the claims of
Adorno's philosophy and the distinctive contentions of the French
post-structuralist thought that emerged in the 1960s.[8] Among the
most obvious points of contact are their shared rejection of systematic
philosophy not only as a model of rationality but in the very practice
of philosophy itself; criticisms of the modern notion of the subject;
complication of the Enlightenment's self-understanding as a casualty-
free process of liberation; a receptivity to forms of truth that lie
outside the discipline of philosophy; the identification of power
structures that determine what is taken as natural in everyday
experience. Negative dialectics and deconstruction are exercised by
their respective theorists as forms of immanent critique. The
category of nonidentity seems to be another name for the notion of
excluded otherness, the retrieval of which is an essential feature of post-
structuralist theory. To what degree can these intriguing convergences
be attributed to Adorno's actual, historical influence?

   Adorno was certainly known among philosophers in France by
the late 1950s. He noted at the end of his Hegel book that the
chapter on the experiential content of Hegel's philosophy had been
presented in French at the Sorbonne in late 1958 (HTS xxxvii).
And in a note at the end of *Negative Dialectics* (which does not appear
in the English translation) Adorno informed his readers that the

core of the book was made up of three lectures – among them the critique of Heidegger – which he had held in the spring of 1961 at the Collège de France in Paris. One of Adorno's biographers records that Adorno offered further lectures in Paris in 1965 and in 1969 (Müller-Doohm 2005: 448 and 469 respectively).

In the work of Jacques Derrida 'striking' affinities with Adorno's philosophy have been observed (Eagleton 1981: 141). Derrida's criticisms of self-presence and constitutive subjectivity, of logocentricism (see DE 51), his notion that the efforts of systems to stabilize themselves by violent exclusion or marginalization are undermined by 'difference' and are inherently 'aporetic' all find sympathetic precedents in Adorno's readings of phenomenology and idealism. The major influence at work in Derrida's development of deconstructive philosophy is Heidegger, and not Adorno, whose name does not appear in Derrida's groundbreaking writings. Yet the question of Derrida's possible debt to Adorno has niggled at his own legacy, as Derrida himself fully appreciated. In a speech upon receiving the Adorno Prize from the City of Frankfurt in 2001 (a prize that has also been awarded to Habermas (1980) and Wellmer (2006)) Derrida chose to address the issue in the following way: 'For decades I have been hearing voices, as they say, in my dreams. They are sometimes friendly voices, sometimes not. They are voices in me. All of them seem to be saying to me: why not recognize, clearly and publicly, once and for all, the affinities between your work and Adorno's, in truth your debt to Adorno?' (Derrida 2005: 176). And Derrida then declares, as though released from a burden: 'I can and must say "yes" to my debt to Adorno, and on more than one count' (Derrida 2005: 176). The speech itself reveals Derrida as a very sensitive and knowledgeable reader of Adorno. It is also evident that he was fascinated by Adorno both as a person and as a thinker. Derrida lists a number of general intellectual commitments and common formative influences that he shared with Adorno, all of which, he claimed, would need to be accounted for in making good on the acknowledgement of what he owed to Adorno (even though supposedly similar philosophical backgrounds do not actually constitute a debt). The only specific declaration of a direct influence Derrida makes is the following: 'What I shared most easily with Adorno, even took from him, as did other French philosophers – although again in different ways – is his interest in literature and in what, like the other arts, it can critically decenter in the field of university philosophy' (Derrida 2005: 180). But this too is, of course, general. Derrida seemed to want to acknowledge in markedly humble terms the influence of Adorno while at the very same time obliquely declining to identify which specific arguments and which concepts in Adorno's work he found valuable. If the question of his debt to Adorno has been prompted by observations of particular conceptual similarities in their philosophies, the 'voices' that Derrida mentioned would be unlikely to have been silenced by the Frankfurt speech.

Among other post-structuralist philosophers the influence of Adorno is a less complex matter. Only late in his career did Michel Foucault come to realize the affinities between his genealogical account of reason and the critique of Enlightenment developed by Adorno and Horkheimer. He shared with them the conclusion that the historical achievement of autonomy comes at the price of the domination of self and nature (McCarthy 1990: 447). Looking back on the efforts of Adorno and Horkheimer he professed: 'If I had known about the Frankfurt School in time, I would have been saved a great deal of work. I would not have said a certain amount of nonsense and would not have taken so many false trails trying not to get lost, when the Frankfurt School had already cleared the way' (quoted by Wiggershaus 1994: 4). Jean-François Lyotard is a quite different case as, among the most prominent post-structuralist philosophers of the 1960s and 70s, he is alone in embracing Adorno's work substantially. His interest is perhaps highlighted by the essay, 'Adorno as the Devil' (1974), in which he elaborately identifies the figure of Adorno behind one of the devil's masks in Thomas Mann's *Doctor Faustus*. But the influence of Adorno

can arguably be seen throughout his work. It has been suggested,
for instance, that Lyotard's notion of the *différend*, which is the conceptual basis of his notion of the 'injustice of translating heterogeneous discourses into a common idiom recalls the violence of
subsumptive procedures analysed in *Negative Dialectics*'. Furthermore,
'Adorno's critique of identity thinking and the philosophy of the
différend both inveigh against the reduction of the heterogeneous to
totality' (Foster 1999: 92). And in an essay of 1981, 'Discussions,
or Phrasing "After Auschwitz"' Lyotard elaborates on the constraints
on theory identified by Adorno in *Negative Dialectics*.

***

The interpretation and philosophical reappropriation of Adorno's
work is an ongoing task. It should not be assumed that further
appropriations of his work will be found only among those who
conceive of philosophy as a task with radical social implications.
The recent interest by 'analytic philosophy' in Hegelianism –
among the 'Pittsburgh' philosophers in particular – appears to be
opening up a space for discussion within the concerns of English
language philosophy of a number of ideas that were important to
Adorno too: for instance, the theory of conceptual mediation, the
status of second nature. And scholars of Adorno have been keen to
articulate his ideas in ways that promote the case for Adorno's
relevance for this new chapter of Anglo-American philosophy.[9]
Whether this new direction has a future remains to be seen.

 Adorno's work, as I have tried to show, contains an enormous
number of conceptions and arguments, many of which might be
notionally separated from their original contexts and put to good
use in new debates. What marks out Adorno as a philosopher,
though, is not simply the range of ideas he developed. It is, as
Wellmer has rightly emphasized, his nonidentity thinking, his
effort to philosophize through the object. This commitment
enabled him to critically expose what he took to be the deceptive

theoretical constructions that form, in large part, the main achievements of modern philosophy. This dimension of Adorno's philosophy – his practice of philosophy – has yet to gain wide appreciation. The continuing interest of contemporary philosophy in abstracted idealizations (of experience or reason or society) – Adorno might well have perceived them as reifications – should suggest, though, that the time for nonidentity thinking has not yet passed. That this possibility is available to us might be seen as the most significant even if least developed part of Adorno's philosophical legacy.

autonomy of art   Art's autonomy consists in its independence from the norms of purposefulness in the era of 'bourgeois' society. This autonomy places it in contrastive relation to conventional society. Adorno interprets this contrast as one of implicit opposition. As opposition autonomous art provides a critical perspective on society and its reified social forms (of experience and reason).

constellation   A notion derived from Walter Benjamin to address the inability of concepts (universal in nature) to do justice to objects (particular in nature). A constellation of concepts is a set of concepts developed by examination of the distinctiveness of the object. The legitimacy of those concepts is their capacity to express what the object is and to refer collectively to the object. The concepts in a constellation are not a system in that they are not inferentially or deductively interconnected.

culture industry   To be distinguished from 'mass culture', which bears connotations of cultural preferences that just happen to be those of the majority. The culture industry refers to the calculated (industrial) production of cultural commodities – popular music and movies most especially – which follow standard patterns. Operating within social ideology the culture industry does not and cannot prompt new experiences in its consumers. Its products resonate with the 'false consciousness' of its consumers: e.g. with the unwarranted belief in a well-ordered community which can resolve all its internal conflicts. The culture industry is therefore accused of perpetuating false consciousness.

dialectics (negative)   The moment in which our judgments are disrupted by a realization that the concepts they contain are inadequate to the object we are attempting to understand is a 'dialectical' moment. Hegel is the original author of this idea. But, according to Adorno, Hegel forced each dialectical moment to become a step in the ongoing process of the systematization of knowledge. Adorno claims that Hegel turned dialectics, in this way, into a 'positive' enterprise. He names his own philosophical procedure a 'negative dialectics' because, in contrast to Hegel's philosophy, it attempts to understand its objects without any presumption that the inadequacy of our conceptualizations of objects can serve as a new level of knowledge upon which we can base further constructions of the object.

exchange   The mechanism of transaction in capitalism in which an abstract token is given in exchange for something which is not that token. Its prevalence distorts all forms of transaction: human interaction, especially, takes on the character of exchange relations.

experience   A process of transformation in which a subject in responsive interaction with the outer world (other people or objects) exercises a capacity to change its conceptualizations of the outer world. Experience is rational: it is a matter of reflective conceptual activity in which a subject is willing to address the limitations – inadequacy of its conceptions, incoherence of its conceptions – of its judgments. This notion of experience originates in Hegel's *Phenomenology of Spirit*.

false consciousness   A term used by Adorno and Horkheimer for ideology. False consciousness is shared by those whose consciousness or intuitive perception of the world is determined by the social totality. Individuals with false consciousness perceive, for instance, exchange relations as natural and think of instrumental reason as the essence of reason. False consciousness is 'necessary' for the perpetuation of society in its current form since it precludes a critical perspective on society's central principles (by assuming that they are natural).

identity   A misunderstanding of the relationship between subject and object in which the concepts or systems of concepts of a subject (person, philosopher, scientist, etc.) are taken to be identical with the object. This misunderstanding is not primarily philosophical: it is determined by the prevailing form of social reason (instrumental reason) which is geared towards 'the domination of nature'.

immanent critique   Transcendent social criticism, in contrast to immanent critique, assumes that the critic is employing standards of evaluation that are free of social influence. This critical perspective is undermined by the notion of social mediation. Criticism can avoid the delusion of social independence if it is immanent. In practice this means testing the claims or explicit commitments of the position to be criticized against the position as it is articulated or realized. No outside standards of the good or the true are introduced in immanent critique.

instrumental reason   A concept conceived by Max Weber and central to *Dialectic of Enlightenment*. Instrumental reason originates in the efforts of human beings to manipulate nature. It gains sophistication in the era of modern science and, according to Adorno, predominates as the preferred form of reason in contemporary society (to the point that the alternatives no longer seem like reason). A form of reason which might take an overall view of society appears meaningless from the perspective of instrumental reason since a social overview – e.g. the critical theory of society – uses none of the methods that are recognizable to instrumental reason.

nonidentity   What concepts or systems of concepts do not capture in an object is its irreducible particularity. In any act of conceptualization, therefore, there will be nonidentity because there can be no final identity between concepts and the object. The nonidentical properties of an object are not indeterminate (in the manner of Kant's thing-in-itself). They are what actually constitute the object's 'own identity' though they are elusive to concepts.

mediation (subject-object)   The process of subject-object interaction. The subject mediates the object through concepts and the object mediates the subject by determining the content of the subject's concepts. This is a constitutive process for both sides since neither is meaningful without the other. Adorno refers to the two sides of the process as the 'how' and the 'what' respectively.

mediation (social)   The notion that all meanings – concepts, ideas, commitments etc. – are determined by the 'social totality' within which they have validity. The idea, for example, that an individual can conceive him/herself as fundamentally independent of social influence is false because the very notion of individuality – how one understands oneself as an individual – is socially mediated: it is inseparable from the forms of freedom and scope of action that are the norms of the society within which the individual is located.

mimesis   A Greek word for imitation that has been a concept in philosophy since the discussion of art as imitation in Plato and Aristotle. Although mimesis is discussed by Adorno mainly within the sphere of aesthetic experience, its significance is more wide-reaching than as a category of aesthetic theory. Imitation is essential to any non-distorted interaction between people, and between human beings and aesthetic objects. In this process of imitation the self is transformed as it begins to imitate and become like the other. Loving relationships are mimetic; genuine engagements with artworks – as creator, performer or experience – are mimetic.

particular   The distinctiveness and uniqueness of each person and object. Particularity is violated with the application of concepts – universal by their nature – that supposedly capture the essence of a person or object.

positivism   A position in social theory and philosophy criticized by Adorno because it investigates only what is apparent or given in facts (appearance). Critical theory, by contrast, needs to go behind the facts (to reality) as it seeks to explain the processes and prevalence of social mediation.

reification   A concept first conceived by Georg Lukács. Reification is a process in which non-things – primarily, human beings, qualitative differences – are turned into things. (*Res* is Latin for thing; *Ding* is the German for thing, the stem of the word in its original conception, *Verdinglichung*.) This process is not simply a misunderstanding or a misapplication of the wrong kind of description. Reification is a mode of perception which is prevalent wherever instrumental rationality and capitalism predominate. Instrumental rationality assumes that the world is made up of things we can manipulate. Capitalism grants each phenomenon an abstract value in order to enter it into 'exchange' relations. The qualities of the phenomenon are, in this sense, reified. Adorno also refers to the reification of consciousness: this is the consciousness of an individual who habitually reifies his/her experience.

social totality   Adorno holds that society is a system that attempts to determine every feature of life within it. In contemporary society this is evident in the increasing reach of the capitalist form of behaviour – exchange – into all relations. In this way, the influence of society becomes total. Human values are increasingly aligned with capitalism's efforts to sustain and reproduce itself. Spaces for individual expression or the appreciation of particularities are excluded within a social totality.

(A glossary of some of Adorno's ideas can also be found in Rose 1978: 149–53.)

One: Adorno's Life and Philosophical Motivations

1 This section draws much of its factual information from Jay 1996, Müller-Doohm 2005 and Wiggershaus 1994.
2 Horkheimer made this observation in a letter which is reprinted in Claussen 2008: 365.
3 For a list of Adorno's compositions see Metzger and Riehn 1989: 144–46.
4 For more positive appraisals of the place of the first *Habilitationsschrift* in Adorno's philosophical development see O'Connor 2004: 102–6 and Wiggershaus 1994: 81–82.
5 In Horkheimer 1999.
6 See, for example, A. J. Ayer's personal view of Adorno in Ayer 1977: 153.
7 The major study from this period was published in Adorno's name as *Guilt and Defense: On the Legacies of National Socialism in Postwar Germany.*
8 See Rolf Tiedemann's editorial postscript in ME 241.
9 The contributions to this debate were published as T. W. Adorno et al, *The Positivist Dispute in German Sociology.*

Two: Society

1 See Benhabib 1986, especially chapter 1, for a discussion of the motivations behind Western Marxism's development of 'critique'.
2 See, for instance, Adorno's essay 'Free Time', in CM.

Six: Aesthetics

1 Früchtl 1986 is the most comprehensive study to date of the concept of mimesis in Adorno's work.
2 As Martin Jay notes, Adorno and Horkheimer 'mourned the loss or withering of a primal and inherently benign human capacity to imitate nature as the dialectic of enlightenment followed its fateful course' (Jay 1997: 30).

3 Adorno does not acknowledge this distinction. He speaks of the 'Platonic-Aristotelian tradition, which distinguished between the semblance of the sensuous world on the one hand, and essence or pure spirit as authentic being on the other' (AT 108).

4 See Adorno and Benjamin 2006: Letter 26, 16 December 1934. For an analysis of this letter see Weber Nicholsen 1997: 183ff. Benjamin's essay appeared as 'Franz Kafka: On the Tenth Anniversary of his Death', in Benjamin 1973.

5 See Adorno's essay 'Alienated Masterpiece: *Missa Solemnis*' in B. O'Connor (ed.) Theodor W. Adorno, *The Adorno Reader*; also in R. Leppert (ed.) Theodor W. Adorno, *Essays on Music*.

6 He makes this argument in 'The Dialectical Composer', in R. Leppert (ed.) Theodor W. Adorno, *Essays on Music*.

7 See Leppert 2002: 349–62 for a useful orientation in the variety of Adorno's criticisms of jazz, his knowledge of the field, and some of its most significant difficulties.

8 'On the Problem of Musical Analysis', in R. Leppert (ed.) Theodor W. Adorno, *Essays on Music*: 167.

Seven: Adorno's Philosophical Legacy

1 See Chapter 1, p. 12.

2 Habermas 1991.

3 See Specter 2010 for an account of Habermas' fraught relationship with the student activists.

4 See Held 1980: 379–80 for a sceptical discussion of Connerton's schematization.

5 This was not the first time Wellmer sought to return attention to the notion of nonidentity thinking. See, for instance, Wellmer 1985. That essay was replaced by one on Kant and Habermas' Discourse Ethics in the English translation of the volume.

6 In 1985, for instance, he claimed that Adorno had given 'the competencies of critical knowledge to art', motivated by the worry that 'philosophical reflection and (especially) scientific research are not able to escape the suspicion of complicity in the civilizing process of reification'. By attempting to aestheticize critical theory itself Adorno 'vacillates helplessly between philosophical reflection and aesthetic experience, not wanting to be the one and not able to be the other' (Honneth 1991: 68–69).

7 See, for example, Honneth 2008 and Honneth 2009.

8 See for instance Dews 1995: 19–38 and Pensky 1997b: 6–12.

9 None more so than Bernstein 2001.

Primary sources in German

Adorno's works have been edited under two groupings: (1) the *Gesammelte Schriften*, which contains books and papers published or completed in some form during Adorno's lifetime (*Aesthetic Theory* being the main exception) and (2) the *Nachgelassene Schriften*, made up of unpublished drafts and lecture courses.

(1) *Gesammelte Schriften*, Frankfurt am Main: Suhrkamp, editor-in-chief, Rolf Tiedemann.

1 (1973) *Philosophische Frühschriften*
   Die Transzendenz des Dinglichen und Noematischen in Husserls Phänomenologie [1924]
   Der Begriff des Unbewußten in der transzendentalen Seelenlehre [1927]
   Vorträge und Thesen [early 1930s]
2 (1979)
   Kierkegaard. Konstruktion des Ästhetischen [1933]
3 (1980)
   (With Max Horkheimer) *Dialektik der Aufklärung. Philosophische Fragmente* [1944]
4 (1979)
   Minima Moralia. Reflexionen aus dem beschädigten Leben [1951]
5 (1971)
   Zur Metakritik der Erkenntnistheorie. Studien über Husserl und die phänomenologischen Antinomien [1956]
   Drei Studien zu Hegel [1963]
6 (1972)
   Negative Dialektik [1966]
   Jargon der Eigentlichkeit. Zur deutschen Ideologie [1964]
7 (1971)
   Ästhetische Theorie [1970]

8 (1972) Soziologische Schriften I (various pieces assembled by the editors)
9.1 (1975) Soziologische Schriften II
The Psychological Technique of Martin Luther Thomas' Radio Addresses [1943]
Studies in the Authoritarian Personality [1950]
9.2 (1975) Soziologische Schriften II:
The Stars Down to Earth [1957]
Schuld und Abwehr [1955]
10.1 (1977) Kulturkritik und Gesellschaft I
Prismen. Kulturkritik und Gesellschaft [1955]
Ohne Leitbild. Parva Aesthetica [1967]
10.2 (1977) Kulturkritik und Gesellschaft II
Eingriffe. Neun kritische Modelle [1963]
Stichworte. Kritische Modelle 2 [1969]
Kritische Modelle 3 (various pieces)
11 (1974) Noten zur Literatur
Part I [1958]
Part II [1961]
Part III [1965]
Part IV (various pieces assembled by the editors)
12 (1975)
Philosophie der neuen Musik [1949]
13 (1971) Die musikalische Monographien
Versuch über Wagner [1952]
Mahler. Eine musikalische Physiognomik [1960]
Berg. Der Meister des kleinsten Übergangs [1968]
14 (1973)
Dissonanzen. Musik in der verwalteten Welt [1956]
Einleitung in die Musiksoziologie [1962]
15 (1976)
(With Hanns Eisler) Komposition für den Film [1944, in English, bearing only
  Eisler's name, and 1969]
Der getreue Korrepetitor. Lehrschriften zur musikalischen Praxis [1963]
16 (1978) Musikalische Schriften I-III
Klangfiguren. Musikalische Schriften I [1959]
Quasi una fantasia. Musikalische Schriften II [1963]
Musikalische Schriften III (unfinished collection)
17 (1982) Musikalische Schriften IV
Moments musicaux. Neu gedruckte Aufsätze 1928–62 [1964]
Impromptus. Zweite Folge neu gedruckter musikalischer Aufsätze [1968]
18 (1984) Musikalische Schriften V (various pieces assembled by the editors)
Musikalische Aphorismen
Theorie der neuen Musik
Komponisten und Kompositionen

Konzert-Einleitungen und Rundfunkvorträge mit Musikbeispielen
Musiksoziologisches
19 (1984) *Musikalische Schriften VI* (various pieces assembled by the editors)
Frankfurter Opern- und Konzertkritiken
Andere Opern- und Konzertkritiken
Kompositionskritiken
Buchrezensionen
Zur Praxis des Musiklebens
20.1 (1986) *Vermischte Schriften I* (various pieces assembled by the editors)
Theorien und Theoretiker
Gesellschaft, Unterricht, Politik
20.2 (1986) *Vermischte Schriften II* (various pieces assembled by the editors)
Aesthetica
Miscellanea
Institut für Sozialforschung und Deutsche Gesellschaft für Soziologie

(2) *Nachgelassene Schriften*, Frankfurt am Main / Berlin: Suhrkamp Verlag, editor-in-chief, Rolf Tiedemann.
Not every volume of the projected series has yet appeared.

Part I. *Fragment gebliebene Schriften*

1. (1993) *Beethoven. Philosophie der Musik*
2. (2001) *Theorie der musikalischen Reproduktion*
3. (2006) *Currents of Music. Elements of a Radio Theory*

Part II. *Philosophische Notizen* (c. 5 volumes)
Part III. *Poetische Versuche* (1 volume)
Part IV. *Vorlesungen* (Square brackets indicate the year in which the lectures were delivered.)

   1. *Erkenntnistheorie* [1957/58]
   2. (2010) *Einführung in die Dialektik* [1958]
   3. (2009) *Ästhetik* [1958/59]
   4. (1995) *Kants »Kritik der reinen Vernunft«* [1959]
   5. *Einleitung in die Philosophie* [1959/60]
   6. *Philosophie und Soziologie* [1960]
   7. (2002) *Ontologie und Dialektik* [1960/61]
   8. *Ästhetik* [1961/62]
   9. *Philosophische Terminologie* [1962/63]
     (A transcription of these lectures has already appeared under a separate edition (Suhrkamp, Vol. I, 1973, Vol. II, 1974).)
 10. (1996) *Probleme der Moralphilosophie* [1963]
 11. *Fragen der Dialektik* [1963/64]
 12. (2008) *Philosophische Elemente einer Theorie der Gesellschaft* [1964]

13. (2001) *Zur Lehre von der Geschichte und von der Freiheit* [1964/65]
14. (1998) *Metaphysik, Begriff und Probleme* [1965]
15. (1993) *Einleitung in die Soziologie* [1968]
16. (2003) *Vorlesung über Negative Dialektik* [1965/66]
17. *Stichworte und Stenogramm-Fragmente zu den nicht erhaltenen Vorlesungen*

Part V. *Improvisierte Vorträge* (c. 2 volumes)
Part VI. *Gespräche, Diskussionen, Interviews*

Primary Sources in English Translation

(Books; cited articles; edited collections)

'The Actuality of Philosophy', trans. B. Snow, in *The Adorno Reader*.

The Adorno Reader, ed. B. O'Connor, Oxford / Malden MA: Blackwells, 2000.

Aesthetic Theory, trans. R. Hullot-Kentor, Minneapolis: University of Minnesota Press, 1997.

Aesthetics and Politics (Adorno et al.) ed. R. Taylor, London: NLB, 1977.

Against Epistemology: A Metacritique. Studies in Husserl and the Phenomenological Antinomies, trans. W. Domingo, Oxford: Basil Blackwell, 1982.

Alban Berg: Master of the Smallest Link, trans. J. Brand and C. Hailey, Cambridge: Cambridge University Press, 1991.

'Alienated Masterpiece: *Missa Solemnis*', trans. D. Smith, in *The Adorno Reader* (also in *Essays on Music*).

Aspects of Sociology, The Frankfurt Institute of Social Research, trans. J. Viertel, Boston: Beacon Press, 1972.

The Authoritarian Personality (with E. Frenkel-Brunswick, D. Levinson and R. N. Sanford) New York: Harper & Brothers, 1950. Abridged edition, *The Authoritarian Personality*, New York: W. W. Norton & Company, 1982.

Beethoven: The Philosophy of Music, trans. E. Jephcott, Cambridge: Polity Press / Stanford CA: Stanford University Press, 1998.

Can One Live after Auschwitz? A Philosophical Reader, ed. R. Tiedemann, Stanford CA: Stanford University Press, 2003.

The Complete Correspondence 1928–1940, Theodor W. Adorno and Walter Benjamin, ed. H. Lonitz, trans. N. Walker, Cambridge / Malden MA: Polity Press, 2nd edn, 2006.

Composing for the Films (with H. Eisler) New York / London: Continuum, 2007.

Correspondence 1925–1935, Theodor W. Adorno and Alban Berg, ed. H. Lonitz, trans. W. Hoban, Cambridge / Malden MA: Polity Press, 2005.

Correspondence 1943–1955, Theodor W. Adorno and Thomas Mann, ed. C. Gödde and T. Sprecher, trans. N. Walker, Cambridge / Malden MA: Polity Press, 2006.

Critical Models: Interventions and Catchwords, trans. H. W. Pickford, New York: Columbia University Press, 1998.

The Culture Industry: Selected Essays on Mass Culture, ed. J. M. Bernstein, London: Routledge, 1991.

'Culture Industry Reconsidered', trans. A. G. Rabinbach, in *The Adorno Reader* (also in *The Culture Industry*).

Dialectic of Enlightenment: Philosophical Fragments (with M. Horkheimer) trans. E. Jephcott, Stanford CA: Stanford University Press, 2002.

'The Dialectical Composer', in *Essays on Music*.

'Education for Maturity and Responsibility' (with H. Becker) trans. R. French, J. Thomas and D. Weymann, *History of the Human Sciences*, Vol. 12, No. 3, 1999.

Essays on Music, ed. R. Leppert, Berkeley CA: University of California Press, 2002.

'On the Fetish-Character in Music', trans. A. Arato and E. Gebhardt, rev. R. Leppert, in *Essays on Music*.

Guilt and Defense: On the Legacies of National Socialism in Postwar Germany, trans. J. K. Olick and A. J. Perrin, Cambridge MA / London: Harvard University Press, 2010.

Hegel: Three Studies, trans. S. Weber Nicholsen, Cambridge MA / London: MIT Press, 1993.

History and Freedom, trans. R. Livingstone, Cambridge / Malden MA: Polity Press, 2006.

'The Idea of Natural History', trans. R. Hullot-Kentor, *Telos*, No. 60, 1984.

In Search of Wagner, trans. R. Livingstone, London: NLB, 1981.

'Introduction' to (Adorno et al) *The Positivist Dispute in German Sociology*.

Introduction to Sociology, trans. E. Jephcott, Cambridge: Polity Press / Stanford CA: Stanford University Press, 2000.

Introduction to the Sociology of Music, trans. E. B. Ashton, New York: Seabury Press, 1976.

The Jargon of Authenticity, trans. K. Tarnowski and F. Will, London: Routledge & Kegan Paul, 1973.

Kant's 'Critique of Pure Reason', trans. R. Livingstone, Cambridge: Polity Press / Stanford CA: Stanford University Press, 2001.

Kierkegaard: Construction of the Aesthetic, trans. R. Hullot-Kentor, Minneapolis MN: University of Minnesota Press, 1989.

Lectures on Negative Dialectics. Fragments of a Lecture Course 1965/1966, trans. R. Livingstone, Cambridge / Malden MA: Polity Press, 2008.

Letters to his Parents 1939–1951, ed. C. Gödde and H. Lonitz, trans. W. Hoban, Cambridge / Malden MA: Polity Press, 2007.

'On the Logic of the Social Sciences', in (Adorno et al) *The Positivist Dispute in German Sociology*.

Mahler: A Musical Physiognomy, trans. E. Jephcott, Chicago IL: University of Chicago Press, 1992.

Metaphysics: Concept and Problems, trans. E. Jephcott, Cambridge: Polity Press / Stanford CA: Stanford University Press, 2000.

Minima Moralia: Reflections from Damaged Life, trans. E. Jephcott, London: NLB, 1974.

Negative Dialectics, trans. E. B. Ashton, London: Routledge & Kegan Paul, 1973.

Notes to Literature, Vol. I, trans. S. Weber Nicholsen, New York: Columbia University Press, 1991.

Notes to Literature, Vol. II, trans. S. Weber Nicholsen, New York: Columbia University Press, 1992.

Philosophy of New Music, trans. R. Hullot-Kentor, Minneapolis MN: University of Minnesota Press, 2006.

The Positivist Dispute in German Sociology (Adorno et al), trans. G. Adey and D. Frisby, London: Heinemann, 1976.

Prisms, trans. S. Weber and S. Weber, Cambridge MA / London: MIT Press, 1981.

'On the Problem of Musical Analysis', in *Essays on Music*.

Problems of Moral Philosophy, trans. R. Livingstone, Cambridge: Polity Press / Stanford CA: Stanford University Press, 2000.

Quasi una Fantasia: Essays on Modern Music, trans. R. Livingstone. London: Verso, 1992.

'Society', trans. F. R. Jameson, *Salmagundi*, Vols. 10–11, 1969–70.

'Sociology and Empirical Research', in (Adorno et al) *The Positivist Dispute in German Sociology*.

Sound Figures, trans. R. Livingstone, Stanford CA: Stanford University Press, 1999.

The Stars Down to Earth and Other Essays on the Irrational in Culture, ed. Stephen Crook, London: Routledge, 1995.

'Theory of Pseudo-Culture', trans. D. Cook, *Telos*, No. 95, 1993.

Towards a Theory of Musical Reproduction: Notes, a Draft and Two Schemata, trans. W. Hoban, Cambridge / Malden MA: Polity Press, 2006.

Secondary sources

(Selected studies of Adorno in English; other works cited).

Albert, H. (1976) 'The Myth of Total Reason', in (Adorno et al) *The Positivist Dispute in German Sociology*.

Ayer, A. J. (1977) *Part of My Life*, London: Collins.

Benhabib, S. (1986) *Critique, Norm and Utopia: A Study of the Foundations of Critical Theory*, New York: Columbia University Press.

Benjamin, W. (1973) *Illuminations*, ed. H. Arendt, trans. H. Zohn, London: Fontana.

Berman, R. (2002), 'Adorno's Politics', in Gibson and Rubin 2002.

Bernstein, J. M. (1993) *The Fate of Art: Aesthetic Alienation from Kant to Derrida and Adorno*, Cambridge: Polity Press.

Bernstein, J. M. (ed.) (1995) *The Frankfurt School: Critical Assessments*, London, Routledge, Vols 3 and 4.

Bernstein, J. M. (2001) *Adorno: Disenchantment and Ethics*, Cambridge: Cambridge University Press.

Bredin H. and Santoro-Brienza, L. (2000) *Philosophies of Art and Beauty*, Edinburgh: Edinburgh University Press.

Bronner, S. E. (1994) *Of Critical Theory and Its Theorists*, Oxford: Blackwell.

Brunkhorst, H. (1999) *Adorno and Critical Theory*, Cardiff: University of Wales Press.

Buck-Morss, S. (1977) *The Origin of Negative Dialectics: Theodor W. Adorno, Walter Benjamin, and the Frankfurt Institute*, Sussex: The Harvester Press.

Claussen, D. (2008) *Theodor W. Adorno: One Last Genius*, trans. R. Livingstone, Cambridge MA / London: Harvard University Press.

Connerton, P. (1976) 'Editor's Introduction', in *Critical Sociology*, ed. P. Connerton, Harmondsworth: Penguin.

Connerton, P. (1980) *The Tragedy of Enlightenment: An Essay on the Frankfurt School*, Cambridge: Cambridge University Press.

Cook, D. (1996) *The Culture Industry Revisited: Theodor W. Adorno on Mass Culture*, Landham MD: Rowman and Littlefield.

Cook, D. (2004) *Adorno, Habermas, and the Search for a Rational Society*, London / New York: Routledge.

Cook, D. (ed.) (2008) *Adorno: Key Concepts*, Stocksfield: Acumen.

Cook, D. (2011) *Adorno on Nature*, Durham: Acumen.

Corngold, S. (2002) 'Adorno's "Notes on Kafka": A Critical Reconstruction', *Monatshefte*, Vol. 94, No. 1.

Derrida, J. (2005) 'Fichus: Frankfurt Address', in J. Derrida, *Paper Machine*, trans. R. Bowlby, Stanford CA: Stanford University Press.

Dews, P. (1995) *The Limits of Disenchantment: Essays on Contemporary European Philosophy*, London / New York: Verso.

Eagleton, T. (1981) *Walter Benjamin: Or, Towards a Revolutionary Criticism*, London / New York: Verso.

Finlayson, J. G. (2002) 'Adorno on the Ethical and the Ineffable', *European Journal of Philosophy*, Vol. 10, No. 1.

Foster, R. (1999) 'Strategies of Justice: The Project of Philosophy in Lyotard and Habermas', *Philosophy and Social Criticism*, Vol. 25, No. 2.

Foster, R. (2007) *Adorno: The Recovery of Experience*, Albany NY: SUNY Press.

Freyenhagen, F. (2008) 'Moral Philosophy', in Cook 2008.

Früchtl, J. (1986) *Mimesis: Konstellation eines Zentralbegriffs bei Adorno*, Würzburg: Königshausen und Neuman.

Gabel, J. (1975) *False Consciousness: An Essay on Reification*, trans. M. A. Thompson and K. A. Thompson, Oxford: Blackwell.

Geuss, R. (1981) *The Idea of a Critical Theory: Habermas and the Frankfurt School*, Cambridge: Cambridge University Press.

Geuss, R. (2005) *Outside Ethics*, Princeton NJ: Princeton University Press.

Gibson, N. C. and Rubin, A. (eds) (2002) *Adorno: A Critical Reader*, Oxford / Malden, MA: Blackwells.

Habermas, J. (1983) *Philosophical-Political Profiles*, trans. F. G. Lawrence, Cambridge MA / London.

Habermas, J. (1984) *Theory of Communicative Action*, Vol. I, trans. T. McCarthy. London: Heinemann.

Habermas, J. (1990) *The Philosophical Discourse of Modernity: Twelve Lectures*, trans. F. G. Lawrence, Cambridge MA / London: MIT Press.

Habermas, J. (1991) *The Structural Transformation of the Public Sphere: An Inquiry into a Category of Bourgeois Society*, trans. T. Burger and F. Lawrence, Cambridge MA / London: MIT Press.

Hammer, E. (2005) *Adorno and the Political*, London: Routledge.

Harding, J. M. (1997) *Adorno and 'A Writing of the Ruins': Essays on Modern Aesthetics and Anglo-American Literature and Culture*, Albany NY: SUNY Press.

Hegel, G. W. F. (1975) *Aesthetics*, Vol. I, trans. T. M. Knox, Oxford: Clarendon Press, 1975.

Hegel, G. W. F. (1977) *Phenomenology of Spirit*, trans. A. V. Miller, Oxford: Oxford University Press.

Hegel, G. W. F. (1991a) *Elements of the Philosophy of Right*, trans. H. B. Nisbet, Cambridge: Cambridge University Press.

Hegel, G. W. F. (1991b) *The Encyclopaedia Logic* trans. T. F. Geraets, W. A. Suchting and H. S. Harris, Indianapolis IN: Hackett.

Held, D. (1980) *Introduction to Critical Theory: Horkheimer to Habermas*, Berkeley CA: University of California Press.

Hohendahl, P. U. (1995) *Prismatic Thought: Theodor W. Adorno*, Lincoln NE: University of Nebraska Press.

Honneth, A. (1979) 'Communication and Reconciliation: Habermas' Critique of Adorno', trans. V. Thomas and D. Parent, *Telos*, Vol. 39.

Honneth, A. (1991) *The Critique of Power: Reflective Stages in a Critical Social Theory*, trans. K. Baynes, Cambridge MA / London: MIT Press.

Honneth, A. (2007) 'The Possibility of a Disclosing Critique of Society: The Dialectic of Enlightenment in Light of Current Debates in Social Criticism', in A. Honneth, *Disrespect: The Normative Foundations of Critical Theory*, Cambridge MA: Polity Press, 2007.

Honneth, A. (2008) *Reification: A New Look At An Old Idea*, Oxford: Oxford University Press.

Honneth, A. (2009) *Pathologies of Reason: On the Legacy of Critical Theory*, trans. James Ingram, New York, Columbia University Press.

Horkheimer, M. (1999) *Critical Theory: Selected Essays*, trans. M. J. O'Connell, New York: Continuum (includes 'Traditional and Critical Theory' and 'The Latest Attack on Metaphysics').

Huhn, T. (1985) 'Adorno's Aesthetics of Illusion', *The Journal of Aesthetics and Art Criticism*, Vol. 44, No. 2.

Huhn, T. (ed.) (2004a) *The Cambridge Companion to Adorno*, Cambridge: Cambridge University Press.

Huhn, T. (2004b) 'Introduction: Thoughts beside Themselves', in Huhn 2004a.

Huhn, T. and Zuidervaart, L. (eds) (1997) *The Semblance of Subjectivity: Essays in Adorno's Aesthetic Theory*, Cambridge MA / London: MIT Press.

Hullot-Kentor, R. (2008) *Things Beyond Resemblance: Collected Essays on Theodor W. Adorno*, New York: Columbia University Press.

Jäger, L. (2004) *Adorno: A Political Biography*, trans. S. Spencer, New Haven CN / London: Yale University Press.

Jameson, F. (1990) *Late Marxism: Adorno, or, The Persistence of the Dialectic*, London: Verso.

Jarvis, S. (ed.) (2006) *Theodor Adorno: Critical Evaluations in Cultural Theory*, Abingdon: Routledge.

Jarvis, S. (1998) *Adorno: A Critical Introduction*, Cambridge: Polity Press.

Jay, M. (1984a) *Adorno*, London: Fontana.

Jay, M. (1984b) *Marxism and Totality: The Adventures of a Concept from Lukács to Habermas*, Berkeley: University of California Press.

Jay, M. (1996) *The Dialectical Imagination: A History of the Frankfurt School and the Institute of Social Research 1923–50*, 2nd edn, Berkeley CA: University of California Press.

Jay, M. (1997) 'Mimesis and Mimetology', in Huhn and Zuidervaart 1997.

Jenemann, D. (2007) *Adorno in America*, Minneapolis MN: University of Minnesota Press.

Kant, I. (1991) 'An Answer to the Question, "What is Enlightenment?"' in H. Reiss (ed.) I. Kant, *Political Writings*, Cambridge: Cambridge University Press, 1991.

Kant, I. (1997) *Groundwork of the Metaphysics of Morals*, trans. M. Gregor, Cambridge: Cambridge University Press.

Kant, I. (2001) *Critique of the Power of Judgment*, trans. P. Guyer and E. Matthews, Cambridge: Cambridge University Press.

Kant, I. (2011) *Lectures on Pedagogy* in R. B. Louden and G. Zöller (eds) I. Kant, *Anthropology, History, and Education*, Cambridge: Cambridge University Press.

Krahl, H.-J. (1974) 'The Political Contradictions in Adorno's Critical Theory', *Telos*, Vol. 21.

Krakauer, E. L. (1998) *The Disposition of the Subject: Reading Adorno's Dialectic of Technology*, Evanston IL: Northwestern University Press.

Lee, L. Y. (2005) *Dialectics of the Body: Corporeality in the Philosophy of Theodor Adorno*, New York / Abingdon: Routledge.

Leppert, R. (2002) 'Editorial Commentary' in R. Leppert (ed.) *Theodor W. Adorno, Essays on Music*.

Lunn, E. (1982) *Marxism and Modernism: A Historical Study of Lukács, Brecht, Benjamin, and Adorno*, Berkeley CA: University of California Press.

Lyotard, J.-F. (1974) 'Adorno as the Devil', *Telos*, Vol. 19.

Lyotard, J.-F. (1989) 'Discussions, or Phrasing "After Auschwitz"', in *The Lyotard Reader*, ed. A. Benjamin, Oxford / Malden MA: Blackwells.

Macdonald, I. and Ziarek, K. (eds) (2007) *Adorno and Heidegger: Philosophical Questions*, Stanford CA: Stanford University Press.

Mann, T. (1961) *The Genesis of a Novel*, trans R. and C. Winston, London: Secker & Warburg.

Marcuse, H. (1956) *Eros and Civilization: A Philosophical Inquiry into Freud*, London: Routledge & Kegan Paul

McCarthy, T. (1990) 'The Critique of Impure Reason: Foucault and the Frankfurt School', *Political Theory*, Vol. 18, No. 3.

Menke, C. (1998) *The Sovereignty of Art: Aesthetic Negativity in Adorno and Derrida*, trans. N. Solomon, Cambridge MA /London: MIT Press.

Metzger, H.-K. and Riehn, R. (eds) (1989) *Theodor W. Adorno: Der Komponist*, Munich: edition text + kritik.

Morgan, A. (2007) *Adorno's Concept of Life*, London / New York: Continuum.

Müller-Doohm, S. (2005) *Adorno: A Biography*, trans. R. Livingstone, Cambridge: Polity Press.

O'Connor, B. (2004) *Adorno's Negative Dialectic: Philosophy and the Possibility of Critical Rationality*, Cambridge MA / London: MIT Press.

O'Connor, B. (2011) 'Adorno's Reconception of the Dialectic', in S. Houlgate and M. Baur (eds) *A Companion to Hegel*, Oxford / Malden MA: Blackwells.

O'Neill, M. (ed.) (1999) *Adorno, Culture and Feminism*, London: Sage.

Paddison, M. (1993) *Adorno's Aesthetics of Music*, Cambridge: Cambridge University Press.

Paddison, M. (1996) *Adorno, Modernism and Mass Culture: Essays on Critical Theory and Music*, London: Kahn and Averill.

Pensky, M. (ed.) (1997a) *The Actuality of Adorno: Critical Essays on Adorno and the Postmodern*, Albany NY: SUNY Press.

Pensky, M. (1997b) 'Editor's Introduction: Adorno's Actuality', in Pensky 1997a.

Plato (2000) *The Republic*, ed. G. R. F. Ferrari, trans. T. Griffith, Cambridge: Cambridge University Press.

Popper, K. R. (1976) 'Reason or Revolution?' in (Adorno et al) *The Positivist Dispute in German Sociology*.

Rescher, N. (1993) 'Idealism', in J. Dancy and E. Sosa (eds) *A Companion to Epistemology*, Oxford: Blackwell.

Richter, G. (ed.) (2009) *Language Without Soil: Adorno and Late Philosophical Modernity*, New York: Fordham University Press.

Roberts, D. (1991) *Art and Enlightenment: Aesthetic Theory after Adorno*, Lincoln NE: University of Nebraska Press.

Rose, G. (1978) *The Melancholy Science: An Introduction to the Thought of Theodor W. Adorno*, London: Macmillan.

Rosen, M. (1982) *Hegel's Dialectic and its Criticism*, Cambridge: Cambridge University Press.

Scanlon, T. M. (1972) 'A Theory of Freedom of Expression', *Philosophy and Public Affairs*, Vol. 1, No. 2.

Schmidt, J. (ed.) (2007) *Theodor Adorno* (International Library of Essays in the History of Social and Political Thought) Surrey: Ashgate.

Schultz, K. L. (1990) *Mimesis on the Move: Theodor W. Adorno's Concept of Imitation*, New York: Peter Lang.

Schweppenhäuser, G. (2009) *Theodor W. Adorno: An Introduction*, trans. J. Rolleston, Durham NC: Duke University Press.

Schweppenhäuser, G. (2004) 'Adorno's Negative Moral Philosophy', in Huhn 2004a.

Sherratt, Y. (2002) *Adorno's Positive Dialectic*, Cambridge: Cambridge University Press.

Specter, M. G. (2010) *Habermas: An Intellectual Biography*, Cambridge: Cambridge University Press.

Tar, Z. (1977) *The Frankfurt School: The Critical Theories of Max Horkheimer and Theodor W. Adorno*, New York: John Wiley.

Thyen, A. (1989) *Negative Dialektik und Erfahrung: Zur Rationalität des Nichtidentischen bei Adorno*, Frankfurt-am-Main: Suhrkamp Verlag.

Vogel, S. (1996) *Against Nature: The Concept of Nature in Critical Theory*, Albany NY: State University of New York Press.

de Vries, H. (2005) *Minimal Theologies: Critiques of Secular Reason in Adorno and Levinas*, trans. Geoffrey Hale, Baltimore MD: Johns Hopkins University Press.

Weber, M. (1978) *Economy and Society: An Outline of Interpretive Sociology*, trans. G. Roth and C. Wittich, Los Angeles CA: University of California Press.

Weber Nicholsen, S. (1997) *Exact Imagination, Late Work: On Adorno's Aesthetics*, Cambridge MA: MIT Press.

Wellmer, A. (1985) 'Adorno, Anwalt des Nicht-Identischen. Eine Einführung', in *Zur Dialektik von Moderne und Postmoderne*, Frankfurt: Suhrkamp.

Wellmer, A. (1991) 'The Dialectic of Modernism and Postmodernism: The Critique of Reason since Adorno', in A. Wellmer, *The Persistence of Modernity: Essays on Aesthetics, Ethics and Postmodernism*, trans. D. Midgley, Cambridge: Polity Press.

Wellmer, A. (1998) *Endgames: The Irreconcilable Nature of Modernity*, trans. D. Midgley, Cambridge MA / London: MIT Press.

Wellmer, A. (2007) 'Adorno and the Problems of a Critical Construction of the Historical Present', *Critical Horizons: A Journal of Philosophy and Social Theory*, Vol. 8.

Whitebook, J. (1996) *Perversion and Utopia: A Study in Psychoanalysis and Critical Theory*, Cambridge MA / London: MIT Press.

Wiggershaus, R. (1994) *The Frankfurt School: Its History, Theories and Political Significance*, trans. M. Robertson, Cambridge: Polity Press.

Wilson, R. (2007) *Theodor Adorno*, Abingdon / New York, Routledge.

Witkin, R. W. (1998) *Adorno on Music*, London: Routledge.

Zuidervaart, L. (1991) *Adorno's Aesthetic Theory: The Redemption of Illusion*, Cambridge MA / London: MIT Press.

Zuidervaart, L. (2007) *Social Philosophy after Adorno*, Cambridge: Cambridge University Press.

Index

www.routledge.com/sociology

Adorno in the *Routledge Classics*

The Jargon of Authenticity
2nd Edition

Theodor Adorno

'A volume of Adorno's essays is equivalent to a whole shelf of books on literature.' – *Susan Sontag*

Theodor Adorno was no stranger to controversy. In *The Jargon of Authenticity* he gives full expression to his hostility to the language employed by certain existentialist thinkers such as Martin Heidegger. With his customary alertness to the uses and abuses of language, he calls into question the jargon, or 'aura', as his colleague Walter Benjamin described it, which clouded existentialists' thought. He argued that its use undermined the very message for meaning and liberation that it sought to make authentic. Moreover, such language – claiming to address the issue of freedom – signally failed to reveal the lack of freedom inherent in the capitalist context in which it was written. Instead, along with the jargon of the advertising jingle, it attributed value to the satisfaction of immediate desire. Alerting his readers to the connection between ideology and language, Adorno's frank and open challenge to directness, and the avoidance of language that 'gives itself over either to the market, to balderdash, or to the predominating vulgarity', is as timely today as it ever has been.

September 2002: 176pp
Pb: 978-0-415-28991-7

www.routledge.com/sociology

Adorno in the *Routledge Classics*

The Culture Industry
Selected Essays on Mass Culture, 2ⁿᵈ Edition

Theodor Adorno
Edited by **J.M. Bernstein**

'Adorno expounds what may be called a new philosophy of consciousness. His philosophy lives, dangerously but also fruitfully, in proximity to an ascetic puritanical moral rage, an attachment to some items in the structure and vocabulary of Marxism, and a feeling that human suffering is the only important thing and makes nonsense of everything else ... Adorno is a political thinker who wishes to bring about radical change. He is also a philosopher, with a zest for metaphysics, who is at home in the western philosophical tradition.'
– Iris Murdoch

The creation of the Frankfurt School of critical theory in the 1920s saw the birth of some of the most exciting and challenging writings of the twentieth century. It is out of this background that the great critic Theodor Adorno emerged. His finest essays are collected here, offering the reader unparalleled insights into Adorno's thoughts on culture. He argued that the culture industry commodified and standardized *all* art. In turn this suffocated individuality and destroyed critical thinking. At the time, Adorno was accused of everything from overreaction to deranged hysteria by his many detractors. In today's world, where even the least cynical of consumers is aware of the influence of the media, Adorno's work takes on a more immediate significance. *The Culture Industry* is an unrivalled indictment of the banality of mass culture.

May 2001: 224pp
Pb: 978-0-415-25380-2

For more information and to order a copy visit:
http://www.routledge.com/9780415253802

Available from all good bookshops

www.routledge.com/sociology

Adorno in the *Routledge Classics*

The Stars Down to Earth
2nd Edition

Theodor Adorno

'There is no question of the contemporary importance and relevance of these essays. T. W. Adorno is one of the great critics of the role of irrational authoritarianism in contemporary society.' – *Douglas Kellner*

The Stars Down to Earth shows us a stunningly prescient Adorno. Haunted by the ugly side of American culture industries he used the different angles provided by each of these three essays to showcase the dangers inherent in modern obsessions with consumption. He engages with some of his most enduring themes in this seminal collection, focusing on the irrational in mass culture – from astrology to new age cults, from anti-semitism to the power of neo-fascist propaganda. He points out that the modern state and market forces serve the interest of capital in its basic form. Stephan Crook's introduction grounds Adorno's arguments firmly in the present where extreme religious and political organizations are commonplace – so commonplace in fact that often we deem them unworthy of our attention. Half a century ago Theodore Adorno not only recognised the dangers, but proclaimed them loudly. We did not listen then. Maybe it is not too late to listen now.

October 2001: 248pp
Pb: 978-0-415-27100-4

For more information and to order a copy visit:
http://www.routledge.com/9780415271004

Available from all good bookshops

www.routledge.com/philosophy

ROUTLEDGE

The Ideal Companion to *Adorno*

The Continental Aesthetics Reader
2nd Edition

Edited by **Clive Cazeaux**,
University of Wales Institute, Cardiff

'There is a clear need for a Reader in continental aesthetics
and Clive Cazeaux has assembled the readings with great
care.' – *Michael Newman, Slade School of Art, London*

The Continental Aesthetics Reader brings together classic and
contemporary writings on art and aesthetics from the major figures in
continental thought. The second edition is clearly divided into seven
sections:

- Nineteenth-Century German Aesthetics
- Phenomenology and Hermeneutics
- Marxism and Critical Theory
- Excess and Affect
- Embodiment and Technology
- Poststructuralism and Postmodernism
- Aesthetic Ontologies.

Each section is clearly placed in its historical and philosophical context,
and each philosopher has an introduction by Clive Cazeaux. An updated
list of readings for this edition includes selections from Agamben,
Butler, Guattari, Nancy, Virilio, and Žižek. Suggestions for further
reading are given, and there is a glossary of over fifty key terms.

Ideal for introductory courses in aesthetics, continental philosophy, art,
and visual studies, *The Continental Aesthetics Reader* provides a thorough
introduction to some of the most influential writings on art and
aesthetics from Kant and Hegel to Badiou and Rancière.

June 2011: 768pp
Pb: 978-0-415-48184-7

For more information and to order a copy visit:
http://www.routledge.com/9780415481847

Available from all good bookshops